Ancient Wisdom and Modern Science

Ancient Wisdom
and Modern Science

Edited by STANISLAV GROF, M.D.

with the assistance of Marjorie Livingston Valier

State University of New York Press ALBANY

We would like to acknowledge permission to reprint "Morphic Resonance" by Rupert Sheldrake from *A New Science of Life* © 1981 by Rupert Sheldrake, published by J.P. Tarcher, Inc., 9110 Sunset Boulevard, Los Angeles, CA 90069.

Published by
State University of New York Press, Albany

For information, address State University of New York Press, State University Plaza, Albany, N.Y., 12246

The address of the International Transpersonal Association is 3519 Front Street, San Diego, California 92103 USA.

Library of Congress Cataloging in Publication Data

Main entry under title:

Ancient wisdom and modern science.

   Papers from a conference held in Bombay, India Feb. 1982, which was organized by the International Transpersonal Association.
   Bibliography: p.
   1. Science—Philosophy—Congresses. 2. Religion and science—1946-   —Congresses. 3. Psychology—Congresses. I. Grof, Stanislav, 1931-
II. International Transpersonal Association.
Q174.A53 1984   501   83-17877
ISBN 0-87395-848-9
ISBN 0-87395-849-7 (pbk.)

10 9 8 7 6 5 4 3

Contents

Preface

The rapid development of Western science has created a strange paradox. While pursuing a vision of progress and improvement in the human condition, mechanistic science has led to increasing dehumanization and alienation. Psychology and psychiatry—the disciplines studying specifically human phenomena—have tended to reduce the psyche to a complex of neurological reflexes and interacting instinctual forces. In the mid-1950's, academic psychology was dominated by behaviorism and psychoanalysis, two orientations that represent most distinctly this approach to the understanding of mental processes. But in the 1960's, an influential group of professionals were unwilling to reduce the study of the human psyche to that part of it which humans share with animals or with emotionally disturbed individuals, and they launched the movement of *humanistic psychology*, or the *Third Force*, as it was called by Abraham Maslow. The new movement emphasized the central significance of human beings as subjects for study and of human objectives as criteria for determining the relevance of research findings. In direct contrast with behaviorism, the objective of which is to predict and control the behavior of other people, the new movement put a high value on personal freedom and on the ability of the individual to determine his or her life.

While humanistic psychology was rapidly gaining momentum, a new force emerged within its inner circles which held that the humanistic emphasis on personal growth and self-actualization was still too narrow and limited. New emphasis was put on recognition of spirituality and transcendental needs as intrinsic aspects of human nature and on the right of every individual to pursue his or her own spiritual path. Leading humanistic psychologists showed interest in the neglected psychological realms of mystical experiences, transcendence, ecstasy, cosmic consciousness, meditation, and inter-individual and inter-species synergy. These interests culminated in the emergence of a new movement—*transpersonal psychology.*

Transpersonal psychology, established as a discipline in the late 1960's, received impetus from the work of Carl Gustav Jung, Roberto Assagioli and Abraham Maslow, and from clinical work with psychedelics, particularly LSD psychotherapy. The new insights into the human psyche were crystalized and consolidated into a new movement, or Fourth Force in psychology, by humanistic psychologists Anthony Sutich and Abraham Maslow.

Transpersonal psychology has rapidly grown and developed in the last decade. The *Journal of Transpersonal Psychology,* The *Association of Transpersonal Psychology,* The *California Institute of Transpersonal Psychology* were established, and movement activities, centered in the USA, particularly California, generated considerable interest and response abroad. Since 1972 international meetings in transpersonal psychology have reflected its growing influence. The first two international meetings, held in Iceland, the third, in Inari, Lappland, and the fourth, in Belo Horizonte, Brazil, were organized by transpersonally oriented psychologists, particularly Geir Vilhjamssen, Léo Matos, and Pierre Weil.

At the fourth international meeting, in 1978, it was decided that the growing popularity and vitality of these meetings justified launching an international organization. This was the formal beginning of the *International Transpersonal Association* (ITA). Stanislav Grof, nominated the first president of the ITA, was asked to take responsibility for future conferences, and formulate the philosophy, strategy, legal structure, and goals of the ITA.

The conceptual and organizational outline prepared by Stanislav Grof differed from that of the Association for Transpersonal Psychology by stressing the explicitly international structure and interdisciplinary nature of the ITA. The rapid convergence between transpersonal psychology and other scientific disciplines led to the fact that the ITA membership included quantum-relativistic physicists, information and system theorists, biologists, anthropologists, thanatologists, theologians, philosophers, artists. Hence the *International*

Transpersonal Association is defined as a scientific organization that unites individuals of different nationalities, professions, and philosophical or spiritual preferences who share the transpersonal orientation or world view. This means that using the specific methods and observations of their respective areas of interest, they are moving toward or have arrived at the recognition of fundamental unity underlying the world of separate beings and objects, and they are applying this new understanding in their fields.

The ITA supports efforts to bridge the gaps between various disciplines and formulate a comprehensive, integrated image of human nature. It facilitates the development of new scientific paradigms that synthesize previously disparate or contradictory approaches, emphasize the unity of mind and body, and describe human beings in their complex interpersonal, social, ecological, and cosmic context. Based on the recognition that reality is infinitely more complex than any scientific theory or ideological system, and that it is absolutely mandatory to maintain an open-minded approach to the exploration of the world, unimpeded by rigid adherence to the existing paradigms, the ITA supports attempts to reconcile and integrate seemingly disparate approaches—the mystical traditions and quantum-relativistic physics, Western pragmatism and Oriental philosophies, ancient wisdom and modern science, or contemporary medicine and aboriginal healing practices.

In practice, the ITA encourages the application of new principles and conceptual frameworks to therapy, education, economy, ecology, politics, religion, art, and other areas of human life. It stresses inner life, quality of the human experience, self-actualization, and evolution of consciousness. ITA activities emphasize complementarity, synergy and cooperation as opposed to antagonism, competition and self-assertion; a holistic approach rather than selective focus on isolated sectors of reality; and harmonious tuning into natural processes and cosmic cycles in contrast to manipulative intervention and control.

The last three annual conferences organized by the ITA* focused

*The ITA is deeply indebted for the great success of these conferences to several teams of unique coordinators. For the Boston conference, it was Elias and Isa Velonis, for the Melbourne conference Alf and Muriel Foote, and for the conference in Bombay Marilyn Hershenson, Abby Rosen, Ira Rifkin and Ruth Berlin.

on issues that are of critical importance for the transpersonal movement. The 1979 conference in Boston, Massachusetts, entitled *The Nature of Reality: Dawning of A New Paradigm*, brought together important representatives of the transpersonal field to discuss new developments in science and their relevance for the transpersonal orientation. The 1980 conference on Phillip Island near Melbourne, Australia, was based on the main theme *Reality: New Perspectives*, and further explored the relationship between transpersonal theory and revolutionary developments in various scientific disciplines. In addition, it introduced the new movement into Australia and led to consolidation of various individuals and groups interested in the transpersonal field into an integrated and well organized network. The third of these conferences, held in February 1982 in Bombay, India, under the title *East and West: Ancient Wisdom and Modern Science*, represented a culmination of the above efforts. It brought together prominent representatives of science and of the great spiritual traditions to explore, in an open dialogue, the rapidly increasing convergence between the ancient teachings and modern science and between Eastern thought and Western pragmatism.

The ancient tradition of Siddha Yoga was represented by the head of the lineage, the late Gurudev Swami Muktananda Paramahansa, Swami Prajnananda, and Swami Kripananda. The Christian representatives at the conference included one of the world's most honored humanitarians, Mother Teresa of Calcutta, and the Benedictine monk, writer, and philosopher, Father Bede Griffiths. Rabbis Zalman Schachter, Shlomo Carlebach and David Zeller participated jointly in a special evening of Jewish mysticism that combined elements of Kabbalah with Hassidic songs and dances. Al Chung-liang Huang, master of t'ai chi and Chinese dance, theater and calligraphy shared with participants the living Taoist tradition in a series of demonstrations, performances, and experiential workshops. Tantric scholar and writer Ajit Mookerjee introduced the audience to the science and art of Kundalini. The Buddhist Vipassana tradition was represented by the American psychologist and Buddhist monk and teacher Jack Kornfield. Swami Sivananda Radha, founder and spiritual director of the Yasodhara Ashram in Canada, and a Westerner who received spiritual training in India, shared with participants her unique ability to interpret the principles and ideas of yoga to Western audiences. His Holiness the Dalai Lama had planned to open the conference with an introductory speech and blessing, and His Holiness the Karmapa had agreed to close it with a Black Crown ceremony. The untimely death of His Holiness the Karmapa and sudden illness of His Holiness the Dalai Lama meant that Tarab Tulku Ngawang Losang Rinpoche was the representative to the conference of Tibetan Buddhism. An unexpected major contribution to the meeting was an unplanned appearance of the high priest of the Parsees, Dastoor Minocher Homji.

The spectrum of scientific presentations at the Bombay conference was equally rich. Among the speakers were neuroscientist Karl Pribram, who formulated the revolutionary holonomic theory of the brain; physicist Fritjof Capra, known for his work on the convergence of physics and mysticism; and biologist Rupert Sheldrake, who recently shocked the scientific world with his theory of morphic resonance. Biofeedback pioneers Alyce and Elmer Green, and British stress researcher Malcolm Carruthers discussed the relationship between yoga and Western medical research. Psychology was represented by Jungian therapists June Singer, Cecil Burney and Dora Kalff, transpersonal therapist Frances Vaughan, founder of family therapy Virginia Satir, and writer and educator Joseph Chilton Pearce. Psychiatrists Claudio Naranjo and Stanislav Grof explored the relationship between their discipline and the Eastern systems. Uniquely combining his academic education and shamanic training, anthropologist Michael Harner, with Sandra Harner, conducted workshops in which participants had the opportunity to experiment with ancient shamanic techniques.

Among transpersonal artists who added an important dimension to the meeting was Paul Horn, who appeared as a soloist, jointly with Al Chung-liang Huang, and also in the context of his superb multimedia show. The rising Indian star, dancer Alarmel Valli, stunned participants with her breath-taking performance in an evening of Indian classical ballet.

Many of those who could not attend the Bombay conference as well as its participants have been asking the ITA to make the proceedings available in written form. The ITA board therefore accepted with great pleasure the offer of William Eastman from the State University of New York Press to publish a book based on the last ITA conference. Because the program was extremely rich, it was not possible to include all the presentations, and the editors and publisher were confronted with the difficult task of selecting some papers and excluding others. Decision was influenced by considerations of available space and by the nature of the contributions: some were primarily experiential, impossible to represent in printed articles. The general policy was to include those that were most closely related to the theme of the conference and were most comprehensive.

The emergence of the new paradigm and the increasing convergence between science and mysticism seems to be one of the most critical issues the scientific world is facing these days. This book thus transcends the framework of a historical document on the Bombay conference and can be seen as a independent statement of lasting value, anticipating developments in the future.

Part I
INTRODUCTION

1

Stanislav Grof   East and West: Ancient Wisdom
                  and Modern Science

Science and technology have become dominant forces in the modern
world, and Western civilization, pioneering in technological development, is commonly seen as a symbol of progress and enlightenment.
A tendency to glorify progress and evolution and to look down upon
the past as a time of infancy and immaturity is associated with the
view that the ideological and cultural differences between East and
West are absolute and unbridgeable. This view was most succinctly
expressed by Rudyard Kipling in his famous "East is East and West
is West/ and never the twain shall meet."

   A major reason for the incompatibility of the ancient and the
modern, as well as the Eastern and the Western, has been fundamental difference in their dominant world-views and philosophies. Western scientific disciplines have described the universe as an infinitely
complex mechanical system of interacting, discrete particles and separate objects. In this context, matter appears to be solid, inert, passive and unconscious; life, consciousness and creative intelligence are
seen as insignificant accidents and derivatives of material development. They emerged after billions of years of random mechanical evolution of matter and only in a negligible section of an immense
universe.

   In contrast, the spiritual philosophies of the great ancient and

3

Eastern cultures—or "perennial philosophy"[1] as Aldous Huxley referred to them—describe consciousness and creative intelligence as primary attributes of existence, both transcendent and immanent in the phenomenal world. Western science recognizes as real only those phenomena that can be objectively observed and measured; perennial philosophy acknowledges an entire hierarchy of realities—some of them manifest, others hidden under ordinary circumstances and directly observable only in certain special states of consciousness.

Materialistic science and perennial philosophy differ most in their images of human nature. Western science portrays human beings as highly developed animals and thinking biological machines who have a fleeting, insignificant role in the overall scheme of things. Perennial philosophy sees humans as essentially commensurate with the entire universe and ultimately divine. Western science offers psychological and psychopharmacological assistance to people who have difficulties adjusting to the miserable predicament of human life. (Sigmund Freud, the founder of psychoanalysis, described the goal of successful psychotherapy as "changing the extreme suffering of the neurotic into the normal misery of human existence."[2] But perennial philosophy offers a rich spectrum of spiritual techniques through which it is possible to recognize and experience one's own divinity and achieve liberation from suffering.

Materialistic science has developed effective means of alleviating the most obvious forms of suffering—diseases, poverty and starvation—but has done very little for inner fulfillment and genuine emotional satisfaction. Increased material affluence has been associated with a dramatic increase of mental disorders, alcoholism, suicide rates, crime, and violence. On the other hand, perennial philosophy has offered inner liberation to a select few, but has failed to offer solutions for the urgent practical problems of everyday existence or to improve the external conditions of human life. These differences invite us to wonder if Western science and perennial wisdom could be reconciled in a way that would combine their advantages and avoid their drawbacks. Since it is not possible to change the ancient and perennial, any attempt at such synthesis must involve changes in the philosophy of Western science. But is it possible to change the basic assumptions of science while preserving its formidable pragmatic power? Do not the everyday triumphs of mechanistic science constitute a clear proof of the accuracy of its basic philosophical assumptions?

One of the most important achievements of Western philosophy of science is the recognition that scientific theories are but conceptual models organizing the data about reality available at the time. As useful approximations to reality, they should not be mistaken for correct descriptions of reality itself. The relationship between theory and the reality which it describes is like that between a map and territory in Korzybski's sense;[3] to confuse the two represents a violation of scientific thinking—a serious error in what is called logical typing. American anthropologist and generalist Gregory Bateson said that a person committing logical errors of this kind may one day eat the menu instead of the meal. Since it is always possible to formulate more than one theory accounting for the available data, the problem is to find a theory that would be broad enough to incorporate basic assumptions of perennial philosophy and yet preserve the pragmatic power of mechanistic science.

The concept of a *paradigm* is extremely useful here. Coined by the American physicist and historian of science Thomas Kuhn, author of the ground-breaking book *The Structure of Scientific Revolutions,* the term *paradigm* describes conceptual systems that dominate the thinking of scientific communities during certain specific periods of the evolution of science.[4] Initially each new paradigm has a positive and progressive role. It identifies legitimate scientific problems, offers methodology for conducting scientific experiments, and describes criteria for evaluating the data. A paradigm clearly defines not only what reality is, but also what it is not and cannot possibly be. Once the paradigm is accepted, its basic philosophical assumptions are not questioned and scientists focus their attention and efforts on its further elaboration and articulation. However, continued research inevitably will produce data that are incompatible with the leading paradigm, since reality is always much more complicated than even the most sophisticated and complex scientific theory.

At first, all research challenging the dominant paradigm tends to be suppressed, because the current theories are mistaken for a true and exhaustive description of reality. Scientists who are under the spell of the leading paradigm have a strong conviction about the nature of reality. The scientist who generates controversial data is discounted as inept, accused of cheating, or even labeled mentally ill. When the new data hold in subsequent experiments and are further confirmed by independent research, the discipline in question moves into a serious paradigm crisis that Kuhn calls a period of abnormal science. After attempts to create *ad hoc* hypotheses and conceptual adjustments fail, more and more courageous and fantastic theories are generated, and out of this chaos one of these alternatives finally emerges victorious as the new paradigm. In the history of science, this sequence of events is continuously repeated.

The old and the new paradigm typically represent entirely different and mutually incompatible world-views. Historical examples of major paradigm shifts are the transition from the geocentric astronomy of Ptolemaius to the heliocentric system of Copernicus and Galileo, from the flogiston theory to the modern chemistry of Lavoisier, and, most recently, from the Newtonian mechanics to quantum-relativistic physics.

In the past 300 years, Western science has been dominated by the Newtonian-Cartesian paradigm. As Fritjof Capra outlined them in *The Tao of Physics,* the basic philosophical assumptions of this system of thought are derived from the ideas of Isaac Newton and René Descartes.[5] Newton's mechanistic universe is a universe of solid matter made of fundamental building blocks or atoms, which are by definition indestructible.* They influence each other by forces of gravitation and interact according to fixed and unchangeable laws. Their interaction occurs in absolute space, which is three-dimensional, homogeneous, and independent of the presence of matter. Time in the Newtonian universe is uni-dimensional, flowing evenly from the past through the present to the future.

Newton's universe resembles a gigantic supermachine governed by linear chains of causes and effects. It is strictly deterministic: if we knew all the factors operating at present, we should be able to reconstruct accurately any situation in the past or predict any event in the future. Although this determinism cannot be scientifically proven and the complexity of the universe prevents its practical testing, it constitutes one of the cornerstones of mechanistic science.

To this Newtonian model, the French philosopher René Des-

*The Greek *a-tomos* is composed of the negative prefix *a-* and the verb *temnein*—to cut; it means that which cannot be cut or divided any further.

cartes contributed absolute dichotomy between matter (*res extensa*) and mind (*res cogitans*). According to Descartes, the universe exists objectively in the form in which a human observer would perceive it, but its existence is entirely independent of the process of observation.

These ideas of Isaac Newton and René Descartes became the foundations of Western mechanistic science and became the driving force behind the Scientific and Industrial Revolutions. The mechanistic model of the universe was so successful in its pragmatic technological applications that it became the ideal prototype of all scientific thinking, and was emulated by other disciplines, including psychology, psychiatry, sociology, anthropology, and related fields. Freud was a member of the so-called "Helmholtz Society," whose explicit goal was to introduce into science the principles of Newtonian mechanics. While formulating psychoanalysis, Freud quite consciously and rigorously used the criteria of Newtonian thinking. The extreme example of this thinking is behaviorism—an attempt to eliminate the element of consciousness as a legitimate object of scientific interest and research, and to develop scientific psychology without the use of subjective introspective data.

The various scientific disciplines based on the mechanistic model have created an image of the universe as an infinitely complex assembly of passive, inert and unconscious matter, developing without any participation of creative intelligence. From the "Big Bang," through the initial expansion of the galaxies, to the creation of the solar system and Earth, the cosmic processes were allegedly governed by blind mechanical forces. Organic matter and life were thought to have originated in the primeval ocean by accident through random chemical reactions. Similarly, the cellular organization of organic matter and the Darwinian evolution to higher life forms occurred quite mechanically without the participation of an intelligent principle—through genetic mutations and natural selection that guaranteed survival of the fittest.

Then somewhere very high in the evolutionary pedigree, consciousness emerged as a product of highly developed and organized matter, the central nervous system or brain. At a certain point of its development—not clearly identified by mechanistic science—matter, previously blind and inert, suddenly became aware of itself. Although the mechanism involved in this miraculous event entirely escapes even the crudest attempts at speculation, it is taken for granted and represents a fundamental postulate of the materialistic and mechanistic world-view.

The belief that consciousness is a product of matter is not, of course, entirely arbitrary. It reflects a vast mass of observations, particularly from clinical and experimental neurology, showing clear connections between various conscious processes and physiological or pathological processes such as traumas, tumors or infections in the brain. Brain contusions, anaesthesia, or restriction of blood supply will lead to loss of consciousness. A temporal tumor is associated with changes of consciousness that are quite specific and different from those accompanying, for example, a prefrontal tumor. These connections are so consistent and predictable that they can be used in establishing neurological diagnosis. In some instances, the distortions of conscious processes can even be corrected by neurosurgery, pharmacotherapy, or other medical interventions.

Although close correlations between consciousness and cerebral structures or processes have been established beyond any reasonable doubt, mechanistic science tends to misinterpret correlation for cause. The logical inconsistency of its conclusions is analogous to a faulty conclusion that, for example, television programming is caused by components of the TV set. A knowledgeable TV mechanic can correct problems with the picture or sound by repairing the TV components. But since television is a human-made invention, none of us would see these repairs as scientific proof that the program must be, therefore, generated by the components. It simply means that the integrity of the set is a necessary prerequisite for the integrity of sound and picture. To conclude otherwise is to mistake connection for cause, but this is the kind of faulty conclusion that mechanistic science draws from neurological findings. It is worth mention here that in his last book *Mystery of The Mind*, pioneering neurosurgeon Wilder Penfield expressed deep disbelief that consciousness is a product of the brain and can be explained in terms of neurophysiology.[6]

Materialistic psychology explains mental processes as reactions of the organism to the environment and/or recombinations of previous sensory input stored in the brain. In this it adheres to John Locke's empiricist credo that "nihil est in intellectu quod non antea fuerit in sensu." (There is nothing in the mind that was not previously in the senses.) Memories of any kind have to have a specific material sub-strate—the cells of the central nervous system or the physiochemical code of the genes. Access to any new information is possible only through direct sensory input or through combination of old and newly acquired data. Mechanistic science thus tries to explain even such phenomena as human intelligence, creativity, art, religion, eth-ics, and science itself as products of material processes in the brain. But the probability of human intelligence developing all the way from the chemical ooze in the primeval ocean to its present stage solely through random mechanical processes has been aptly com-pared to the probability of a tornado blowing through a gigantic junkyard and assembling by accident a 747 Jumbo-jet.

In the reductionistic world-view of mechanistic and materialistic science, there is no place for mysticism and religion. Spirituality is seen as a sign of primitive superstition, intellectual and emotional immaturity, or even severe psychopathology that science will one day explain in terms of deviant biochemical processes in the brain. Mainstream psychoanalysis, for example, interprets unitive and oce-anic states of the mystics as a regression to primary narcissism and infantile helplessness, and it interprets religion as an obsessive-com-pulsive neurosis of humanity.[8] Psychoanalyst Franz Alexander de-scribed the states achieved by Buddhist meditation as self-induced catatonia.[9] Western anthropologists see shamans as mentally ill who suffer from schizophrenia or epilepsy, and refer to the initiatory ex-periences that mark the onset of the career of many shamans as "shamanic illness." The report of the Group for the Advancement of Psychiatry interpreted mysticism as an intermediate phenomenon be-tween normality and psychosis.[10]

Although Newtonian-Cartesian science has acquired great pres-tige, the mechanistic paradigm, once a progressive and powerful tool for science, has become a strait-jacket, seriously impeding further evolution of human knowledge.

A paradigm is more than just a useful theoretical model for sci-ence; its philosophy has a powerful indirect influence on society. Newtonian-Cartesian science has created a very negative image of human beings, depicting them as biological machines driven by bestial instinctual impulses. This image endorses competition and the principle of "survival of the fittest" as natural and essentially healthy tendencies. Contemporary science, blinded by its model of the world as a conglomerate of mechanically interacting separate units, has been unable to recognize the vital importance of cooperation, synergy, and ecological concerns. Technological achievements that have the potential to solve most of the problems plaguing humanity—nuclear energy, lasers, space age rocketry, cybernetics, and the miracles of modern chemistry and bacteriology—have turned into menaces.

In the last decades, the authority of mechanistic science has also been undermined from within. As Fritjof Capra demonstrated in *The Tao of Physics* and *The Turning Point*, developments in the twentieth century physics have questioned and transcended every postulate of the Newtonian-Cartesian model. Astonishing explorations of both the macro-world and the micro-world have created an image of reality which is entirely different from the seventeenth century model used by mechanistic science. The myth of solid and indestructible matter, its central dogma, disintegrated under the impact of experimental and theoretical evidence that the fundamental building blocks of the universe—the atoms—were essentially empty. Subatomic particles showed the same paradoxical nature as light, manifesting either particle properties or wave properties depending on the arrangement of the experiment. The world of substance was replaced by that of process, event, and relation. In subatomic analysis, solid Newtonian matter disappeared. What remained were activity, form, abstract order, and pattern. In the words of the famous mathematician and physicist Sir James Jeans, the universe began to look less like a machine and more like a thought system.[11]

Newton's three-dimensional space and uni-dimensional time were replaced by Einstein's four-dimensional continuum of space-time. In new physics, the objective world cannot be separated from the observer, and linear causality is not the only and mandatory connecting principle in the cosmos. The universe of modern physics is not the gigantic mechanical clockwork of Newton, but a unified network of events and relations. Prominent modern scientists Eugene Wigner, David Bohm, Geoffrey Chew, Edward Walker, Gregory Bateson, Fritjof Capra, and Arthur Young believe that mind, intelli gence, and possibly consciousness are integral parts of existence rather than insignificant products of matter.[12]

Although quantum-relativistic physics provides the most convincing and radical critique of the mechanistic world-view, important revisions have been inspired by various avenues of research in other hard sciences. Scientific thinking has also been changed by developments in cybernetics, information theory, systems theory and the theory of logical types. According to Gregory Bateson, thinking in terms of substance and discrete objects represents a serious epistemological mistake—error in logical typing.* In everyday life, we deal not with objects but with their sensory transforms or with messages about differences; in Korzybski's sense, we have access to maps, not the territory. Information, difference, form and pattern that constitute our knowledge of the world are dimensionless entities that cannot be located in space or time. Information flows in circuits that transcend the conventional boundaries of the individual and include the environment. This way of scientific thinking makes it absurd to treat the world in terms of separate objects and entities; to see the individual, family or species as the Darwinian units of survival; to draw distinctions between mind and body; or to identify with the ego-body unit (Alan Watts' "skin-encapsulated ego"). Emphasis has shifted from substance and object to form, pattern and process.†

Systems theory has made it possible to formulate a new definition of the mind. This theory holds that any constellation of events that has the appropriate complexity of closed causal circuits and the appropriate energy relations will show mental characteristics, i. e., respond to difference, process information, and be self-corrective. In this sense, cells, tissues, and organs of the body; a cultural group or

---

*Most important aspects of this criticism of mechanistic science can be found in Gregory Bateson's *Steps To an Ecology of Mind* and *Mind and Nature: A Necessary Unity.*

†This conceptual conflict between mechanistic science and the modern revolutionary developments represents a replica of the ancient conflict between major schools of Greek philosophy. The Ionic school—Thales of Miletos, Anaximenes, Anaximandros and others—considered the basic philosophical question to be "What is the world made of?", "What is its basic substance?" In contrast, Plato and Pythagoras believed that the critical issue is its form, patterning and order. Modern science is distinctly neo-Platonic and neo-Pythagorean.

nation; an ecological system; or even the ettire planet (Gaia theory) can be said to have mental characteristics. And when we consider a larger mind that integrates all the hierarchies of the lower ones, even a critical and skeptical scientist like Gregory Bateson has to admit that this concept comes close to that of an immanent God.

Another profound criticism of mechanistic science has emerged from the work of the Nobel laureate Ilya Prigogine and his colleagues in Brussels and in Austin, Texas.[13] Traditional science depicts life as a specific, rare, and ultimately futile process—an insignificant and accidental anomaly involved in a Don Quixotean struggle against the absolute dictate of the second law of thermodynamics. This gloomy picture of the universe, dominated by an all-powerful tendency toward increasing randomness and entropy, and moving relentlessly toward a thermal death, belongs now to the history of science. It was dispelled by Prigogine's study of the so-called "dissipative structures"* in certain chemical reactions and his discovery of their underlying principle—"order through fluctuation." Further research revealed that this principle is not limited to chemical processes but represents a basic mechanism of revolution in all domains—from atoms to galaxies, and from individual cells to human beings, and further to societies and cultures.

These observations enable a unified view of evolution in which the unifying principle is not the steady state, but the dynamic conditions of the non-equilibrium systems. Open systems on all levels and in all the domains are carriers of an over-all evolution which ensures that life will continue to ever newer and dynamic complexity. Whenever systems in any domain become stifled by past entropy production, they mutate toward new regimes. The same energy and the same principles thus carry evolution on all the levels, whether it involves matter, vital forces, information, or mental processes. Micro- and macro- cosmos are two aspects of the same unified and unifying evolution. Life is not seen any longer as a phenomenon unfolding in an inanimate universe; the universe itself becomes increasingly alive.

---

*"Dissipative structures" derive their name from the fact that they maintain continuous entropy production and dissipate the accruing entropy by exchange with the environment. The most famous example is the so-called Belousov-Zhabotinski reaction, which involves oxidation of malonic acid by bromate in a sulphuric acid solution in the presence of cerium, iron, or manganese ions.

Although the simplest level on which self-organization can be studied is the level of dissipative structures which form in self-renewing chemical reaction systems, applying these principles to biological, psychological and socio-cultural phenomena does not involve reductionistic thinking. Unlike the reductionism of mechanistic science, such applications are based on fundamental homology, on the relatedness of the self-organizing dynamics on many levels.

From this point of view, humans are not higher than other living organisms; rather, they live simultaneously on more levels than life forms that appeared earlier in evolution. Here science has rediscovered a truth of perennial philosophy: the evolution of humanity forms an integral and meaningful part of universal evolution. Humans are important agents in this evolution; rather than helpless subjects of evolution, they *are* evolution. Like quantum-relativistic physics, this new science of becoming, replacing the old science of being, shifts emphasis from substance to process. In this context, structure is an incidental product of interacting processes, and, in Erich Jantsch's words, it is no more solid than a standing wave pattern in the confluence of two rivers or the grin of a Cheshire cat.*

The latest serious challenge to mechanistic thinking is the theory of British biologist and biochemist Rupert Sheldrake, expounded in his revolutionary *A New Science of Life*.[14] Sheldrake has offered a brilliant critique of how mechanistic science explains morphogenesis during individual development and evolution of species, genetics, and instinctual and more complex forms of behavior. Mechanistic science considers only the quantitative aspect of phenomena, which Sheldrake calls "energetic causation." It has nothing to say about the qualitative aspect—the development of forms or the "formative causation." According to Sheldrake, living organisms are not just complex biological machines, and life cannot be reduced to chemical reactions. Form, development and behavior of organisms are shaped by morphogenetic fields of a type that at present is not recognized by physics. These fields are molded by the form and behavior of past organisms of the same species through direct connections across both space and time. These fields show cumulative properties; if a certain number of members of a species develop certain organismic

*See Erich Jantsch's *Design For Evolution* (Braziller, New York, 1975) and *The Self-Organizing Universe* (Pergamon Press, New York 1980) for further information.

14   *Stanislav Grof*

properties or learn a specific form of behavior, these are automatically acquired by other members of the species, even if there exist no conventional forms of contact between them. The phenomenon of "morphic resonance," as Sheldrake calls it, is not limited to living organisms and can be seen in such elementary phenomena as the growth of crystals.

However implausible and absurd this theory might appear to a mechanistically oriented mind, it is testable. Even at present, in its early stages, it is supported by experiments with rats and observations of monkeys.* Sheldrake is aware that his theory has far-reaching implications for psychology and has discussed its relationship to Jung's concept of the collective unconscious.

Another dramatic revision of the mechanistic world-view is the holonomic theory of the universe formulated by David Bohm, former coworker of Albert Einstein and author of basic texts on both relativity theory and quantum physics. According to Bohm, the phenomenal world that we observe in our ordinary states of consciousness represents only one aspect of reality—the explicate or unfolded order. Its generative matrix—the implicate or enfolded order—exists on another level of reality and cannot be directly observed, except possibly in episodes of non-ordinary consciousness, such as deep meditative, mystical or psychedelic states. Like many other famous physicists, including Niels Bohr, Erwin Schroedinger, Robert Oppenheimer, and Albert Einstein, Bohm finds modern physics compatible with the mystical world-view.[15]

The famous neurosurgeon Karl Pribram has developed a new model of the brain that in the future might converge with Bohm's theory of holomovement.[16] Pribram was able to demonstrate that, in addition to digital processing, the brain also performs parallel processing which involves holographic principles. Pribram's model not only explains a number of otherwise puzzling aspects of the brain function, but opens entirely new perspectives for speculations

*The most famous example is the anecdotal observation reported by Lyall Watson in *Lifetide* (Bantam Books, New York, 1980), and referred to as the "hundredth monkey phenomenon." When a young female Japanese monkey (Macaca fuscata) on the island Koshima learned an entirely new behavior—washing raw sweet potatoes covered with sand and grit—this behavior was not only transmitted to her immediate peers, but appeared in monkeys on neighboring islands when the number of monkeys reached a certain critical number.

about mystical and psychedelic states, parapsychological phenomena, spiritual healing, and many other problem areas that were previously excluded from serious scientific inquiry. Although it is at this point premature to talk about an integrated holonomic theory of the universe and of the brain, it is very exciting that both approaches are using similar and compatible explanatory principles.

This discussion of new and promising developments in science would not be complete without mention of the work of Arthur Young. His theory of process is a serious candidate for a scientific metaparadigm of the future. It organizes and interprets in a most comprehensive way the data from a variety of disciplines—geometry, quantum theory, theories of relativity, chemistry, biology, botany, zoology, history, psychology, and mythology—and integrates them into an all-encompassing cosmological vision. Young's model of the universe has four levels defined by degrees of freedom and of restraint, and seven consecutive stages: light, nuclear particles, atoms, molecules, plants, animals, and humans. Young was able to discover a basic pattern of the universal process that repeats itself continuously on different levels of evolution in nature. The explanatory power of this metaparadigm is complemented by its predictive power. Like Mendeleyev's periodic table of elements, it is capable of predicting natural phenomena and their specific aspects.

By assigning a critical role in the universe to light and the purposeful influence of the quantum action, Young made it possible to bridge the gap between science, mythology, and perennial philosophy. His metaparadigm is not only consistent with the best of science, but it is also capable of dealing with non-objective and non-definable aspects of reality far beyond accepted limits of science. Since it is not possible to do justice to Young's theory without detailed excursions into a variety of disciplines, those who are interested in this approach are referred to his original writings.

Although it is not yet possible to integrate the various revolutionary developments in modern science discussed here into a cohesive and comprehensive new paradigm, they all seem to have one thing in common: their proponents share a deep belief that the mechanistic image of the universe created by Newtonian-Cartesian science is no longer an accurate and mandatory description of reality. By far the most far-reaching challenges to the Newtonian-Cartesian paradigm have emerged in the fields of depth psychology and modern consciousness research. As the authority of mechanistic science is collapsing, serious researchers are rediscovering and re-evaluating a broad spectrum of data that in the past have been suppressed or even ridiculed because of their incompatibility with the old paradigm. At the same time, vast amounts of new revolutionary observations are being generated by laboratory consciousness research, psychedelic therapy, experiential psychotherapies, field anthropology, parapsychology, and thanatology.

Parapsychological researchers Joseph Banks Rhine, Gardner Murphy, Stanley Krippner, Jules Eisenbud, Charles Tart, Elmer and Alyce Green, Arthur Hastings, Russell Targ, and Harold Puthoff have done meticulous scientific work that suggests the existence of telepathy, remote viewing, psychic diagnosis and healing, Poltergeist, or psychokinesis. This avenue of research has attracted the attention of modern physicists and it has become a serious theoretical challenge to incorporate its findings into the new paradigm.

Another major area of psychology that challenges the Newtonian-Cartesian paradigm and is receiving increasing scientific recognition is Jung's work. The two dominant orientations in Western psychology, behaviorism and Freudian psychoanalysis, have created mechanistic models of the psyche: behaviorism in its extreme form attempts to exclude consciousness from psychology and to reduce mental functioning to reflex activity and to the stimulus-response principle, and Freudian psychoanalysis sees psychological phenomena as derivatives of base instincts and biological functions. But Jung discovered the collective unconscious, myth-forming properties and far-reaching healing potentials of the psyche, and the existence of archetypes—transindividual dynamic patterns in the psyche that not only transcend the boundaries of the individual, but represent an interface between consciousness and matter (psychoids).[18] Whereas Freud's individual unconscious is an inferno of instinctual forces and suppressed and rejected psychological tendencies, Jung's psychology returns the cosmic status to the psyche and re-introduces spirituality into psychiatry.[19] Unlike Freud, who tried all through his life to raise the prestige of psychology by reducing it to Newtonian mechanics, Jung was aware that his findings were incompatible with the existing philosophy of science and required an entirely new paradigm. He followed developments in quantum-relativistic physics with great interest and was deeply influenced by his personal interactions with Wolfgang Pauli and Albert Einstein.[20] Several decades of psychedelic research have also generated data of critical importance for the new paradigm. Various cultural groups throughout the world have long used plants with powerful psychedelic properties for ritual and healing purposes. The legendary plant and potion *soma* played a critical role in the development of Vedic religion and philosophy. Pre-Columbian Central American cultures used a broad spectrum of psychedelic plants; the best known of these are the Mexican cactus *peyote*, the sacred mushrooms *teonanacatl*, and the morning glory seeds, or *ololiuqui*. South American Indians of the Amazon have used for centuries decoctions from the jungle liana *yagé* or *ayahuasca*. In Africa, many tribes know the secret of the psychedelic plant *eboga* and ingest it in smaller doses as a stimulant, and in larger amounts as a sacrament in their rituals. The tomb of a shaman found during the excavations of the New Stone Age settlement from the sixth millennium B.C. in Catal Hüyük in Turkey contained plants that according to pollen analysis were specimens with psychedelic properties. Preparations from several varieties of hemp have been smoked and ingested under various names (hashish, charas, bhang, ganja, kif, marijuana) in the Oriental countries, in Africa, and in the Caribbean area for recreation, pleasure, healing, and ritual purposes. They have been important sacraments for such diverse groups as the Indian Brahmans, several orders of the sufis, African natives, ancient Skythians, and the Jamaican Rastafarians. According to recent research, ergot alkaloids similar to LSD were used in the famous Eleusinian mysteries in ancient Greece. Both Plato and Aristotle were initiates of these mysteries and their systems of thought were deeply influenced by their experiences in them.[21] Swiss chemist Albert Hofmann's sensational discovery of the semi-synthetic psychedelic LSD inspired a wave of interest in psychopharmacology.[22] The alkaloids responsible for the effects of most of the above sacred plants have now been isolated in pure form as mesacaline, psilocybine, psilocin, lysergamid, bufotenin, dimethyltryptamine, tetrahydrocannabinol, harmin, and ibogain.

It has become evident that the Western model of psyche, with its narrow biographical orientation, is inadequate to account for a wide spectrum of phenomena occurring in psychedelic states. Under the catalyzing influence of these remarkable psychoactive drugs, experimental subjects have experienced not only autobiographical sequences, but also powerful confrontations with birth and death, and an entire gamut of phenomena that have been named "transpersonal." The rediscovery of these experiences and the recognition of their heuristic relevance has been one of the major incentives for the development of a new movement in psychology—the transpersonal orientation.[23]

In the ordinary state of consciousness, a person is expected to identify experientially with his or her body image, to be Alan Watts' "skin-encapsulated ego." It is generally possible to experience with all the sensory qualities only the present moment and the present location. Recall of the past is without the sensory vividness of the present moment, and experiencing the future is considered absurd and impossible in principle. Perception of the here and now is limited by the sensory organs' physical and physiological characteristics.

In transpersonal experiences, one, two, or more of the above limitations appear to be transcended. The sense of one's identity can expand beyond the body image and encompass other people, groups of people, or all of humanity. It can transcend the human boundaries and include animals, plants, or even inanimate objects and processes. Events that occurred in personal, ancestral, racial, phylogenetic, geological or astronomical history, and even future events can be experienced with vividness ordinarily reserved only for the present moment and location. In the extremes, one can experientially identify with the whole planet or the entire cosmos at various points of their development.

Experiences of this kind can bring instant intuitive knowledge that by far exceeds the intellectual capacity and educational background of the individual. While consciously identifying with another person, one can gain access to that person's thoughts, feelings, physical sensations, or memories. During episodes of animal identification, one can have detailed insights into animal psychology, instinctual dynamics, reproductive cycles, or courtship dances of the species involved. Plant experiences can similarly mediate new and accurate insights into botanical processes such as photosynthesis, sprouting of seeds, growth, pollination, or exchange of minerals and water in the root system. The same is occasionally true for inorganic processes, such as birth and death of stars, subatomic events, and dynamics of cyclones or volcanic eruptions. Racial memories in the Jungian sense or past incarnation experiences are frequently associated with new information about cultures and historical periods, their architecture, costumes, weaponry, religious rituals, or social structure. Similarly, the content of ESP experiences such as precognition, clairvoyance, or astral projection can frequently be independently confirmed as accurately reflecting reality.

It is even more remarkable that experiences accurately portraying various aspects of the phenomenal world can alternate in unusual states of consciousness with experiences that have no basis in what is called in the West "objective reality" such as archetypal visions of deities or demons and mythological sequences from different cultures. Even these experiences can impart entirely new information; they reflect accurately, and frequently in great detail, the mythologies of the cultures involved. The nature and quality of this information is typically far beyond the educational level or even intellectual capacity of the individual involved. Some of the most encompassing transpersonal experiences are of a cosmic and transcendental nature; here belongs identification with the Universal Mind or Cosmic Consciousness (Sacchidananda) or the experience of the Supracosmic and Metacosmic Void (Sunyata).

Transpersonal experiences are not limited to psychedelic states. They occur in new experiential psychotherapies such as neo-Reichian approaches, primal therapy, psychosynthesis, Gestalt practice, marathon sessions, and various forms of rebirthing. They are particularly frequent in the process of holonomic integration developed by my wife Christina and myself.[24] It is a technique that combines controlled breathing with evocative music and focused body work. That many spiritual practices can induce transpersonal experiences is now being confirmed by an increasing number of Westerners who experiment with transcendental meditation, Zen practice, Tibetan psycho-energetic exercises, or forms of yoga.

The new understanding of transpersonal phenomena mediated deep insights into an important subcategory of non-ordinary states of consciousness labeled and treated by Western science as psychotic and thus indicative of mental disease. These can now be interpreted as "spiritual emergencies" or "transpersonal crises"; if properly treated, they can result in psychosomatic healing, personality transformation, and consciousness evolution. Ancient and Eastern cultures have not only developed elaborate cartographies for these states, but also have powerful techniques to induce them. Various rites of passage of aboriginal cultures, ancient death-rebirth mysteries, spiritual healing ceremonies, shamanic practices and secret initiations are salient examples.[25]

Various transpersonal phenomena have also been described in the context of non-drug laboratory techniques of consciousness alteration such as biofeedback, developed by Elmer and Alyce Green, Barbara Brown, Joe Kamiya and others; sensory isolation and sensory overload; use of various kinaesthetic devices such as the "witches cradle"; use of non-authoritative forms of hypnosis; and the "mind games" developed by Jean Houston and Robert Masters.[26]

Another important source of fascinating data about transpersonal experiences is the young discipline of thanatology, the study of death and dying. Clinical observations of people who are near death and those who have died and been resuscitated confirm essentially the descriptions of death in spiritual literature, particularly from the ancient books of the dead such as *The Tibetan Bardo Thödöl*, the Egyptian *Pert em Hru,* and the European *Ars moriendi* or *Art of Dying*.[27] The original data collected by Karlis Osis in *Death-Bed Observations of Physicians and Nurses,*[28] Raymond Moody in *Life After Life*,[29] and Elisabeth Kübler-Ross are now being confirmed by more systematic studies such as Kenneth Ring's *Life At Death,*[30] and American cardiologist Michael Sabom's *Recollections of Death*.[31] Sabom used a careful scientific approach to re-examine the claims of previous studies and ancient books of the dead that, following clinical death, many people have out-of-the-body experiences in which they accurately perceive near or remote events. He was able to confirm that these people describe in many instances minute details of the circumstances following their deaths, including the use of specific interventions and esoteric gadgets that are not commonly known to laymen. It would be difficult to come up with a more dramatic example of a critical challenge to the Newtonian-Cartesian mechanistic science and its interpretation of the relationship between consciousness and the brain than a situation involving a clinically dead person, lying on the back with the eyes closed and witnessing accurately the events in the room from the vantage point of the ceiling, or even events occurring in another room of the building, or in a remote location.

The most exciting aspect of all the above revolutionary developments in modern Western science—astronomy, physics, biology, medicine, information and systems theory, depth psychology, parapsychology and consciousness research—is the fact that the new image of the universe and of human nature increasingly resembles that of the ancient and Eastern spiritual philosophies—the different systems of yoga, the Tibetan Vajrayana, Kashmir Shaivism, Zen Buddhism, Taoism, Kabbalah, Christian mysticism, or gnosticism. It seems that we are approaching a phenomenal synthesis of the ancient and the modern and a far-reaching integration of the great achievements of the East and the West that might have profound consequences for the life on this planet.

REFERENCES

1. HUXLEY, A. *Perennial Philosophy*. London: Fontana, 1958.
2. FREUD, S. *Civilization and Its Discontents*. New York: Norton Press, 1962.
3. KORZYBSKI, A. *Science and Sanity: An Introduction to Non-Aristotelian Systems and General Semantics*. Lakeville, Conn.: The International Non-Aristotelian Library Publ. Co., 1933.
4. KUHN, T. *The Structure of Scientific Revolutions*. Chicago, Ill.: University of Chicago Press, 1962.
5. CAPRA, F. *The Tao of Physics*. Berkeley, CA.: Shambhala Publications, 1975. See also Capra, F. *The Turning Point*. New York: Simon & Schuster, 1982.
6. PENFIELD, W. *The Mystery of the Mind*. Princeton, N.J.: Princeton University Press, 1976.
7. LOCKE, J. "An Essay Concerning Human Understanding." In *The Works of John Locke*. London: T. Tegg, 1823.
8. FREUD, S. "Obsessive Acts and Religious Practices." *Collected Papers*, vol, 6, Institute of Psychoanalysis, Hogarth Press, London, 1924.

22   *Stanislav Grof*

9. ALEXANDER, F. "Buddhist Training As Artificial Catatonia." *Psychoanalyt. Rev.* 18 (1931): 129.

10. Group for the Advancement of Psychiatry, Committee on Psychiatry and Religion: *"Mysticism: Spiritual Quest or Psychic Disorder?"* Washington, D.C., 1976.

11. JEANS, J. *The Mysterious Universe.* New York: Macmillan, 1930.

12. See WIGNER, E. *Symmetries and Reflections.* Bloomington, Ind.: Indiana University Press, 1967; CHEW, G.F. "Bootstrap: A Scientific Idea?" *Science* 161 (1968): 762; BOHM, D. *Wholeness and the Implicate Order.* London: Routledge and Kegan, 1980; WALKER, E.H. "The Nature of Consciousness." *Mathemat. Biosciences* 7 (1970): 138; BATESON, G. *Mind and Nature: A Necessary Unity.* New York: E.P. DUTTON, 1979; and BATESON, G. *Steps to An Ecology of Mind.* San Francisco, CA.: Chandler Publications, 1972; CAPRA. op. cit.; and YOUNG, A.M. *The Geometry of Meaning.* New York: Delacorte Press, 1976.

13. PRIGOGINE, I. *From Being to Becoming: Time and Complexity in the Physical Sciences.* San Francisco, CA.: W.H. Freeman and Co., 1980.

14. SHELDRAKE, R. *A New Science of Life: The Hypothesis of Formative Causation.* Los Angeles, CA.: J.P. Tarcher, 1981.

15. See BOHM. op. cit.

16. PRIBRAM, K. *Languages of the Brain.* Englewood Cliffs, N.J.: Prentice-Hall, 1971. See also PRIBRAM, K. "Non-Locality and Localization: A Review of the Place of the Holographic Hypothesis of Brain Function in Perception and Memory." Preprint for the Tenth ICUS, November 1981.

17. See YOUNG. op. cit.

18. JUNG, C.G. "On the Nature of the Psyche." *Collected Works*, vol. 8, Bollingen Series XX. Princeton, N.J.: Princeton University Press, 1960.

19. JUNG C.G. *"Symbols of Transformation." Collected Works* vol. 5., Bollingen Series XX. Princeton, N.J.: Princeton University Press, 1956.

20. See PAULI, W. "The Influence of Archetypal Ideas on the Scientific Theories of Kepler." In *The Interpretation of Nature and the Psyche.* Bollingen Series LI. New York: Pantheon Books, 1955.

21. See WASSON, R.G. et al. *The Road to Eleusis: Unveiling the Secrets of the Mysteries.* New York: Harcourt, Brace Jovanovich, 1978; Croissant, J.: *Aristôte et les mystères.* Faculté de Philosophie et Lettres, Liège, 1932; and Plato, "Phaedrus." In *The Collected Dialogues of Plato.* Bollingen Series LXXI. Princeton, N.J.: Princeton University Press, 1961.

22. HOFMANN, A. "The Chemistry of LSD and Its Modifications." In

D.V. SIVASANKAR et al. *LSD: A Total Study*. Westbury, N.Y.: PJD Publications Ltd., 1975.

23. Sutich, A. "The Emergence of the Transpersonal Orientation: A Personal Account." *J. transpersonal Psychol.* 8 (1976): 5.

24. GROF, S. Journeys Beyond the Brain. Manuscript pending publication.

25. GROF, S., GROF, C.: *The Concept of Spiritual Emergency: Understanding and Treatment of Transpersonal Crises*. Mimeographed manuscript. See also GROF, S. HALIFAX, J.: *The Human Encounter with Death*. New York: E. P. Dutton, 1977 and GROF, S., GROF, C., *Beyond Death*. London: Thames and Hudson, 1980.

26. MASTERS, R.E.L., Houston, J. *Mind Games: The Guide to Inner Space*. New York: Dell Publ. Co., 1972.

27. See RAINER, R. Ars Moriendi: *Von der Kunst des heilsamen Lebens und Sterbens*. Koeln, Graz: Boehlav Verlag, 1957.

28. New York: Parapsychology Foundation, 1961.

29. Atlanta, GA.: Mockingbird Press, 1975.

30. New York: Coward, McCann, & Geoghegan, 1980.

31. New York: Harper & Row, 1981.

2

Frances Vaughan   The Transpersonal Perspective

It is said that when Robert Oppenheimer, who was credited with the invention of the atomic bomb, witnessed the first nuclear explosion, what flashed through his mind were two lines from the Bhagavad Gita in which God speaks: "I am become death, the shatterer of worlds;/ Waiting that hour that ripens to their doom."[1]

In the past, we believed Kipling's refrain that "East is East and West is West/ And never the twain shall meet." But today we think more of the next two lines: " 'Till earth and sky stand presently/ At God's great Judgment Seat." Kipling's "presently" has arrived with the nuclear age, and it is human beings who now have the power of judgment and the power to shatter the world. It has now become our responsibility to find the wisdom that will enable us to step back from the brink of destruction and to create a viable global society.

Will we be able to find that wisdom? Only in joining our efforts, in joining East and West, can we hope to turn this time of fear into a time of transformation. We will never, however, be able to build a desirable human society on an inadequate picture of human nature. So we must pay attention to the ancient wisdom and attempt to incorporate into our lives what we have learned from the ancient traditions.

The transpersonal perspective is a meta-perspective, an attempt to learn from all different perspectives. It does not attempt to impose a new belief system or a new metaphysics, but rather to see the relationship between existing world views, in order to create something that can be truly transformational in our world. The transpersonal perspective is what has been emerging from the needed integration of ancient wisdom and modern science. Science without wisdom can destroy the world; wisdom without science remains ineffectual. The transpersonal perspective sees the eastern and western approaches as complementary, and recognizes the transcendental mystical unity of all religions. Mystical teachings all agree that the source of wisdom is within. We need to have access to this source of wisdom if we are going to turn the tide of destruction in this time and age. Each tradition has a different way of saying this. In Christianity, it is: "The Kingdom of God is within." In Buddhism, enlightenment is the discovery of our own true nature. In Hinduism, the inner search culminates in Self-realization as Atman. In psychology, we speak of the Transpersonal Self as that part of us which has access to the perennial wisdom.

We need to recognize that there comes a time when we can no longer rely on external teachings and teachers to tell us what to do. The transpersonal movement is unique in that it has no charismatic leader. Rather, it is an organic movement that has grown by networking, a movement that has drawn people to it who share a concern, a purpose, and a vision of what is possible for humanity. It is a movement in which all are equal participants, all equal co-creators of our realities. It is an organic, interrelated form of working in which considerable emphasis is placed on self-determination, self-actualization, self-realization, and self-transcendence. It is cross-cultural and interdisciplinary: though it has roots in the ancient perennial philosophy, it makes use of modern science because science, like mysticism, is a search for truth. It is simply a different way of looking.

I like to think of wisdom as a blending of consciousness and love. The Dalai Lama often speaks of our need for compassion in the world, and Mother Theresa speaks about our need for love. We discover this not from any outside picture, but only in our direct experience, when we are willing to remove the obstacles to awareness of love's presence in our lives. We can then become participants in our personal transformation and in the transformation of society. We all need to find the source of wisdom in our own inner experience, and then join together to share it with each other. My own experience of the transpersonal movement is that it has been empowering.

Part of the transpersonal purpose is to evoke the higher potential in human beings. It aims at the wise use of technology and resources, recognizing that the human mind is one of our greatest, inexhaustible resources, and it attempts to understand the transformational process so that it can be facilitated and encouraged. It sees the possibility of growth towards wholeness, and that means growing beyond ego. It does not mean moving into transcendence instead of ego, but sees ego development as a stage along the way. We can use the ego strength that we develop in normal, healthy adult development, and go beyond it, seeing ego development as midpoint on the great chain of being. As conscious beings emerging out of the pre-personal, less conscious aspect of our lives, we move through ego development—and all of the alienation that is associated with being indentified with ego—into a transpersonal awareness which extends beyond the personal goals of ego development. The transpersonal orientation recognizes that we all exist in a web of mutually conditioned relationships based on awareness of our interdependence with each other and with the environment. We see that we are not only shaped by our environment, but that we are also the shapers of that environment.

It is important to emphasize the difference between pre-personal and transpersonal states, because not all non-ego states are transpersonal. Charles Tart defines higher states of consciousness as those states in which attributes and functions in addition to all those of the normal waking state are available.[2] These higher states should not be confused with altered or sub-optimal states. Transpersonal development is development beyond ego, not a substitute for ego or regression to pre-egoic states.

Transpersonal psychology has attempted to expand the field of inquiry to include the spiritual dimension of our lives. The term "transpersonal" means, literally, "beyond the personal," or "beyond the personality." We recognize, therefore, that who and what we are is not limited to personality, and that when we are identified solely with the body, the ego, or the personality, we have a limited, constricted view of ourselves. Transpersonal psychology seeks to bring about a balance of inner and outer experience and awareness, recognizing that these are two sides of a mutually interdependent reality. Before transpersonal psychology became a separate branch of psychology, the term "transpersonal" had been used by Jungians to describe the underlying ground of ego psychology. It had also been used by Stanislav Grof to describe experiences he observed in research of LSD psychotherapy. In his *Realms of the Human Unconscious,* Grof describes transpersonal experiences as those in which ego boundaries are dissolved and awareness is extended beyond the ordinary confines of time and space.[3]

In the late 1960's Stanislav Grof, Anthony Sutich, and Abraham Maslow, among other psychologists, began to integrate some of their understanding of humanistic psychology with Eastern traditions. Abraham Maslow and Anthony Sutich felt that the term "transpersonal" would be appropriate to this new branch of psychology, and Sutich, editor of the *Journal of Humanistic Psychology,* launched the *Journal of Transpersonal Psychology* in 1969.

Tony Sutich was a remarkable man. When he died in 1976 at 62 years of age, he had lived an amazingly active life in spite of the fact that a baseball injury had totally paralyzed him in his teens, and he had spent the rest of his life flat on his back on a gurney. But he could read and talk, and he talked by telephone with people all over the world. He was active in civil rights and made a living as a psychotherapist. He started both the humanistic psychology movement and the transpersonal psychology movement, not as a charismatic leader, but as a facilitator. Tony knew how to empower others to actualize their potential. When I first met him in 1965, at a seminar on humanistic psychology at Esalen Institute, I had not known that the leader of the workshop I was attending would be totally paralyzed. I was surprised, impressed, and never more inspired than I was at that time. I then decided to go back to school for a Ph.D. to become a psychologist. I learned a lot from Tony and from working on the *Journal* as an associate editor in the early years.

Now under editor Miles Vich, the *Journal* continues to publish original empirical research and theoretical articles that probably would not be published by mainstream journals. It has always sought to build on what has been done before; specifically, to build on both western psychology and on eastern mysticism. I was impressed by the fact that the editors of the *Journal* engaged in very lively discussion about papers that were submitted. Sometimes editors would have totally opposing viewpoints, and diversity of opinion was encouraged. Everyone was heard, and nobody seemed attached to opinion. All were great friends despite their differences. This was my first experiential contact with the idea of not being attached to an opinion or a point of view, seeing how powerful that kind of diversity could be, how much love came out of it, and how an organization could work with cooperation and caring.

Perhaps the leading theoretician in the field of transpersonal psychology is Ken Wilber, whose remarkable work compares with Jung's, Freud's and William James'. His first book, *The Spectrum of Consciousness,* compares the transpersonal with other views of consciousness. His second book, *The Atman Project,* is a transpersonal view of human development from infancy to Self-realization, as Atman. His most recent publication, *Up From Eden,* is a transpersonal view of human evolution. It is useful to make a distinction, as Ken Wilber has, between the different realms of knowledge: the empirical or sensory realm; the mental or rational realm, which is concerned with values and meaning; and the spiritual or transcendent realm, which is concerned with insight and truth. Each realm of knowledge has its own way of acquiring information; each has its own rules for validation. We make a category error if we attempt to reduce one to the other, and attempt to interpret the findings of one in terms of the other. For example, we need to recognize that we can never find empirical validation for the truth of mathematical theorems or values such as meaning and purpose and love in the world. Likewise, we can never hope to appreciate the spiritual insights of those people who have undertaken the rigorous disciplines of contemplation and meditation merely by an intellectual understanding of what they have attempted. These different realms of knowledge can only be understood in and of themselves. To attain any of them requires training. Most of us would not dream of visiting a physics lab and pretending to evaluate what is being done there if we are not trained as physicists; yet we are all quite happy to evaluate spiritual teachers without having done any homework at all. We need to acknowledge that each realm of learning requires training if we want to really delve into what it has to offer us.

In the realm of empirical research in transpersonal psychology, much work is being done on the physiological correlates of altered states of consciousness, and the therapeutic effects of meditation. Stanislav Grof's work and Elmer and Alyce Green's biofeedback research at the Menninger Foundation is notable. While I was traveling in India, I had the opportunity to visit a laboratory of the Institute of Mental Health in Bangalore, where study of the physiological correlates of yoga and an interesting consciousness project are being conducted. Daniel Brown, at Harvard, is studying the effects of meditation on perceptual sensitivity. In addition, the Institute of Neotic Sciences* is funding studies of exceptional human abilities, optimum health, and well being. Work is also being done on the effects of what we have come to call the consciousness disciplines, essentially the eastern meditative disciplines. Social scientist Duane Elgin, in *Voluntary Simplicity,* collects evidence that when people undertake some of these consciousness disciplines, changes in lifestyle and values result.[4] Elgin has found a large movement, in the United States, of people whose lifestyles are changing in the direction of voluntary simplicity, mainly as a result of their having incorporated some of the eastern disciplines into their lives. More evidence of the social transformation that is underway can be found in Marilyn Ferguson's *The Aquarian Conspiracy.*[5]

Applications of transpersonal psychology are being reflected in developments in education and psychotherapy. Transpersonal education takes an expanded view of human capacities, emphasizing the integration of physical, emotional, mental and spiritual aspects of well being. It also emphasizes service as the application of this learning in the world. At the California Institute of Transpersonal Psychology, where I teach, there are five areas of emphasis: physical, emotional, mental, spiritual, and community. Every student does some physical discipline, such as Aikido or T'ai Chi, and all do emotional work, or have clinical training and participate in group process. They study the theory of transpersonal as well as general psychology, and they all are expected to have some spiritual discipline of their own choosing. No one belief is supported; rather, there is an emphasis on a willingness to question beliefs, and a willingness to have not only an intellectual understanding of more than one tradi-

* "Noetics" is from the Greek word for mind.

tion, but also an experiential knowledge of a tradition. Transpersonal theory needs to be informed by that experience. We cannot just talk about spirituality; it needs to be an experiential realization. Enlightenment does not come simply from following the wisdom teachings. It comes through direct experience. In order for the experiential component to inform the theory that comes through us, there needs to be the experiential work as well. This work is also important in our emphasis on community, which translates intellectual work and personal transformation into community service.

In transpersonal psychotherapy, as in education, many new developments have come from the work of therapists who were trained traditionally and who then became interested in Eastern disciplines. Born from the experience of therapists who felt that greater exploration of their own spiritual growth could have a profound effect on their work, transpersonal psychotherapy distinguishes the context of therapy, which is established by the beliefs, values, and attitudes of the therapist, from the content of therapy, which is established by the client. A transpersonal therapist may not necessarily deal with transpersonal content, but may facilitate the growth of the client from a pre-personal state of disintegration to an integrated ego state.

A transpersonal therapist can also be expected to be qualified and capable of working with people who are ready to grow beyond ego, people who come to therapy because they have been disillusioned or disappointed with the attainment of ego goals. There are two ways of arriving at disappoinment: One is by not getting what one wants; the other is by getting what one wants. We all know how success often can leave one feeling empty and depressed. An existential crisis is sometimes precipitated by a brush with death, sometimes by an experience of loss, or sometimes by the experience of success. That point, when we are really willing to confront death and aloneness and the nature of our existence in the world, often is the beginning of a transpersonal awakening that can lead us through the existential crisis of despair. What we have called the dark night of the soul is perhaps better renamed the dark night of the ego.

The transpersonal content of therapy, then, is that which comes from a client who is having transpersonal experiences or who is ready to move into transpersonal areas of exploration. Sometimes people feel disturbed by transpersonal experiences which have happened spontaneously, as the result of meditative practice, or as the result of unsupervised use of psychedelics. Whatever the cause, therapists who have some understanding and knowledge of the transpersonal dimension are increasingly needed. People who are experiencing a spiritual emergency do not feel adequately cared for by therapists who have not explored their own spirituality and who are not prepared to deal with it in their practice.

It should be emphasized that the transpersonal perspective is open-ended, and that it is in process—not fixed, finished or done with. Each one of us is participating in a process that is unfolding, an evolution of consciousness. The holonomic theory is a wonderful metaphor because it implies that all exists in each of us, and each exists in all of it. We only imagine that we are separate from all that is. This is the illusion. When we wake up to who and what we really are, we discover that we are all in it together. Each of us has an important part to play, and each of us has to learn to discover what our unique part will be. We find that sometimes under the guidance of teachers, but finally we find it in turning inward and getting in touch with our inner guidance. Our teachers tell us that, too. Our gurus remind us that we need to contact the universal Self within our hearts in order to find the wisdom that will guide our personal growth as well as our social transformation.

None of our leaders has any source of wisdom that is not available to each one of us. They, too, must look within, to find access to that universal source. We all need to take responsibility for our own lives and relationships.In the words of the great Indian teacher, Gautama Buddha:

Do not believe in what you have heard. Do not believe in traditions because they have been handed down for many generations. Do not believe anything because it is rumored and spoken of by many. Do not believe merely because the written statement of some old sage is produced. Do not believe in conjectures. Do not believe merely in the authority of your teachers and elders. After observation and analysis, when it agrees with reason and it is conducive to the good and benefit of one and all, then accept it, and live up to it.

Kalamas Sutra[6]

32   *Frances Vaughan*

REFERENCES

1. As cited in SMITH, H. *The Religions of Man.* New York: Harper & Row, 1958.
2. TART, C. *Transpersonal Psychologies.* New York: Harper & Row, 1975.
3. GROF, S. *Realms of the Human Unconscious.* New York: Viking, 1975.
4. ELGIN, D. *Voluntary Simplicity.* New York: Morrow, 1981.
5. FERGUSON, M. *The Aquarian Conspiracy.* Los Angeles: J.P. Tarcher, 1980.
6. KALAMAS SUTRA. As cited in *Transpersonal Psychotherapy,* edited by S. Boorstein. Palo Alto, CA.: Science and Behavior Books, 1980.

Part II

ANCIENT SPIRITUAL
TRADITIONS

3

Swami Muktananda   Understanding Your Own
Mind

Many psychologists, psychiatrists, scientists, and philosophers have
come from all over the world to attend this conference. You are all
interested in the mind, and the mind is the subject which I have been
given for my talk. If you understand your own mind through psychology, if you come to know the nature of the mind, then you also
come to know the Truth. Once you know that Truth, you see the
same Truth in everyone, and you welcome everyone with great love.
Bearing this in mind, I welcome you all.

The mind is a great gift from God. Without the mind, you are not
a human being. You are called a human being only because you
have a mind. Therefore, through your own mind, understand your
own value. The mind is so strong. Understand its power. Allow the
mind to become one-pointed, because when the mind is concentrated, it turns within and taps the source of serenity and tranquility.
When the mind becomes peaceful, it is able to give that peace to the
world. That serenity prevails everywhere and is able to help other
people.

In order to strengthen the mind and to help other people, a psychologist should meditate. He should make his own mind very clean
and very pure. In this way, he should identify with his own inner
power and should become very strong from within. When a psychol-

ogist meditates on his own inner Self, when he understands his own true nature, he becomes filled with incredible compassion for other people, and as a result of the kindness that he feels he is able to help them. Through compassion and kindness, he can make others improve and become free from addictions. It is very important for a psychologist to develop these qualities.

If your mind is not pure and clean, if you do not take joy in others' good fortune, if you do not experience pain in others' misfortune, then your life is totally meaningless. Not only that, as long as your own mind does not become free from all its defects, whatever effort you make to teach others or to console them will remain only a play of your mind. It will not benefit anyone. We have a habit of constantly teaching others. All our effort goes into teaching and helping others, and we let ourselves deteriorate more and more. A person does not understand his own condition. He imagines that he has improved himself and then tries to improve others. However, he has not really improved himself.

While I was in Piedmont, California, during my second world tour, a group of healers came to see me. All of them complained about one thing or another. One said, "After doing so much healing my arms have become exhausted." Another said, "My legs have become so weak." Still another said, "My mind is so upset." All of them lacked luster; there was no radiance in their faces. When I had heard their complaints I said, "Your problems are totally authentic. You really deserve to experience what you are experiencing." Then I laughed. Because I laughed and said such things, the healers became upset. I explained to them, "I speak the truth. I do not speak for the sake of pleasing you. The truth of the matter is that every person's vibrations, every person's feelings, constantly flow out of his body. A healer's vibrations are transmitted into a patient, and a patient's vibrations are transmitted into a healer. As you work with a patient for a long time, his vibrations enter your body, and you are affected by them. As a result, you yourself become a patient." This is what had happened to the healers. They had performed healings on thousands and thousands of people, but they themselves had become patients.

In the same way, if you try to practice psychology without understanding your own mind, you only run into difficulties. Many years ago, an article from *New Age* magazine was read to me. It said that more psychologists and psychiatrists were mentally ill than people of any other profession. Many psychologists have self-doubt. They are filled with self-contempt. A psychologist does not try to attain his own power, the power of the mind, through which he would be able to affect a patient immediately in a very powerful way. Instead, he only talks to a patient for hours on end, not realizing how much he himself is being affected by the patient's illness.

How can a healer or a psychologist overcome his predicament? If a psychiatrist realizes the power of his own mind, if through meditation he actually contacts the energy which powers the mind, then he can become strong enough so that his patients' vibrations do not affect him, and he can really help them. In our ashram in India, we try to keep the atmosphere very clean and pure through chanting, through the repetition of God's name, and through meditation. The environment in the ashram is so strong that no outsiders can affect it through their feelings and vibrations. Instead, they themselves are uplifted. Visitors to the ashram sometimes complain, saying, "If you go to that ashram you have to chant all the time. You have to become so totally immersed in chanting and meditation that you have no time to gossip and socialize with other people." But it is through these practices of chanting and meditation that a person makes his mind strong.

The sages of ancient India were the greatest psychologists. They understood that there is nothing more important in the life of a human being than the mind. The mind is the source of all knowledge. Whatever you understand, you understand only through the mind. Although you have five senses of perception and five organs of action, without the help of the mind no sense in this body can work. One thing is certain: all the senses are under the control of the mind. If somebody is talking to you while your mind is wandering, you will not hear what the person is saying. Only when your mind is engaged do you receive the information gathered by the senses.

The location of the mind is the heart, and the mind is supported by the *prana shakti,* the vital force. A great Upanishadic sage said, "O my son, the mind is bound by the prana." The Upanishads say that the vital force arises from the Self. This vital force moves constantly and the mind is one with it. As a result, the mind thinks and thinks endlessly. The mind is so active. In this world there is no human being who has escaped his mind. The mind harasses even the highest yogis until they reach the nirvikalpa state, the state free from thoughts. The mind is so tricky, so treacherous. You never know how the mind will torture you, how the mind will trick you, how the mind will make you fall into any pit. The *Bhagavad Gita* says that when the mind pursues the senses, which continually bring in information from outside, a person becomes like a ship which is driven everywhere by the storm of his own mind. Eventually, the mind makes him sink.

It is said that a human being is what he thinks. Whatever he feels and thinks is what he becomes. We are so careful about so many things in our lives. We take care of all our files; we have so many counselors; we receive so much advice of all kinds. Yet we do not think about our own minds. We never try to keep our minds under our control. If you allow your mind to run free without reins, then it becomes totally immersed in your negative feelings. It becomes filled with anger, shame, and all kinds of petty feelings, and you identify yourself with that pettiness. Whatever thought you entertain, whatever thought you harbor, is what you become. If you think of yoga, you become a great yogi. If you think about the psychology of the mind, you become a great psychologist. If you have inferior thoughts all the time, then you fall into that pettiness. So be very vigilant regarding your thoughts. A great being, Tukaram Maharaj, said, "It does not matter whether you are among multitudes or in solitude, you will receive the fruits of whatever thoughts are in your mind." God dwelled in Tukaram's mind, and for this reason he saw only God everywhere. In a very beautiful poem, he said, "O Lord, I offer my salutations to everybody with the understanding that everybody is You." Tukaram had this kind of experience because of the power of his own mind. He said, "I have given up all feelings of difference, all distinctions. I have not done this because I am whimsical, but because I want to experience the Truth. This Truth was proclaimed by all the scriptures, all the Vedas. These scriptures were not manmade: they emanated from God." Due to the power of his own thought and of his constant contemplation, Tukaram attained the awareness that God pervades everywhere. A person always attains what he constantly contemplates.

This reminds me of a story. Once Sheik Nasrudin had a neighbor who was taking care of a buffalo. The buffalo had two beautifully curved horns. Every day Sheik Nasrudin watched the buffalo. He admired its strength and beauty, and he particularly admired its beautiful horns. He began to think, "If I were to sit on the buffalo's forehead right between its two horns, I would feel as though I were sitting on the throne of Delhi!" Day after day Nasrudin thought about this. His obsession grew more and more intense. He thought about the buffalo's forehead even in his dreams. As luck would have it, one day the buffalo went and sat down in Nasrudin's courtyard. Immediately, Nasrudin jumped on the buffalo's forehead. He sat there and held on to the horns. Immediately the buffalo stood up, shook itself and threw Nasrudin off. Nasrudin fell to the ground and broke his back. He began to scream for his beloved wife. He cried, "O my beloved, I am so hurt. Please take me inside and give me a massage." Nasrudin's wife Fatima helped him inside and began to give him a warm towel treatment. As she was treating him, she talked to him. She said, "Darling, why didn't you think before you sat on the forehead of that buffalo?"

"O my dull-witted wife," replied Nasrudin, "I have been thinking about sitting on that buffalo's forehead for a whole year!"

This is how the mind affects your life. You think and think, and then you get the fruits of your thoughts. The mind is the source of all calamities, of all pain and all pleasure. You have bad thoughts and you have good thoughts. Sometimes you see what is bad as good and what is good as bad. You continually revel in the movements of the mind. You can control the mind only by knowing the mind. You will know the mind when you know the source of the mind, when you discover how the mind has come into existence.

What is the source of the mind? The philosophers of Kashmir Shaivism say, "Do not think that the mind is a material substance. The mind is simply a contracted form of the universal consciousness." This universal consciousness has given rise to the splendid world full of sentient beings and insentient objects. Consciousness has not used any external materials to create this cosmos. It has created it out of its own being upon its own screen. It is this same universal consciousness which has become the mind. In the *Bhagavad Gita* the Lord says, "This entire world is the product of My own mind." Therefore, know the mind. Know the value of the mind; know the worthiness of the mind; know the sublimity of the mind. If you understand your own mind completely, then you are not just a human being: you yourself are God.

The sages who knew the Truth said, "Every human being is nothing but God." Nevertheless, this is not our experience. Our experience is that we are limited. And our sense of limitation is because of the mind. The *Katha Upanishad* says that the Self becomes the limited experiencer when it is equipped with the senses and the mind. The sages of Kashmir Shaivism explain this very well. Kashmir Shaivism states that when the supremely free consciousness, in the process of creating the world, descends from its lofty and sublime state it becomes more and more limited, and takes the form of the objects of perception. Operating through the senses of perception, it considers itself an individual experiencer. Operating through the organs of action, it considers itself an individual doer. When it is in this limited form, it is called the mind. So the human mind is nothing but consciousness in a contracted form. When that contracted consciousness separates itself from outer objects and turns inside through meditation, then it again becomes pure consciousness. This is the true greatness and power of the mind.

In its limited state, the mind is plagued by all kinds of feelings, thoughts, and imaginings. These are called *vikalpas*. From one thought, many thoughts arise, and from one thought, all thoughts are destroyed. *Vikalpas* are the source of all kinds of feelings and emotions, such as attachment, aversion, envy, hatred, jealousy, and greed. They make a person believe that what is true is false and what is false is true. However, if you use the power of the mind to create positive thoughts, to create within yourself the understanding that your true nature is consciousness, then your own mind can lead you towards the truth. When you make your mind pure through right understanding, you can attain the thought-free state. And then you will experience your own inner power. The great sage Maharishi Patanjali, who was also a great psychologist, said in his *Yoga Sutras: yogash chitta-vritti nirodaha*—"Yoga is the stilling of the modifications of the mind." When the mind is controlled through meditation and right understanding, then the inner Self which is the source of the mind reveals itself on its own.

For this reason the Upanishads say that the same mind which is the cause of bondage is also the cause of liberation. The mind gives birth to so many kinds of suffering. However, if you free the mind from thoughts, you perceive this world as a paradise. To free your mind from thoughts, turn within and meditate. Through the power of thought you can become a great scholar and give many lectures. You can read many books, and you can also write many books. But to give your mind its true power, you should maintain the stability of your mind through meditation. If you maintain the strength of your mind, then you can really help many people; other people will benefit from the power of your mind. If a psychologist maintains the stability of his mind, he becomes a treasured gift to the world.

4

Mother Teresa   Love Until it Hurts

Make us worthy, Lord, to serve our fellow men
    throughout the world
who live and die in poverty and hunger.
Give them to our hand this day their daily bread
and by our understanding love, give peace and joy.

We read in the scripture that God loved the world so much that He gave His son, Jesus, to come and bring the good news. The greatest science in the world, in heaven and on earth, is love. He came to give that good news to you and me and to proclaim it to the poor: that God is love and that He loves you and He loves me. Jesus Christ proved that love by giving His life, and again and again he kept saying, "Love one another as I have loved you."

I think this loving is the greatest science that we have to learn: to love until it hurts. To be able to love, we need to pray, because prayer gives a clean heart and the fruit of prayer is the deepening of faith. If we have a clean heart we can see, we can understand, we can accept each other, and we begin to love. When we really love, we begin to serve. We all want to love God because we have been created for that. The same loving hand of God has created you, created me, and created that man dying in the street.

This morning two people died in our home. They were picked up from the streets of Bombay, brought to our home, and died. They really went home to God. The other day in Calcutta, I had brought a man from the street, and he was at his last. After being given tender love and care, he looked at the sister and he said, "I'm going home to God," and he died. The sister had prepared him to die in peace with God, to go home to God, and that was the last word in his mouth. That man understood what is love. This is something we must pray for, to bring in our life that real oneness with God. To be able to do that we need a clean heart, to be able to see God in each other. Jesus said very clearly that at the hour of death we are going to be judged on what we have been to each other. And he says:

> I was hungry, you gave me to eat. I was naked, you clothed me. I was homeless, you took me in. I was lonely and you spoke to me. I was sad and you smiled at me.

This is a great science. The greatest science in the world is love. Science is a gift of God, given to you—for what? It is to give to others, to share. It is His gift to you and what we have to do is to use that to be His love and compassion. Today God loves the world through us. He has given you this gift and each one of you has got something special. To do what? To destroy? No, it is His tender love and care that God is concerned about. We need science not to destroy, but to come to know better, to help each other better, to love not by words but by living action.

I will never forget an experience we had some time ago in Calcutta. We did not have sugar for some time and a little Hindu child, four years old, heard that Mother Theresa had no sugar and he went home and told his parents, "I will not eat sugar for three days. I will give my sugar to Mother Theresa." It was so little, what he brought after three days, but it was great love. He taught great science: to love until it hurts.

This is something for what you have gathered here. You must pray for that gift of God, to allow God to use you to proclaim the good news. The world is dying of hunger for that love, for that knowledge. You have come from so far, from everywhere, to help each other, to know, to be able to love and to exchange means and ways of that greater love, the love that Christ has shown to each one of us. We all know that; let us put that into action and let us get to know where that love begins—at home.

Today people have no time—they are so busy. They have no time even to smile at each other. Let us bring back God into our lives, bring back prayer into the family life, for the family that prays together, stays together. If you stay together, you will pray, and you will love one another as God loves each one of us. It is very important for us to be able to have a life of peace, of joy, of unity. I do not know if there is any greater science than the science of love for one another. We must learn like that little child that it is not how much we give but how much love we put into the giving. God does not expect extraordinary things. After I had received that Nobel prize, many people came and gave; they fed our people, they brought clothes, they did beautiful things. One afternoon I met a beggar in the street, and he came up to me and he said, "Mother Teresa, everybody is giving to you. I also want to give to you, but today, the whole day, I have just got ten pais and I want to give you that."

I cannot tell you the joy, the radiant joy on his face, because I took that ten pais, knowing that if he does not get anything today, he will have to go to bed without eating; but also knowing that it would have hurt him so much if I did not take it. The joy and expression of peace and love in his face, I cannot express to you. I can tell you one thing, that in accepting that ten pais, I felt it was much greater than the Nobel prize because he gave all that he had and he gave with so much tenderness.

This is the greatness of love. Let us try to find that love and put it into action. Where is God? We know God is everywhere. Deep down in our hearts we all have that desire, that flame burning there, that desire to love God. How do we love God whom we do not see, if we do not love one another whom we do see? When you see a person in the street, who is he to you? Your brother, your sister, because the same loving hand that has created them has created me and you. And that is where I would like you today.

Let us pray, because that is the greatest science when we may learn the fruit of that love. To be able to love is important, especially today, in this world where there is so much killing, so much hatred, so much destruction. Why? Because people do not know each other, do not have time for each other, and do not pray. If we pray, we will naturally come to know each other, because we will have a clean heart and we will truly see each other. We will see God in each other, and then we will begin to love with a tender love. We read it in the scriptures where God speaks:

I have called you by your name. You are mine. Water will not drown you. Fire will not burn you. I will give up nations for you. You are precious to me. I love you.

This is God speaking and we must speak that language to each other. Where? At home first. I feel that gift of God that God has given to each one of you. It has been given to you not to keep, not to destroy, but to bring joy, peace, unity and love. This is what I say about abortion. Science that has discovered all kinds of things has also found ways of destroying the unborn child. What a terrible thing! What a terrible murder of an innocent, helpless child, who has been created in the image of God, to love and to be loved. So let us pray that we do not use the gift of God—our brain—to work alone. The brain, to work, must be the fruit of the heart. To be able to work we must listen, for God speaks in the silence of the heart. Then only do we speak from the fullness of our heart. Whatever God has given you, those wonderful brains, he has given to you to use for His glory and the good of all people. Let us pray that none of you ever use that gift to destroy God's image, never to use that gift to break love, to destroy love, to destroy unity, to cause hatred or greed, but to use it to bring people together into greater love, greater peace and greater unity. And where we learn these things very well is from our poor people.

We, the sisters and I, have visited people who have nothing and nobody, who are unwanted, unloved, uncared for—and not only in India. In India and in Africa we have people who are hungry for bread, but in the United States, Europe and in all the places where our sisters are working, people are hungry for love: to be wanted, to be loved, to be somebody to somebody. Once in the streets of London or New York I took the hand of somebody sitting in the street. He took my hand and said, "Oh, for so many years this is the first time I feel the warmth of a hand. Nobody has ever, for so many years, touched my hand. I have not felt a human love or warmth of a hand." I will never forget that. We see yet we pass, and we pass so many whom we see. Maybe in our own homes we have somebody lonely, somebody feeling unwanted, somebody crippled.

The last time I went to Venezuela, I found that a very rich family had given us a plot of land on which to build a home for our crippled children. When I visited the family to thank them, there was their first child, terribly crippled, terribly disabled. When I asked the mother, "What is his name?" she said, "We call him 'Professor of Love' because he continually teaches us how to love." Professor of Love—such a beautiful name given by the mother herself, and by the family. I learned from him how to smile; there was a big smile on that child's face. Why? Because he was teaching the whole time. This is where love begins, at home.

Love begins at home, and comes home. Much of the suffering of our children today is of children who come home from school and find no one there. There is no grandmother or grandfather, mother and father are very busy, and there is no one to receive the child. The child needs that tender love, that tender appreciation, that tender embrace from mother or father; without it, the child goes back to the street. Let us bring that love home. If we love one another as God loves each one of us, then there will be peace. We do not need bombs and guns and all kinds of things to bring peace. We need tender love and compassion and the sharing, the joy of loving one another, as God loves each one of us. God bless you.

5

Dastoor Minocher Homji   The Cows are Many
Colors, But the Milk
Is the Same

Yatha ahū vairyō
athā ratush ashat-chit hachā
Vanheush dazdā mananhō
shyaothenanam anhēush Mazdāi
Kshathrem-chā Ahurāi ā
yim drigubyō dadat vāstāram.

As the Lord is best to be adored, so is the Prophet, on account of
his being ever-associated with Righteousness, with the uprightness of
pure mind acquired of the deeds of life unto Mazdā, and whom the
power of self-control from Ahurā gives protection for the self-
restrained.

Ahuna-Vairya (Yasna 27.13)

The priest follows the prince. In ancient times, the priest and the
prince ruled the roost. We are here to sow. The ancient Indian
wisdom says, "gavām anekavarnānām kśīrasyāstu ēkavarnatā":
"The cows are of many colors, but the milk, the nourishing element, is the same." Let us not fight about the color and the size of
the cows. Let us mix the nourishing element.

An American wit has said it well when he was asked questions on
matter and mind. "What is mind? No matter. What is matter? Never
mind." I am not telling this only to laugh away your blues, but to

47

ask you to please think over this American sutra. I am personally thinking upon this, the mutual bond between matter and mind. We must not brush aside matter as something bad. It is the foundation; it is that clay pot in which the thinking, the feeling, the sympathizing spirit dwells. Let us make the most of this matter and mind.

I also always dwell upon the Chinese wisdom, especially the wisdom of Kung Fu, otherwise known as Confucius. He said that "reading without thought is useless, but thought without study is dangerous." All around, especially in the field of religion, we see thought without study, and that really is dangerous. I would like to address those who Albert Einstein called the "custodians of religion." Afraid to incur the wrath of the priests, he used this happy term. As custodians of religion, let us always talk sense. Let us always be reasonable. Science keeps within the limits of thought, always basing its inference on evidence. We can also do that in the field of religion. Somebody has defined religion as "an insurance in this world against fire in the next, for which honesty is the best policy."

Of course, I do not substantiate this definition of religion. I have held all along, in my working life of forty-six years, that religion is really the way of good life. Nothing more. All the rest is commentary. In the *pater noster* of Zoroastrianism, with which I began, religion fixes three goals. The first is truth, *satyam*, the second is wisdom, *prajñā*, and the third is service, *sēva*. I think it is for her service that Mother Teresa is respected and revered, not for her thought, or for her words. It is her dedicated service to the cause of humanity for which she has been respected and will always be respected.

In Zoroastrianism, the accent is likewise on action, not on thoughts and words. This is the order: words are good, thoughts are better, but actions are the best. When I say that in religion truth is the most important plank, I am very fond of quoting Mark Twain. Mark Twain was once told that "several prophets have come and gone, several apostles have followed them, and all have taught by their personal example and their teachings, that truth is the best. How is it that man is still resorting to lies?" In his characteristic manner, Twain said, "Well, well, truth is so very precious that man is naturally economical in its use." Let us not be economical in truth. I think the world suffers because we are economical in truth, in wisdom.

The ancient Persian wisdom said, "Look at the composition of the head of man. God has given me two shining eyes, two ears, but only one tongue, so that I may see twice, I may listen to words of wisdom twice, and speak but once. But our affairs are in the reverse gear. We see but once, we listen to the words of wisdom but once, and make up for the loss with our tongues." I think the world suffers for want of deliberation of thought.

Ancient Iranian wisdom said that man's first stage is dormancy. Neither the Hindus nor the Parsees are fire worshippers. We worship light, which is the visible symbol of the invisible Supreme Being, who is all light. In the Bhagavad Gita, God is called, "jyotiśam jyoti." In the Koran, Allah is called, "nur ulanuar." We also say that God is the "light of lights," and we have the famous Vedic prayer, "Oh, light divine, guide us on the path of truth." The Muslim prays: "Oh Allah, lead our steps firm on the path of truth."

These are the sutras of common heritage upon which we shall build our future civilization with the marriage of science and religion. Science cannot step out of its boundary, but religion, unfortunately, does. Let us end by asking, "Is not religion, rightly understood, the pledge of peace and bond of brotherhood?"

6

Father Bede Griffiths   Science Today and the New
Creation

What light can modern physics and evolutionary theory throw on
the doctrine of the New Creation? St. Paul derived his doctrine from
the Jewish tradition. The Bible begins with the words, "In the beginning God created the heaven and the earth," and ends with the
words of the Apocalypse, "I saw a new heaven and a new earth."
Thus the whole Christian revelation is set between these two poles
of the first and second creation. In Jewish tradition, this new creation was conceived in terms of a new age, the Messianic age, which
would be inaugurated by an intervention of God in history, described in symbolic language in the Apocalypse. St. Paul inherits this
tradition, but gives it a new interpretation by affirming that in the
death and resurrection of Jesus, this new age has begun, and the new
creation has actually come into being. So he is able to say, "If anyone is in Christ, there is a new creation," a *Kaine Ktisis*.

To be "in Christ" for St. Paul is to participate in this new creation, to enter into a new mode of existence in which the old world
of this creation has passed away, and a new world has come into being. St. Paul expresses this dramatically in the letter to the Romans
in which he says that "the whole creation has been groaning in travail until now." This introduces a new note of dynamic movement:
the creation is seen not merely as waiting for an intervention of God,

50

but as actually "groaning in travail"—undergoing a kind of gesta-
tion by which it is being prepared for this great event. St. Paul then
describes exactly what this preparation is for, saying that "the creation waits with eager longing for the revealing of the sons of God."
We can now see the purpose of this travail; it is to bring to birth a
new humanity, a New Man, which will be revealed when man becomes a "son of God"; that is, when the human nature is united
with the divine. This event, St. Paul believes, has already taken place
in Christ, when Jesus was raised from the dead and his human nature was finally transfigured by the divine.

The New Creation, we can therefore say, is a further stage in evolution, when our present mode of human existence is transcended.
Man begins to "partake of the divine nature," to transcend the limits of the present space-time universe, and to experience a new mode
of existence and consciousness as far beyond our present mode of
existence as ours is beyond that of an animal. This event, St. Paul
believes, has already taken place in Christ, but it is destined to extend to all mankind and to the whole creation. So it was the plan of
God to "bring all things to a head in him, everything in heaven and
on earth." We can now see the full scope of St. Paul's thought. The
whole creation, from the beginning, is moving towards a fulfillment
when man will be raised to a higher level of existence and consciousness. With him the whole universe will be transfigured, passing beyond its present level of existence in space and time and participating in an external and infinite mode of existence, understood as the
divine.

Let us now see what light modern physics can throw on this. According to Fritjof Capra in *The Tao of Physics*, the division between
matter and mind, between existence and consciousness, which has
prevailed from the time of Descartes and Newton, has now been
overcome. The universe is now conceived as a "web of relations between various parts in a unified whole" of which the human mind is
an essential part. We live in what has been called a "participatory
universe." Nature is not an "extended substance," outside the human mind, but an integrated whole. "What we observe," as Heisenberg said, "is not nature itself, but nature exposed to our method of
questioning." In other words, the object of all scientific knowledge is
not nature itself—or the "thing as such," as Kant called it—but na-

ture mirrored in the human mind and senses, with the instruments we use to extend the range of the senses. We can, therefore, no longer maintain a separation between mind and matter. Just as we ourselves are a psychosomatic unity, so the universe as a whole, as far as we can know it, is a psychosomatic unity.

This means we must consider that consciousness is present in the universe in some way from the beginning. The mathematical order in the structure of the atom, for instance, is a sign of an intelligence at work in matter. In the ancient world, Aristotle and the Arabian philosophers considered that the stars were intelligences, an idea with which the teaching of Sri Aurobindo is related. I consider Sri Aurobindo the greatest philosopher of modern India. Responsible for introducing the theory of evolution into Vedantic philosophy, Sri Aurobindo maintained with all Vedantic philosophers that Ultimate Reality is also pure consciousness. It is *sachidananda*, or absolute Being (*sat*) in pure consciousness (*cit*) which is experienced as perfect bliss (*ananda*). This is the ideal state of being according to all Vedantic philosophy, the state of being in pure consciousness. But according to Aurobindo, the Absolute Being, *Sachidananda*, becomes "involved" in matter. It withdraws its consciousness and allows matter to appear as being, without consciousness. As matter evolves through the *shakti*, the energy inherent in it, and develops more complex organisms, the divine consciousness manifests itself as life. There is evidence today of a kind of consciousness in plants, and in animals consciousness is beginning to manifest itself in sensations, feelings and instinctive intelligence. Finally, in man, we emerge into rational, or what Sri Aurobindo calls "mental," consciousness. The distinctive theory of Aurobindo is that mankind today is in a state of evolution from mental consciousness to supramental consciousness.

The Western world has for centuries developed the rational, analytical consciousness, and this has now reached the limits of its development. We are beginning to discover the need to develop the other form of consciousness, the intuitive consciousness that has been developed in the East from the time of Buddha and the Upanishads through the present day. The intuitive consciousness has been developed by Muslim and Christian as well as Hindu and Buddhist mystics, but the western world has concentrated for two centuries almost exclusively on the rational activity of the mind, and it now has to learn the opposite process by contact with the thought and the meditative techniques of the East. In Sri Aurobindo's thought, various stages lead from the first awakening of the intuitive mind, to the development of what he calls the "overmind," to the attainment of the supreme consciousness with the "descent of the Supermind."

Sri Aurobindo's conception of the Supermind as a "descent" is particularly interesting. In Hindu thought the growth of consciousness is normally seen in terms of an ascent from man to God. But Sri Aurobindo introduced two extremely interesting and original ideas. He conceived that as the mind ascends towards God or the Divine, it is met with a corresponding movement of descent from above, and, further, the Supermind descends not only into the soul or psychic consciousness, but also into the body or physical consciousness. Both Aurobindo and the Mother, who accompanied him in all his work, were attempting to transform the body so that it would not be subject to death. Their attempt was not successful, but it corresponds to a deep human instinct which urges us to seek for an immortal body, a diamond body, as it has been called in Buddhist tradition.

I want to suggest that these two ideas of Sri Aurobindo, though unusual in the Hindu tradition, correspond very closely with what I have described of the Christian tradition in St. Paul. In the Christian belief, the body of Jesus in the resurrection underwent precisely this transformation, which was followed by a descent of the Spirit at Pentecost when the divine Spirit released by the resurrection of Jesus was communicated to his disciples. The doctrine of the resurrection of the body and the descent of the Spirit are, of course, traditional Christian doctrines, but we can now see how these doctrines can be illuminated in the light of modern physics. Once we conceive of the human body not simply as an extended substance but as a "field of energies," it becomes much less difficult to understand how a dead body could be transformed in such a way that the energies which had been structured in a particular way to form that human body could be so penetrated by consciousness that they would begin to obey a different law. Here I would like to introduce a quotation from Whitehead that seems to throw light on this subject.

The doctrine which I am maintaining is that the whole concept of materialism applies only to very abstract entities, the product of logical discernment. The concrete enduring entities are organisms so that the plan of the whole influences the various subordinate organisms, which enter into it. In the case of an animal the mental states enter into the plan of the total organism and thus modify the plan of those successive organisms such as electrons. Thus an electron within a living body is different from an electron outside it by reason of the plan of the body, that is, the general plan of the body including its mental states.

I am suggesting that as consciousness enters into matter, it gradually transforms the structure of the field of energies which makes up that material form. In the resurrection we can conceive of the divine consciousness—the sachidananda—taking possession of a human body and transforming it from within so that the very electrons and other particles begin to obey a new law. This idea links up with Rupert Sheldrake's theory in *A New Science of Life* that there must be formative causes as well as energetic causes in nature. Energy of itself is indeterminate; it has no specific structure. Sheldrake suggests, therefore, that just as there are fields of energy, whether gravitational or magnetic, so there must be what he calls "morphogenetic fields," which are responsible for the organization of matter. The complex organization of atoms and molecules and cells cannot be due to chance; there must be powers of organization in the universe—what Aristotle called formal causes—that are distinct from material causes. We can conceive of a hierarchy of causes which is responsible for the organization of atoms, molecules, cells and organisms in ever greater complexity. In human beings these formative causes become conscious, so that to some degree we can take responsibility for the organization of our bodies. I suggest that as consciousness develops in man, this power of organization increases until conscious organization can take control of the body, and the atoms, molecules, cells and other organs begin to obey a new law.

It is conceivable, then, that the Spirit, or the divine power, took possession of the body of Christ at the resurrection, so that it was no longer subject to the normal laws of space and time. His body in the resurrection could appear and disappear, no longer conditioned by space and time. Finally, the bodily appearance ceased altogether and it became a "spiritual body," as St. Paul calls it, a body in which the elements have been brought totally under the control of consciousness, and matter and mind are integrated.

In this view, the resurrection of the body is the destiny of all mankind. From the beginning of history, the human body has been undergoing a gradual evolution as it comes more and more under the control of consciousness that is not the merely rational, scientific consciousness, but the deep intuitive consciousness that transforms the whole person. In the body of Jesus this final transformation took place, but it was not confined in its effects to Christ alone. No breakthrough in the spiritual sphere occurs in isolation. We are members of a "participatory universe," where every action in space and time, both physical and mental, affects every other organism. Every mystic who rises to a higher level of consciousness affects all human consciousness. The Enlightenment of the Buddha, for instance, released a power of consciousness that transformed a large part of the world and continues to do so in our own time. In the same way, the resurrection of Jesus released a power of transformation in the universe, the effects of which continue to be felt today. Considered the "mystical body of Christ," the Church is a kind of social organism in which this power of transforming consciousness, or supermental consciousness, as Sri Aurobindo calls it, is always present. This new consciousness is destined in the course of time to extend to all mankind.

Here we come to another important Pauline concept; that human society is an organism, modelled on the organization of the human body. In this view, all mankind forms one organic whole. As the great medieval Christian philosopher St. Thomas Aquinas said, "Omnes homines unus homo"; that is, all men are one man. This finds an echo in many ancient traditions. In the Hebrew tradition, Adam is Man, not just an individual man, but collective man, Man in his integral wholeness. We are all members of one another. No action throughout time and space is without effect on all men. Just as Sin disintegrates this body of mankind and causes conflict and destruction like a cancer in the body, so every movement towards truth and love, and every advance in human consciousness affects this total body of mankind. This concept of a Universal or Archetypal Man is found in the Muslim tradition of Ibn al Arabi, and in the Rig Veda it appears as Purusha, the Cosmic Man, of whom it is said, "one quarter is here on earth, three quarters are above in heaven." In other words, one quarter belongs to the physical world of matter, and three quarters to the transcendent world of consciousness. We have to conceive, therefore, that man is united not only by physical heredity, but also by a psychic heredity. There is a universal consciousness of which we all partake in varying measures. This is known as the *Mahat* in the Hindu tradition. It is a cosmic consciousness into which we enter as our normal consciousness expands, and we become aware of the transcendent dimension of humanity beyond space and time.

This transcendence of space and time is a key concept in all mystical experience. In our present mode of mental consciousness, we experience the world in terms of space and time; we experience everything separated in space and going from point to point in time. It is well known that modern physics calls this whole space-time system into question, and the transcendence of the space-time dimension is central in mystical experience. I suggest that this transcendence is the nature of the New Creation; that is, the world of the resurrection. Bodies will no longer be limited by space and time. Universal divine consciousness will so penetrate the human organism that the body will become as if transparent. All bodies in the universe will be seen as one Body, all the separate centers of consciousness will coalesce in the supreme consciousness, and in the end, as St. Augustine said of the Mystical Body of Christ in its final state, there will be "Unus Christus amans seipsum"—One Christ loving himself. That is, Christ will be loving himself in all his members, as though all humanity formed one Body, one organic whole, made up of innumerable cells, each distinct in itself yet all sharing in the one Consciousness of the whole Body.

If we conceive, then, of humanity converging on a new mode of consciousness in which the barriers of space and time are overcome, we also have to conceive of the whole universe as transcending space and time in the same way. This is what is implied in St. Paul's conception of the New Creation. It is to "bring everything to a head," everything in heaven and on earth, both matter and consciousness. Just as the material elements of the human body are transformed by the new consciousness, so also will the elements of the universe be transformed. This is what is meant by the "new heaven and the new earth" of the Apocalypse. If we want to form some idea of this final state of the universe, we have to appeal to the experience of the mystics.

Many people have had the experience of a unifying vision in which the whole creation seems to come together in unity. It is recorded in the life of St. Benedict that, one day when he was meditating, he saw the whole creation gathered together in a single ray of light. Plotinus gives perhaps the most profound description of this ultimate state in his description of the Archetypal world. Soul, he says—that is, the ordinary mental consciousness—"deals with one thing after another—now Socrates, now a horse, always some one entity among beings—but the Intellectual Principle," the *Nous* or pure consciousness, "is all, and therefore its entire content is simultaneously present in that identity. This is pure being in eternal actuality"—the *sachchidananda* of Hindu tradition. "Nowhere is there any future, for every then is a now; nor is there any past, for nothing there has ceased to be, everything has taken its stand forever." This intuition of absolute reality is identical in Hindu, Buddhist, Muslim, and Christian tradition.

A conception of the ultimate unity in being and consciousness of man and the universe, therefore, is common to all the main religious traditions and is based on the experience of the mystics in each tradition. What is novel today is that western science, which for centuries has been confined to a materialist conception of the universe, has now begun to discover in the light of relativity and quantum physics that time, space and matter are not absolutes, having an existence independent of the human mind. Matter and mind are interrelated and interdependent, and it is therefore not difficult to conceive how an eventual transformation of matter in consciousness could take place, verifying the experience of the mystics of both East and West. This, I have suggested, has its bearing on the Christian doctrine of the resurrection and the new creation. What the Christian doctrine would perhaps bring to the understanding of the final destiny of man and the universe is that in the final state, the world does not just pass away, and the human individuality is not lost. In the New Creation the whole universe is realized in the fullness of being, in the "pleroma," as St. Paul calls it, and every human being realizes his full stature as a member of the Mystical Body of Christ. Each person is united with every other person in the communion of the Spirit which is the Spirit of Love, and all persons together form one Person in the Supreme Person, the Purusha or Cosmic Person, or the Word of God, who draws all men and all things into unity of the one supreme consciousness, indivisible Being, Knowledge and Bliss—the divine Sachidananda.

7

Karan Singh   The Evolution of Consciousness
and Human Survival

Man today is at a crucial crossroads in his long and tortuous history upon this planet. The old is dying, the new is struggling to be born, and our generation, in particular, finds itself precariously poised between the past and future. Science and technology have given man tremendous, unprecedented power, but the question is whether this power will be used for creation or for destruction; whether, as Mother Teresa put it, it is going to be the power of love or the other power that is the dark side of the human psyche, the power of hate. Let us not forget that where there is sunshine, there is dark shadow also; where there is daylight there is night also, and today this essential ambivalence within the human psyche is coming more and more to the surface.

If we use science for beneficent purposes, it should be possible by the end of this century to abolish poverty, ignorance, illiteracy, disease, unemployment and hunger from the face of this earth. We have the resources today; we have the technological capacity; we have the administrative infrastructure. On the other hand, if this power continues to be used for destruction, we can abolish not only the human race but all life upon this planet. Man is surely the most destructive of all the species that has ever inhabited planet earth. The dinosaurs dominated this earth for millions of years, but when they left they

59

went comparatively quietly, and the world was still fit for habitation. But if and when we leave, we may leave this earth a charred cinder incapable of supporting any form of life whatsoever.

It seems to me that the future of the human race today is gravely threatened. Arthur Koestler has put forward the chiling hypothesis that man is a creature programmed for self-destruction, that there is something within the human psyche that will ultimately cause disaster. In this context I am fascinated with the ancient myth of Atlantis. Atlantis was a great and glorious civilization, prosperous beyond imagination, glittering with all the achievements of science and technology. And one day, we are told, Atlantis sank below the waves, unable to survive its own technological ingenuity. Could it be that we are the new Atlantis? I would ask you to ponder this question, because once again science and technology have given us all the glittering wonders but wisdom is languishing. Knowledge grows and wisdom languishes.

We have in the Hindu scriptures these two words: *jñāna* and *vijñāna*, *jñāna* being wisdom and *vijñāna* being knowledge. When there is a divergence between the two, there is a real danger for the human race. There is another great myth* in the Hindu scripture of the churning of the milky ocean, the *samudra manthana asuras*, when the *devas* and *asuras*, the divine forces and the hostile forces, between them churned the ocean of consciousness. We are told that great wonders emerged: a beautiful cow, a noble horse, a divine elephant, the wishfulfilling tree, the beautiful damsel. But then a stage came when a terrible poison suddenly sprang up. Nobody was expecting it, because the ultimate goal of that churning of the ocean of consciousness was the pot of nectar of immortality. But before they could come to the nectar, this terrible poison spread throughout the three worlds, and all the *devas* and *asuras* fled in terror because the whole of creation was on the verge of being destroyed. It was then, we are told in this great myth, that Shiva the Great Lord appeared and drank the poison and kept that poison within his throat. In other words, he integrated that poison into the divine consciousness. Only then did the churning proceed, and finally the nectar appeared.

It seems to me that man today has reached the poison. There are

*I use the word "myth" to mean one of those deep overriding ideas that are embedded in the human psyche.

great and glittering triumphs of civilization; there is television, there
is space travel. Man is reaching out literally into the stars, and the
fabulous achievements of medicine, of engineering, are there for all
to see. Yet man seems to have now reached this terrible poison: the
hatred, the envy, the fear, the lack of inner peace, the constant conflict between hostile forces that seem to dominate the world today. It
seems to me that here lies the crux of the problem. Do we now await
another great divine descent in order to integrate this poison? If so,
will it be an automatic descent or do we have to strive for it? Will
our own striving make the critical difference between destruction
and survival?

I think the key lies in the future of human consciousness. This
great gift of the Gods, the gift of consciousness, has grown from uni-
cellular organisms down through millions of years, and has now
come to the human state. Where do we go from here? Is there any
reason to assume that the evolution of consciousness ends with our
present human state? Or are we, in fact, poised on the threshold of a
leap into a new level of consciousness? Why should evolution stop
with us? It seems that something within the whole evolutionary process is pushing the consciousness towards a new leap, which alone
can insure human survival. It is important to remember the great difference between the previous leaps in consciousness and this one.
Animals had nothing to do with their evolution into human beings;
it was a blind evolution. But today, for the first time, we have a species that is able to cooperate with the evolutionary force, and that
can make a contribution to bringing about that greater consciousness. We are not simply blind instruments. We are self-conscious individuals, and it is there that we find the key to the importance of
spiritual endeavor.

The mystic consciousness is part of the heritage of the human
race. In every religion, creed, country, and language one finds the
mystics who have had this greater consciousness; among them Pad-
masambhava and Nagarjuna, St. John of the Cross and Meister
Ekhart, Mansur al Halaj and Jetaluddin Rumi, and the great seer of
the Upandishads, Svetasvatara, who said: "I have seen the greater
consciousness, shining like the sun on the other shore beyond the
darkness. By knowing that alone can one overcome recurrent death;
there is no other path to immortality."

Whether it is a Ramakrishna, a Maharishi Ramana, or a Sri Aurobindo; or whether it is, in our own lifetime, people like Mother Teresa or Swami Muktananda; all of these have tasted the nectar of the higher consciousness. There are clear indications that there *is* a greater consciousness, and that this is part of our heritage. I submit that only if there is a substantial movement into that consciousness will the human race ultimately be able to survive the present crisis.

Simply remaining on this level of consciousness with the accretion of nuclear technology is to invite disaster. Though Fritjof Capra is making valiant efforts for an appeal to ban nuclear technology, I do not think it is possible to prevent its development, because the technology is there. Today, I understand, there is enough fissionable material circumambulating the globe to kill each human being twelve times over. How anybody can be killed twelve times I do not know. We believe in rebirth, but even that takes a little time! Nonetheless, science has given us this power. How do we go back to pre-nuclear technology? An egg can never be unscrambled. Nuclear technology today, whether we like it or not, is part of the human heritage. The question is whether it is going to be used for good or for evil.

The Indian concept of *shakti* power is that the shakti can be *divine* or *asuric*, the power of creation or the power of destruction; it can be the sovereign power of love or it can be the corrosive power of hate as symbolized by Adolf Hitler in our own lifetime. Nuclear technology is like this power. Is it going to be utilized for good? It can move mountains, create electricity, and illuminate the lives, the hearts, and the homes of millions of people. On the other hand, it can totally destroy the human race.

Now this is the question: does the key to human survival lie in the growth of the greater consciousness? Many great hypotheses support this. Sri Aurobindo has put forward the theory of the supramentalization of consciousness. He has written that consciousness has reached this present stage, and the next step—the great divine descent—is now ready. It is necessary for us to aspire to that, to raise our consciousness to a higher level so as to integrate, incorporate the power and the light and the glory of the supramental, and bring it down to bear upon this terrestrial consciousness. In the work of the great Jesuit priest Teilhard de Chardin, it is very clear that the entire thrust is towards the movement of mankind to the "Omega point," as de Chardin calls it, or the Christification of consciousness—the great development of the human race in an evolving and not static once-and-for-all creation, but a creation in which we are at this moment participating. The original idea emerges from Teilhard de Chardin's writings that the creation is not completed once and for all; it is evolving and we are all working it out in our consciousness.

The Kundalini hypothesis, which Swami Muktananda, Gopi Krishna and others have written about, is that the Kundalini is a great spiritual force which lies coiled at the base of the human spine, and which, under certain conditions, can be made to rise and illuminate and irradiate the brain. According to this hypothesis, when the Kundalini power enters the brain, the transformation of consciousness takes place. From the time of Patanjali's *Yoga Sutras*, thousands of years ago, right down to the present day, the Kundalini hypothesis has linked with a broad spectrum of meditational yogic practices.

Another fascinating convergence is between post-Einsteinian physics, subatomic and cosmic physics, and the Eastern wisdom. Fritjof Capra's *The Tao of Physics*, Gary Zukav's *Dancing Wu Li Masters*, and Amaury de Reincourt's *The Eye of Shiva* number among recent books that show that we have now come the full circle. Science and spirituality originally started together. All the great explorations into the material world took place as a result of the religious impetus. Then they diverged and for centuries grew apart from each other. It seems now that again they are converging. This is tremendously important because, as I see it, the time frame is critical. If one looks upon the whole problem from a cosmic point of view, then time of course loses its importance, but from a human point of view, the time frame is crucial.

Something is happening deep within the human collective consciousness. Science and spirituality, the two greatest forces that the human race has known, are coming together again. People are beginning to realize that even in the midst of the battle, when the battle presses the thickest, the divine spark is there. Let us not forget the message of the Gita. The Gita was given at the time of tremendous conflict, when the two opposing forces were locked in conflict and the flight of missiles had begun. It was at that moment that within the human heart the desire for divine enlightenment arose, and it is at that moment that the voice of Krishna was heard. Not only science and spirituality, but also the different religions can start converging. We have a verse in the *Rig Veda*: "Ekam sad viprah bahuda vadanti"—"The truth is one; the wise call it by many names." There is also a beautiful mantra from the *Mundaka Upanishad*:

> Yathā nadya syande mānāsamudre astam
> gacchanti namrupē vihāya tatha vidvan
> nāmarūpatvemukta paratparam pursusham upeiti
> divyam.

This means that in the same way as the rivers and streams arise from different places but ultimately flow into the same ocean, so do all these different religious sects and communities and denominations arise according to historical, geographical and ethnic reasons but, ultimately, reach the same goal.

There cannot be, in the ultimate analysis, different Gods for different religions. We may look upon God differently, we may have different approaches to the divine, but this force or power that we call God must be there for all, irrespective of caste or creed.

The *Ishavāsyā Upanishad* opens with the beautiful line:

> "Ishāvasyamidam sarvam yatkinchya jagatyām
> jagat."

Or, whatever there may be in the Universe, whether it is this little planet or whether it is the hundreds of billions of galaxies, they are all pervaded by the same Divine Power. The dichotomy between matter and energy has broken down. The sages have always known there are not two; in the ultimate analysis, there is only the One.

It is clear, therefore, that the time has now come when we have not only to reaffirm our faith in this greater consciousness, but also to reaffirm our own personal commitment to reflect this consciousness in our daily lives and in our own minds. In the ultimate analysis, it is in the crucible of the individual consciousness that the greater consciousness has to be forged. It may be outside us, but until it is reflected in our own psyche, in our own hearts, it will not become operative.

Mother Teresa speaks of the importance of the head and the heart, these two aspects of the human psyche. Let us try to bring about a new and glowing synthesis, a new, higher consciousness that brings together the East and the West, the head and the heart, science and spirituality, and knowledge and wisdom—that does not compartmentalize the human consciousness but brings it together in a great global thrust. The most remarkable picture ever taken is the one of Planet Earth from the moon. It shows our earth as it really is, a tiny speck against the vastnesses of outer space, a beautiful and fragile flower against the desert of endless time. We are privileged that at this time we are living upon this beautiful earth. Let us try not only to preserve it outwardly, but to bring down that Greater Power so that this earth can really shine like a jewel amid the galaxies, and beings living on other galaxies and other planets can point to the earth and say, "It is here that the greater consciousness has descended."

This needs divine grace, and I would therefore like to end with a prayer. My prayer is addressed to Mahalakshmi, the great goddess. She is known sometimes as the Goddess of Wealth, but it is not only the outer wealth that she symbolizes; she symbolizes the inner wealth of the spirit, the inner capacity, the inner graciousness of consciousness. The prayer to her is that she may bring her grace and her blessings upon all of us, so that in our effort to build a new global consciousness we have the backing of the Divine Force itself:

> May the great, full-breasted lotus-eyed goddess, clothed in white raiments, seated upon the lotus and with lotus stalks in her hands, bathed with water poured from gold pitchers, by divine elephants, always reside with you, accompanied by all that is noble and auspicious.

8

Swami Prajnananda (Amma)   The Mystery of
                             Karma

Although Karma is a mysterious subject I shall make it as clear and
simple as possible. The concept of karma is very interesting. In fact,
it seems to be of universal interest. Recently when I was in America
with Swami Muktananda, who is my Guru, I came across many
books and articles on karma and reincarnation.*

Indian scriptures and sages emphasize the importance of understanding karma because they say it gives meaning to our lives and
explains our involvement in this world. Without this understanding,
there seems to be only one end in life. In other words, it seems that
we are born just to die, because that is what we see happening to
us—we are born, we grow up, we have certain good and bad life experiences and we die. Everything happens so fast! We may call this
the natural process of life. We may even wonder, "What is the use of
this life, in which death seems to be the sole end?" It appears as
though someone has played a big joke on us. Because of this, the
modern attitude is that one should try to derive the most from life,
feel free, and be happy. This attitude also existed in ancient India.

*Some of these books include: *Karma and Rebirth in Classical Indian Traditions*,
edited by O'Flaherty, *Reincarnation in Christianity*, by MacGregor, *Astrology,
Karma and Transformation*, by Arroyo, and *Reincarnation: The Phoenix Fire Mystery*, edited by Head and Cranston.

Some of our scriptural texts make reference to a person named Charvak whose followers were considered heretics and who preached that the goal of human life is:

> "yāvat jivet sukham jivet rinam kritvā dhritam pibet bhasmi-
> bhutasya dehasya punarāgamanam kutah."
>
> "As long as you live, live happily. Incur debt but drink ghee. Once the
> body is reduced to ashes, how can it come back again!"

He advised people, therefore, not to worry about the consequences of their actions or the future. But our sages have pointed out a flaw in this kind of thinking. They have asked, "If this life is our first one, how can we explain the differences, inequalities, and disparities in life-situations and even inherent traits and dispositions that exist among human beings?" For example, the lives of two boys born to the same parents and brought up in the same environment with the same advantages may go in entirely different directions. One boy may become a famous actor, while the other may hardly be able to earn a living. Moreover, some people are naturally beautiful, while some are ugly. Why? Some are born geniuses, some are stupid. When a car carrying two persons meets with an accident, one dies, another does not receive a scratch. How can we justify this? Some religions rationalize these differences as being the will of God. Yet the same religions teach that God is merciful and full of love and forgiveness. If this is really God's nature, then how could He create such inequalities? Therefore, the cause of differences seems to lie not in God, but somewhere else.

Our strong sense of justice and morality forces us to seek a basis in the past for differences in people's lives. We are aware that in the world our society generally punishes a person who commits a bad action, like theft or murder, and rewards one who does good work. We have courts and prisons as well as Nobel Prizes. This means that there are grounds for reward as well as punishment in one's life. If this is true on the mundane level, it must also be true on the spiritual level. The innate disparities that exist among human beings must also have a past cause. In our Indian philosophical tradition that cause is called karma. Karma is an action performed sometime in the past, usually in a previous life, which bears fruit in the present. This means that if there is a past there is also a future, that there is rebirth.

There is an interesting true story about the rebirth of a girl called Shanti. The incident took place in 1935. I remember having read about it in newspapers and magazines. Lama Govinda has also mentioned it in his book, *The Way of the White Clouds*. Shanti lived in Delhi. When she was three years old she began to say that she was married and that her husband, Kedarnath, and her son were living in Mathura, about 80 miles from Delhi. The girl's parents considered her words to be no more than playful childish talk, but when she was eight years old Shanti still insisted that what she said was true. Her grand uncle, Professor Chand, took an interest in the story and found that there was a man named Kedarnath in Mathura who had a son and whose wife had died nine years before. He decided to verify the truth of Shanti's story with several tests. First, Kedarnath was asked to come casually to a shop to which Shanti had been sent to buy something. Shanti immediately recognized Kedarnath and called to him. Then she was taken to Mathura and was told to find the way to her house. She walked through many narrow lanes and winding roads until she reached the exact place. She even recognized the members of her former family and reminded her husband of small, intimate occurrences and conversations known only to the two of them. After many other tests, the proof of Shanti's rebirth was complete. In an interesting book entitled *Twenty Cases Suggestive of Reincarnation*, Ian Stevenson has collected similar cases. Sometimes a person who meditates deeply has a glimpse of his past lives. Great beings, too, have insight into a person's past life. The experience of a past life is sometimes available in the form of intuition; for example, a strong sense of having been to a certain place or an affinity for a particular person.

The way in which karma works is called the law of karma. It is a law of cause and effect, action and reaction. It is said *kāranena vinā káryam na bhavati*, which means that an effect cannot exist without a cause. Even scientific principles and mechanisms, such as Voyagers and computers, operate by this law, and action and reaction are considered to be equal and opposite. In fact, karma is a reaction to an action. Like a tennis ball thrown against a wall, our action rebounds on us in the same way and with the same force with which it is performed. If it is mild, the result is mild; if violent, the result is also violent, like a scratch versus a deep wound on the body. Similarly, if the action is positive or negative, the result is also positive or negative, respectively. In science, the reaction of an action exists on the physical level; in our life, it is on the subtle level. Thus, our own actions determine the future pattern or situations of our lives. We call it destiny, for which no one is responsible but ourselves. It is an automatic process, a computerized system created by nature or a supermind or perhaps God, to run the universe by keeping everything in order. The ancient philosophy of Vedanta even says that the world is created to carry out this karmic process. The law of karma, therefore, does not contradict the belief in God's will. On the contrary, it helps us to understand the ways of God towards human beings. The law of karma *is* the will of God, and He is just.

In this way, karma is a great teacher. It grants us the freedom of choice. We can shape our own future of happiness or unhappiness by performing good or bad actions. However, the working of karma is so complicated that it is difficult to know precisely when and in what manner we will experience the result of a particular good or bad action. This is the mystery of karma. We can scan the depth of the ocean or explore outer space, but no one can unravel the intricate workings of karma.

Swami Muktananda often tells the following story to illustrate this point.

Once there lived a very devoted couple. One day a saintly person named Haridas came to their town, and every day they went to hear his discourses. They were extremely impressed by this saint. They invited him to their house for lunch and asked him to stay with them for a couple of days. Usually Haridas was content within himself and did not go anywhere. But since the time had come to fulfill his karma Haridas was moved by the love and devotion of this couple and accepted the invitation. They served him with great love and devotion. They ate a very delicious meal and then all retired for the night. Now the wife had a lustful attraction for Haridas, so at midnight she went to his room. She told him that she loved him very much and asked him to sleep with her. Haridas saw that the lady was very passionate and that she would not listen to any of his words. In order to discourage her he said to her that people like him, sadhus and sages, did not sleep with married women. When the lady heard this she went away, but after about twenty minutes she returned and said, "I have no husband. Now you can sleep with me."

Haridas wondered at her words and asked, "How can it be that you have no husband?"

She said, "I have killed my husband with an axe."

Haridas was shocked. He told the woman that she had misunderstood him and what she had done was wrong. He immediately prepared to leave. Hearing this and seeing that Haridas was going to leave, she became furious and rushed into the street, wailing and lamenting and calling for help. "This Haridas is a scoundrel," she cried. "He killed my husband and tried to rape me!"

When the people heard this, they grabbed Haridas and beat him with stones and sticks. Then they took him to the police station. The next day he was presented to the judge. The judge knew Haridas was a pious man. He had a feeling that Haridas was innocent. But all the evidence was against him and the judge could not do anything. Nevertheless, he spared his life and ordered that since Haridas had killed the man with an axe in his hand, his hands should be cut off below the elbow. This was done and Haridas was set free.

But Haridas was not angry with God. On the contrary he did intense *tapasya*, meditation and *sadhana*. Ultimately he attained Self-realization, and God appeared before him. God was very pleased with him and told him to ask a boon. Haridas said, "Since I have had Your *darshan* I don't want anything. I am satisfied with myself. I have no desire, but I am curious about one thing. I have led a very pious life. I have not done anything wrong. Why did this happen to me? Why were my hands cut off?"

God said, "What happened was a good thing, because if your hands had not been cut off you would not have seen Me. Your karma had to be worked out."

Haridas said, "How is it possible? What did I do?"

Then God explained to him, "In your past birth you were a very pious brahmin and once, after taking a bath in the river, you were sitting nearby doing your mantra. After some time a cow went running by. A few minutes later a man came along with a very big knife in his hand and asked you whether you had seen a cow. You said that you had seen the cow running in a certain direction. Immediately the man ran after the cow and killed her. In that birth you were the brahmin, the wife was the cow, and the man who killed the cow was the husband. Since the man killed the cow with the knife, in this life the wife killed the husband with an axe. Since you were involved in the incident and indicated where the cow had gone with your hands, in this life your hands were cut off. Since you had to work out your karma, all these things happened. Then you saw Me and attained Self-realization."

According to the law of karma, we come back to this world again and again to settle our karmic accounts. There is a true story to illustrate this. A wealthy man named Biharimal was a devotee of a Guru called Nirvan Saheb. The time came when Biharimal's daughter was to be married. Before the wedding, as is the custom in some communities, Biharimal displayed the gold and diamond ornaments and other valuable things that he was to give his daughter in her dowry. He was proud of his wealth and wanted everyone to know how much he had given to his daughter. With a lurking desire for praise, he also invited Nirvan Saheb to bless the gifts. The Guru was very much aware of Biharimal's pride. He went to his house and was received with great respect, looked at the display and blessed it. Then Biharimal called his daughter to receive the Guru's blessings. When she bowed, Nirvan Saheb said, "My child, be happy with your husband," and then added, "You are taking with you what is yours." These words were a blow to the devotee's pride and he was very upset. He thought, "Does he not know that this wealth is not hers, but mine, which I am giving to her?" But he was intelligent and felt that there must be some meaning behind his Guru's words. One day after the wedding Biharimal went to Nirvan Saheb and with folded hands asked him to explain the meaning of his words. So the Guru revealed the mystery. "When you were married," he said, "your wife brought great wealth with her. You used her money to become wealthy and never bothered to return it to her. After some time your wife died and you married again. Your first wife was born as your daughter. So now you are paying back to her what was hers. It is not yours."

I cannot help telling you another similar story. There was a man in Poona who contracted a mysterious heart ailment. No doctor could diagnose or cure it and the man spent all his money on doctors and hospitals. When he became completely desperate, someone suggested that he consult *Bhrigu Samhita*, a book in which the ancient rishis had written down the destiny of those people who consult it. There it was written that in his past birth this man had been a greedy doctor who cheated his patients by telling them that they had contracted incurable diseases and should take his treatment. He would give them injections of water, take large sums of money and tell them that they were cured. Thus he had amassed a large bank account. Now, in this life, he was paying back all his karmic debts. As with the ricocheting balls in a billiard game, many inter-related forces are at work in the working of karma. This is because life itself is so complex. At the most, if you want to know your past look at your present circumstances, and if you want to know what your future will be look at what you are doing now.

The *Bhagavad Gita* refers to this mysterious nature of karma as *gahanā karmano gatih*, "The working of karma is unfathomable," and *kavayo pyatra mohitāh*, "Even the wise are bewildered by it." Karma may be obscure, but it is irrevocable. It is said: "avash-yameva bhoktavyam kritam karma shubhāshubham," "Good or bad karma, once formed, will absolutely be experienced." Here, perhaps, one may pose a question. Why do we sometimes see a person performing bad actions but getting good results and vice versa? This can be illustrated by a story of a man who had two sons. One was very pious and went to the satsang of a saint every day. Another son was a wayward boy, who did not study but stole money and enjoyed life. One day the pious son met with a terrible accident and broke his hand. The next day the other son found a lump of gold on the street. The father could not understand this and asked the saint why God was so unjust. The saint explained that every good or bad action must give its fruit. All people have mixed karmas, both good and bad. These have their own time of coming to fruition. If a person is performing bad actions now, but seems to be enjoying good results, it does not mean that he is enjoying the good fruits of his bad actions. It is simply his time to enjoy the good fruits of his past good actions. The moment the bank account of his past good actions is depleted, he will receive the fruit of his other actions. It works in the same way with those who perform good actions but seem to get bad results. So this is what happened with the two sons.

Sometimes mixed karmas work simultaneously. For example, a person may become wealthy because of his past charitable actions, but he may suffer from bad health because of some past bad actions. Thus it is said that the law of karma rules our lives. It is very powerful. No one can avoid it, hide from it or escape from it like one can do in the case of mundane laws. One may cross a street against a red light and nothing will happen to him. One can even escape the mundane consequences of committing a theft or murder if one has a clever lawyer. But the law of karma is said to be infallible. Here, one may be tempted to ask, "If this is so, then there is no point in trying to help anyone, because whatever is meant to happen to him is going to happen no matter what you do for him." This is not correct. Once a man was attacked by robbers and left on the street for dead. Several people passed by, looked at him and went on their way. After a while a man saw him, picked him up and took him to the hospital. The victim survived. It was his karma to be saved. But those who missed the opportunity to help him were unfortunate, while the man who picked him up by becoming the voluntary instrument through whom the victim's karma was fulfilled became fortunate by earning some merit for himself.

Now, what should be our attitude towards karma? We are advised by the Indian sages to accept it with gratitude, understanding that it is just. We should regard it as redemption and not as punishment or reward. The working out of karma is a process of purification. Saint Tulsidas says that if a child has a bad boil on his body, the mother mercilessly squeezes it to expel all the impurities. In the same way, God is merciful and compassionate by being seemingly merciless. He has given us a chance to work out our karma and to become free.

The idea of sin in Christianity is very similar to that of karma, except that it refers only to bad actions. According to Indian tradition, both bad and good actions are bondage. One is a hard iron chain which gives pain, while the other is a soft, golden chain of which one is not even aware. Both are chains, however, and one must shake them both off in order to become free from this worldly prison of continuous life and death. The sages tell us that once we have freed ourselves from the shackles of karma, we enjoy eternal bliss. Yet many of us are frightened by the idea of this kind of freedom. We are afraid of the unknown. We prefer to hang on to that with which we are familiar rather than to take a risk, even for something that may be better. In 1979, when I was in Boston with Swami Muktananda, some Catholic monks came to see him. They told him that they talk to people and make them aware of the sufferings of life. Swamiji replied, "People are already familiar with suffering. What they need is a reminder of their true identity, which is bliss." This is the point of view of Indian philosophy. The purpose of un-

74   *Swami Prajnananda*

derstanding the theory of karma is to break this chain of cause and effect and transcend all the worldly sufferings, present or future, with which we are so familiar.

Now the question is: can we end this karmic game in which we pay for the past and create the future? Can the karmic mechanism be made inoperative? To answer this is the real goal of Indian philosophy. It says that we must first understand the three kinds of karma, which are explained in Vedantic philosophy. The first kind of karma is called *prārabdha*, or destiny. It consists of the results of our past actions which are unfolding in this very lifetime as our present experiences. The second kind of karma is called *sanchita*, or accumulated. This consists of actions lying dormant, as if kept in a storehouse or deposited in a bank account, waiting to ripen and manifest in another lifetime. The third kind of karma is called *kriyamāna*, or current. It consists of actions that we are performing now. Sooner or later, some of them will have results in this very lifetime, while the rest will be stored as *sanchita*, until they ultimately become *prārabdha*, or destiny. We can see, therefore, that all three kinds of karma are really the same but have different names due to the differences in their ripening times. Actions are often compared to seeds. It is said, "As you sow, so shall you reap." We are free to sow the seeds, but the ripening times differ depending on the nature of the seeds. For example, wheat seeds, barley seeds, and rice seeds, even fruit seeds have their own time and season for ripening.

Now we shall see how we can deal with these three kinds of karma. Let us first look at *prārabdha* karma, or destiny. It is said that this kind of karma cannot be erased, so one has to face the consequences of one's past actions. In this sense, one's fate is sealed. The science of astrology, which Swami Muktananda calls a natal birth chart, the map of a person's life, shows that there is such a thing as destiny. You cannot avoid your destiny. The road you take to try to avoid your destiny is usually the one on which you meet it. There is a humorous Sufi story which illustrates this. Once a man was standing in the market of the Turkish town of Samarkand. Suddenly a ghostlike being appeared before him, stared at him for some time and then disappeared. The man, frightened, ran to a saint to ask him about the being, and the saint said that this was the angel of death, that the man's time to die had come. Terrified, the man ran away that night to the town of Samara. When he saw the same angel of death following him, he turned around and asked, What are you doing here?" The angel said, "Yesterday I came to look at you in Samarkand, wondering what you were doing there. I did not know what to do because my orders were to grab you tonight in Samara. Now I have no problem."

If we cannot change our destiny, we can definitely remove or lessen the pain of bad karma by changing our attitude toward it. What is happening to us is less important than how and what we think about it. Though we are not free to change the inevitable, we are free to cultivate an attitude. Usually there are three ways in which a person reacts to his destiny. Suppose that a young boy dies of cancer. His mother feels miserable, but if she understands that nothing can be done and that her son was destined to die in this way—in short, if she makes peace with her karma and accepts it—she will find some relief from pain. Another mother may dwell on her son's death continually, blaming God or perhaps the doctors for not yet having found a medicine for curing a terrible disease like cancer, and in that way she will be constantly experiencing mental torture. A third mother may, out of frustration, become violent and beat her other children. Here, the actions of the last two mothers create further karma. The best way to deal with destiny, therefore, is to accept it with the understanding that one's karma is being worked out and will eventually come to an end. If we have this attitude, we will not create new karma through our reaction to what happens.

To deal with *sanchita*, or accumulated karma, we have to first understand how karma produces its result. In yoga philosophy it is said that an action performed with intention or emotion creates *samskāras*, or impressions, which are then stored in the sub-conscious mind. These impressions impel a person to perform actions which bring experiences of pain or pleasure. They are like grooves in a record, waiting to be played back. The *samskāras* are so deeply rooted that we do not know how they operate, but they affect us and shape our experiences in the world. They are like rocks in a stream, diverting the flow of thought waves in a certain direction. Once there was an extravagant person who was sick. The doctor informed him that his test results showed that he had incurable leukemia. Since death was certain, the man immediately set off to spend all of his money travelling lavishly and rapidly all over the world, visiting beautiful holiday resorts and making merry. Returning home he found a letter from the doctor waiting for him. The letter said that the test results sent to him indicating leukemia actually belonged to someone else. In other words, the time had come for him to lose money and so the idea of living extravagantly had arisen in his mind. He might have thought, "Why did I do this?" *Sanchita*, or accumulated karma, exists in the form of *samskāras*, or impressions. These, along with the mind, accompany the soul to its next life in order to give rise to their results. If the mind is purified of these impressions, the accumulated karma comes to an end.

Our scriptures have described many techniques and methods for purifying our mind, such as meditation, mantra repetition, worship, practice of witness-consciousness, and so on. When gradually the mind is completely purified, knowledge of the true identity of one's own Self arises. This is called Self-knowledge. What I mean by Self is the I-awareness which is beyond body, mind and ego. A person has many doubts, but he never doubts the existence of the doubter. This is the I-awareness. There is another means of destroying accumulated karma. According to Vedantic philosophy a direct experience of the Self, without the practice of techniques, immediately destroys all accumulated karma. It is as if a person dreams that he commits a murder and is sentenced to prison for ten years. After three hard years in prison he is beaten severely one day by a prison guard. At that moment he screams and wakes up, realizing at once where he is and who he is. He is neither a murderer, nor is he in prison. Just as when he awoke from his dream he was freed from the remaining seven years of his sentence, in the same way when we awake to the knowledge of the Self, all our accumulated karma is destroyed.

Now let us examine *kriyamāna* karma. This consists of the actions we are performing now. We have full freedom of choice in performing them, but we have to learn the skill of carrying out these actions so that they do not produce results and become binding. The *Bhagavad Gita* is the text from which we can learn how to do this. It says, "yogah karmasu kaushalam," which means that "the art of performing action is yoga." It also shows us what that art or skill is: "samatvam yoga uchyate," which means, "yoga is evenness of mind in the success or failure of an action." It is inner poise, resulting from the conquest of emotions and desires. In order to attain this poise the *Gita* commands, "mā karmaphalaheturbhu." "Let not the fruits of actions be your motive." It also points out the reason for this in the famous lines: "karmanyevādhikāraste mā phaleshu kadāchana," meaning that one has the right to perform an action, but never to demand its particular fruit. One is independent when it comes to performing actions, but dependent when it comes to experiencing results.

If a person remains unattached to the results of his actions and performs them with a sense of duty, he does not create new karma. It is not the physical action but the mental attitude which produces the result of an action. For example, a doctor with his sharp instruments opens the diseased stomach of a patient, but the patient dies because the disease is in an advanced stage. Or suppose a thief stabs a person in the stomach, kills him, and runs away with his possessions. On the mundane level both actions and their results are similar, but the thief's action is binding on him while that of the doctor is not, because the motives behind the two actions were different. In one case it was to kill; in another it was to help. Thus, an action performed without attachment, ego, selfishness, or involvement and with attention to moral codes will not become binding.

Having said all this about karma, the *Bhagavad Gita* gives a final warning: "mā te sangostu akarmani," "Let not you be attached to inaction." In other words, it does not mean that we should stop performing actions, even if we do not desire the fruits of actions. We have to be aware of the fruits of actions and make an effort to perform actions in the best manner we can, playing our part well without getting involved. The important thing is that we concentrate on the action we are performing rather than on its fruit. There is also a practical reason for doing so: if a person is involved in doing his work perfectly he may not have time to worry about the future.

The theory of karma, however, is not fatalistic. One cannot use it to justify one's situation by saying, "Oh, what can I do? It was my karma." Karma is not inconsistent with freedom. In fact, a person has full freedom to act because it is his free will which creates his future: "purvajanmakritam karma daivamiti kathyate," "Destiny is the action done in past life." In other words, it is *kriyamān* karma which creates *prārabdha* karma. There is no conflict between these two karmas as one might think, because their fields of operation are different. They work on separate levels. *Prārabdha* gives experiences while *kriyamāna*, according to one's attitude, brings liberation or rebirth. That which happens to us is *prārabdha*; thinking and deciding what we should do is *kriyamān*. These two karmas are the two wheels of the journey of life. On one hand we experience *prārabdha* over which we have no control, and on the other hand we have full freedom to create the future. We have to remember, however, that although we are free to act, we are also responsible for our actions for which we will have to answer at some time, somewhere, and in some manner.

As explained before, a person has the capacity to free himself totally from karma, to attain Self-knowledge and to enjoy eternal bliss.

9

Swami Kripananda   Kundalini—The Energy of
Transformation

A few months ago someone sent me a copy of a racing chart from
the Del Mar Race Track in southern California. There was a horse
named Kundalini which was entered in the race. The chart said,
"Kundalini lacked speed early but finished well in heavy traffic on
the inside." (This is good news for those whose Kundalini is a bit
slow starting!) The only problem was that Kundalini was beaten by
a horse named Delusion. It is supposed to be the other way around;
it is the job of Kundalini to lead us from delusion and ignorance to
knowledge and enlightenment.

I have been very fortunate to be able to study for a number of
years with Swami Muktananda, or Baba, as we call him, a great
Master and Adept of the science of Kundalini and Shaktipat. I
would like to share with you not only theoretical material but also
some actual case studies and personal experiences.

Although many people may not be familiar with the term Kundalini, they may know it as that essential healing power that we all
have. Some people experience it as a healing force flowing through
their hands, or as an intuitive ability to know what a sick person
needs. Kundalini may often manifest in this particular way, but it is
also much more than this. It is less commonly known for healing
mental and emotional disorders than diseases of the physical body.

79

Kundalini is a transforming energy whose job is to move us from fragmentation to wholeness on all levels. It eventually brings us to the total integration of our being.

The subject of Kundalini and its awakening was traditionally the most closely guarded secret of the ancient sages. It was known only to a tiny fraction of humanity—the initiates, the elect, the elite—and knowledge of it was conferred only in the strictest privacy. The poet-saints and the mystics of all traditions have alluded to it, but only in the most veiled and symbolical terms.

Even the most eminent psychologists are mystified by Kundalini. Fifty years ago in a seminar on Kundalini, the great Swiss psychologist Carl Jung and his colleagues declared that the rising of this force had rarely been seen in the West. They calculated that it would take a thousand years for the Kundalini to be set in motion by depth psychological analysis.

Jung once said, "When you succeed in awakening the Kundalini, so that it starts to move out of its mere potentiality, you necessarily start a world which is totally different from our world. It is a world of eternity" ("Psychological Commentary on Kundalini Yoga," *Spring*, 1975).

Variations of Kundalini Yoga have been studied and used for thousands of years. In Egypt as well as India, initiates practiced specific, strict disciplines for awakening the Kundalini. The secret knowledge was also known and practiced by Western brotherhoods, such as the Freemasons, the Rosicrucians, and the medieval alchemists.

The Masons, for example, taught that there was an energy which was a symbol of Spirit Fire moving through the spinal column. According to the Masons, the science of human regeneration consists of moving the Spirit Fire up through thirty-two degrees, or segments, of the spinal column whereupon it enters the skull. There are twenty-nine "true" vertebrae and three "false" vertebrae, making a total of thirty-two.

The Cabala, the system of esoteric Hebrew theosophy, throws some interesting insights into the episode of the serpent in the Garden of Eden in the Book of Genesis in the Old Testament (from *The Cipher of Genesis—The Original Code of the Qabala as Applied to the Scriptures*, by Carlo Suares). "The book of Genesis was originally a cabalistic script. The twenty-two graphs which are used as letters in the Hebrew alphabet are twenty-two proper names originally used to designate different states or structures of the one cosmic energy, which is the essence of all there is. The decoding of Genesis is not a mere matter of transposing from A-B-C to Aleph-Bayt-Ghimel, but a process of penetrating an unknown world (of cosmic energies). The text is intended to project living universal forces into our being. The Book of Genesis, when read according to custom, appears in the form of a story relating the facts of such people as Adam, Eve, Cain, Abel, and so forth, but whose names when read in the light of the cabalistic code reveal that they are abstract formulas of cosmic energy focused in the human psyche. In the original meaning, woman does not issue from a rib of Adam, she is not called Eve in the Garden of Eden, she does not disobey, there is no question of sin, and the woman is not expelled from Eden."

Concerning the serpent in the Garden of Eden, Suares says: "In certain [traditions] his name is Kundalini. He is the resurrection of Aleph, the principle of all that is and all that is not, from its earthly entombment. [At this point where the serpent appears] Adam and Esha are not wholly there, as if they were just emerging from oblivion. Adam especially is almost entirely asleep. The mission of the serpent is to plunge them into evolution. When Esha is questioned concerning this event, she does not reply, as the translations assert, 'The serpent beguiled me.' What she says is that the serpent blends his earthly fire with her lost heavenly fire, which comes to life again." He breathes the cosmic breath of life into her.

As Joseph Campbell says in *The Mythic Image*, "The usual mythological association of the serpent is not, as in the Bible, with corruption, but with physical and spiritual health. . . . In America, a serpent god, the Feathered Serpent, was recognized as symbolic of the power that casts off death to be resurrected." He was worshipped by the Olmec, Aztec, and Mayan cultures.

The *Gnostic Gospels*, by Elaine Pagels, stated, "In each human being dwells an infinite power, the root of the universe. That infinite power exists in two modes: one actual, the other potential. This infinite power exists in a latent condition in everyone."

The Hopi Indians of North America have always known about Kundalini and the chakras, the subtle energy centers in the spine.

From *Book of the Hopi* by Frank Waters, we learn that they taught: "the living body of man and the living body of the earth were constructed in the same way. Through each ran an axis, man's axis being the backbone, the vertebral column, which controlled the equilibrium of its movements and his functions. Along this axis were several vibratory centers which echoed the primordial sound of life throughout the universe or sounded a warning if anything went wrong.

"The first of these in man lay at the top of the head. Here, when he was born, was the soft spot, the 'open door' through which he received his life and communicated with his Creator. Just below it lay the second center, the organ that man learned to think with by himself, the organ called the brain. The third center lay in the throat, the fourth center was the heart, and the last of man's important centers lay under his navel.

"The first people knew no sickness. Not until evil entered the world did persons get sick in the body or head. It was then that a medicine man, knowing how man was constructed, could tell what was wrong with a person by examining these centers. First, he laid his hands on them: the top of the head, above the eyes, the throat, the chest, the belly. The hands of the medicine man were seer instruments; they could feel the vibrations from each center and tell him in which life ran strongest or weakest."

The Hopis believe that "man is created perfect in the image of his Creator. Then after 'closing the door' (at the top of the head) and 'falling from grace' into the uninhibited expression of his own human will, he begins his slow climb back upward. With this turn man rises upward, bringing into predominant function each of the higher centers. The door at the crown of the head then opens, and he merges into the wholeness of all Creation, whence he sprang."

A number of other so-called primitive peoples know about Kundalini. A researcher by the name of John Marshall led an expedition, under the auspices of Harvard University, into the Kalahari Desert in Africa to study the !Kung people. They produced several documentary films, the most interesting of which is *N/um Tchai: The Ceremonial Dance of the !Kung Bushmen.*

The !Kung dance for many hours to heat up the *n/um* (Kundalini) so that the *kia* state (transcendence) can be attained, allowing them to participate in eternity. The *n/um* rises from the base of the spine to the skull where *kia* then occurs. There is a *n/um* master who puts *n/um* into the student and controls the process. The !Kung believe that *n/um* is not a physical substance. It is instead energy or power, a kind of supernatural potency whose activation paves the way for curing. Some people describe the trance by saying it feels as though they have a hole in their heads, perhaps two inches wide, which extends like an empty column down their spines.

One of the medicine men describes *n/um* by saying: "You dance, dance, dance, dance. *N/um* lifts you in your belly and lifts you in your back, and then you start to shiver. *N/um* makes you tremble; it's hot. When you get into trance, you see everything. You see what's troubling everybody. Rapid shallow breathing, that's what draws *n/um* up. Then *n/um* enters every part of your body, right to the tip of your feet and even your hair.

"*N/um* is put into the body through the backbone. It boils in my belly and boils up to my head. The thing comes up after a dance; then when I lay my hands on a sick person, the *n/um* in me will go into him and cure him.

"In your backbone you feel a pointed something, and it works its way up. The base of your spine is tingling, tingling, tingling; and then it makes your thoughts nothing in your head."

Almost every tradition speaks of Kundalini in one form or another and describes Kundalini in its own way. Here in India it has many names, but it is known mainly as Shakti, or cosmic energy. There is a vast literature in Sanskrit on the subject of Kundalini Shakti. Shakti is the dynamic aspect of Shiva, the formless and attributeless supreme Absolute. Shakti is the creative force or energy through which Shiva, or the Absolute, brings everything into existence.

This energy has two aspects, one external and the other internal. The external aspect of Kundalini supports our lives; it is the vital energy that makes everything in the body work. It makes the heart beat, the blood flow, and the breath come in and go out.

But Kundalini also has an inner, spiritual aspect which ordinarily lies dormant. According to the yogic scriptures, it is located at the base of the spine in the form of a wound-up spring or a coiled, sleeping snake. In this form it is known as Kundalini because the word Kundalini actually means "the coiled one." Once it is awakened and activated, we usually call it Shakti, which means energy, force, or power.

It is located in the subtle body, which is an energy body interpenetrating the physical body. The subtle body is the seat of the mind, the feelings, the emotions. The yogic scriptures say that in this subtle body there are 720 million *nadis,* subtle channels through which *prana,* or vital force, flows. *Nadis* cannot be seen with the physical eyes because they are a part of the subtle body.

Three of these *nadis* are of the utmost importance. The *sushumna* is the principal *nadi,* and it is located in the subtle body in the center of the spinal column from the base of the spine to the crown of the head. The other two important *nadis* are *ida* and *pingala,* which wind around on the outside of the *sushumna.* The caduceus of Hermes, the guide of souls to rebirth into eternal life, is a representation of these three *nadis.* The *sushumna* is also called the *Brahmanadi* (the channel of the Absolute) or the *madhya nadi* (the central channel).

The *Pratyabhijnahridayam,* one of the fundamental texts of Kashmir Shaivism, says: *madhyavikā sacchidānanda lābhāha—*"When the central channel or *sushumna* is unfolded, one experiences the bliss of Consciousness." The dormant Kundalini Shakti lies in the mouth of the *sushumna,* at the base of the spine. When the Kundalini is awakened, it enters the *sushumna.* The *sushumna* opens up and begins to unfold. As the Kundalini moves upward, it pierces the six *chakras,* or centers of subtle energy, which are found in the *sushumna.*

The word *chakra* means "wheel" in Sanskrit, referring to their appearance, as the *chakras* are junction points of the various *nadis.* The first *chakra* is called *muladhara* and is located at the base of the spine. The second *chakra* is the *svadhishthana* at the base of the reproductive organ. The third is *manipura* at the navel. The fourth is *anahata* at the heart. The fifth is *vishuddha* at the throat. The sixth is *ajna* at the space between the eyebrows. Finally, above all the chakras is the *sahasrara* at the crown of the head. It is the most important spiritual center because it is the seat of Shiva, or the Universal Consciousness. When this center opens, a person realizes his oneness with the Shiva principle, the Universal Consciousness.

The *chakras* are often described as lotuses with varying numbers of petals: *muladhara* 4, *svadhishthana* 6, *manipura* 10, *anahata* 12, *vishuddha* 16, *ajna* 2, and *sahasrara* 1,000. The number of petals in any *chakra* is determined by the number and position of the *nadis* around that *chakra*. For instance, four *nadis* surrounding and passing through the *muladhara chakra* give it the appearance of a lotus of four petals.

The Kundalini Shakti unites with the prana and moves through the entire subtle and physical system, purifying all of the *nadis* and strengthening the body. *Tato nadi shuddhihi*—"Through Shaktipat, the purification of the *nadis* takes place." *Shatchakra vedhāt*—"Then the six *chakras* are pierced." Physical diseases as well as negative mental and emotional qualities are caused by impurities blocking the flow of *prana* in the *nadis*. Once the *nadis* are purified and the *prana* can run smoothly through the body, the body is rejuvenated and the mind becomes pure.

While this purification process is taking place, latent mental tendencies are often brought to the surface and expelled. As they arise, we experience them. If your mind has a tendency to become agitated, for example, your agitation may seem to be worse for awhile. If you have a tendency to be fearful, you may feel more fear for awhile. The Kundalini is simply working to expel these tendencies from your system. As a result, your mind will be purified and these negativities will leave you permanently. There is a *sutra* which describes the effects of this process: *Divya bhāvairmatto bhavati raudrādibhāvairapi sampanno bhavati*—"One becomes intoxicated with divine feelings and becomes free from anger and other negativities."

The awakened Kundalini also expels latent physical diseases from the system. That is why, if you have a latent illness, you may be sick for a short time after Kundalini awakening. Again, it is a part of the process of purification.

There are a number of methods to awaken the dormant Kundalini. Some of the most common methods involve concentration techniques. If a person concentrates his attention deeply enough, there may be at least a partial awakening of the Kundalini. Scientists, artists, and poets supposedly owe their talents and genius to an awakening of this force, usually through one-pointedness or concentration of mind. Some of the techniques of concentration are: mantra repetition, chanting, self-inquiry ("Who am I?"), and solving a difficult riddle, as in Zen Buddhism. In addition, hatha yoga employs certain techniques which force the pranic current to enter the *sushumna* and awaken the Kundalini. *Pranayama* or breathing techniques may accomplish the same purpose.

There is another way to awaken the Kundalini, however, and this is through receiving Shaktipat from a Guru. The Shaivite scriptures say that God, or the Absolute, performs five functions: creation, preservation, dissolution, concealment, and bestowal of grace. The *Shiva Sutra Vimarshini* says: *Gururvā pārameshvari anugrahikā shaktihi*—"The Guru is the grace-bestowing power of God." The Guru is not an individual; it is a cosmic force functioning through that individual. The Guru is the cosmic power of grace, the Shakti.

The way the Guru bestows grace is through a process known as Shaktipat, which literally means "descent of Shakti, or grace." There in a *sutra* which says: *Shaktipāta eva dīkshā*—"Shaktipat alone is initiation." Another *sutra* says: *Brahmanishto vedhakaha shaktipāta kshamashcha guruhu*—"The Guru should be enlightened, he should pierce all the blocks, he should have the power of Shaktipat: he should transmit and control the Shakti."

The *Hatha Yoga Pradīpikā* also says:

Suptā guruprasādena yadā jāgarti kundalī
tadā sarvāni padmāni bhidhyante granthayo'pi cha

"When the Kundalini is sleeping, it will be aroused by the grace of the Guru. Then all the *chakras* and knots are pierced."

What the Guru does at the moment of Shaktipat is to transmit a bit of his own fully unfolded Shakti directly into the seeker, activating the dormant Kundalini and setting it into full operation. *Tatapātaha shishyeshu*—"The Shakti is transmitted into the disciple." It is like a lit candle lighting an unlit candle.

Shaktipat was the secret initiation of the greatest sages, and it has been passed down from Guru to disciple since before recorded time. It is not the monopoly of the Indian tradition. Great beings of every tradition had their inner energy awakened and could awaken it and control the intensity of its functioning in others.

There are four classical ways in which the Guru traditionally gives

Shaktipat: *Darshanād bhāshanāt sparshāccha*—"Through look, mantra, touch." Also, *Siddha sankalpādvā*—"By the will of a Siddha, a perfected Master." The Siddha Guru has completely unfolded his own Kundalini energy so that it fills his whole body. Shakti continually flows from him and passes into anyone he touches. The Shakti also pervades the atmosphere around him, including the things he has used or worn. If a person is receptive, all he has to do is to come near the Guru to receive Shaktipat.

Several years ago a young woman from Greece spent a few months in Swami Muktananada's Ashram. As she was leaving, Baba gave her a shawl, which he wrapped around her shoulders. She returned to her mother's home in Greece and resumed her normal daily routine. One day as the mother was ironing the shawl Baba had given her daughter, she felt an electrical current pass from the shawl into her hands and run throughout her body, and she went into meditation over the ironing board!

The effects of Shaktipat vary from person to person. Although the same Shakti is given to everyone, people's capacities are not the same. When the Shakti is awakened, it manifests differently within different people.

Some people react in a very physical way: their heads shake, their bodies sway, they scream, cry or laugh. Some people make animal sounds or cry out mantras. They may perform spontaneous hatha yoga postures with which they were unfamiliar. They may feel a burst of energy, or they may feel like sleeping for days. All these manifestations are called *kriyas*.

Other people may experience *kriyas* of a more subtle nature—they may see lights or visions, or they may hear different kinds of inner sounds. They may experience inner fragrances or tastes.

Many people experience an emotional reaction to Shaktipat—the heart may open and reveal previously unknown depths of love. Sometimes people experience a surge of negative emotions for no apparent reason.

All these various kinds of *kriyas* occur as a part of the process of purification of the *nadis*. They serve to remove the various impurities and blocks which we have accumulated, not only in this lifetime but throughout countless lifetimes.

The intensity with which a person receives Shaktipat depends on the practices he has performed, on his openness and receptivity, and on his *samskaras*. *Samskaras* are old ingrained habits and impressions that we have accumulated, the things that cause us to act and react in certain patterns. There is a *sutra* which says: *Tā necchātantrāha samskāratantratvāt*— "*Kriyas* occur, not because of the will, but because of the *samskaras*." The Shakti works to remove these old *samskaras* and programmed behavior.

Quite a number of psychotherapists are now familiarizing themselves with the Kundalini process and are utilizing mantra in their therapy. A therapist in Washington, D.C. began to work with a thirty-two year old former jet pilot who was manic-depressive and had been hospitalized for a year. After doing the traditional interview, the therapist asked him to try to meditate and to mentally repeat the mantra *Om Namah Shivaya*. Very soon the patient entered a deep state, his head arched back automatically, and his body began to vibrate. He later said that he had gone to a place deep within himself that felt alive, real, and very familiar. It felt as though he had come home within himself. He began using mantra and meditation to stay focused and centered in his inner Self. He would have *kriyas* of spontaneous hatha yoga postures and *pranayama*, and his body would vibrate with intense energy.

He soon gained control over his moods without the aid of lithium, and after several months he spontaneously began to relive his entire life while in meditation. He would begin by repeating the mantra, but then he would be drawn deep inside where he would no longer be saying the mantra but rather experiencing the vibration of the mantra. From this internal position of mantra vibration, he would directly witness his early experiences and developmental conflicts. He was not remembering back reflectively, but instead he was directly perceiving the experience and the meaning of the experience. The therapist had almost nothing to do because the meaning and significance would automatically come to the patient. He relived his psychotic experiences and understood the meaning behind his bizarre behavior. He experienced his inner Self as being different from his ego identifications.

He attended a local Siddha Meditation Center, developed great interest in chanting, and was eventually able to live in the world in an ordinary and successful manner. He became a well-paid professional and married. The entire three and a half year therapy process had taken place spontaneously and had unfolded in an orderly and intelligent manner. The therapist noted that whatever was presented to the patient by the awakened Kundalini process was always assimilatable, perfectly timed, and appropriate.

In some people, the awakened Shakti works immediately and with great intensity; in others, it may take some time to manifest and may work less intensely. The Shaivite scriptures say that there are twenty-seven degrees of intensity with which a person can receive Shaktipat, depending on his capacity to hold the Shakti. Once a person has received Shakti, it will always stay with him and sooner or later it will begin to manifest.

When I returned from my first trip to India in 1973, I told my former Stanford roommate, Linda, about my experiences with Baba. She was intrigued and took an Intensive with him when Baba went to northern California during his second world tour. She received Shaktipat and began to have very dramatic experiences: Baba and his Guru, Bhagawan Nityananda, would appear to her in visions in her home and would then vanish in explosions of white light, and she would be lulled to sleep at night by beautiful inner symphonies.

Her husband, Bill, was fascinated by her experiences and took an Intensive, but did not notice any effect from it. Several months later he took a second Intensive, and again nothing happened. Six months later he took a third, with no apparent results. However, he faithfully kept up his practice of meditation at home every evening in their meditation room. Suddenly and without any warning, one evening he exploded into powerful *kriyas*—the classical *bandhas* and *pranayamas* of hatha yoga took place spontaneously as an inner force seized him. The Shakti, which had been working subtly within him, finally manifested in a very obvious physical manner.

The process that begins once the Kundalini is awakened by a Siddha Guru is known as Siddha Yoga (the perfect yoga) or Maha Yoga (the great yoga), because after the Shakti is awakened, all the classical yogas happen spontaneously within. This is why it is said that Siddha Yoga encompasses all the other yogas. For example, hatha yoga postures, locks, and breathing techniques may occur automatically during meditation. The specific postures and movements that occur in a person are exactly the ones that he needs for the purification of his system.

A young man who was a professional dancer contracted rheumatoid arthritis at the age of nineteen. By twenty-two he was unable to continue his career and when he was twenty-four he walked with a cane and was stooped over. He had been to many hospitals and had taken many drugs to get rid of his pain and suffering, but to no avail.

At this point he received Shaktipat, and felt a bolt of energy enter him right between his eyebrows. As it began to circulate throughout his whole body, powerful physical *kriyas* took place. His legs locked into a lotus posture, he started bouncing up and down like a frog, and every joint in his body began to crack. His back lurched backward and his head bent back all the way to the floor.

After about four months, he could straighten up his body. After six months, he put his cane away. His horrible ordeal was over, and he was completely healthy again.

In bhakti yoga, love wells up within. In jnana yoga, knowledge of the Self begins to arise on its own. In laya yoga, a person in meditation may see inner lights or hear inner sounds. Finally, in raja yoga, when the Kundalini reaches *sahasrara* at the crown of the head, the *samadhi* state occurs.

During the course of this whole process, a total transformation of one's being takes place on every level. Addictions disappear, and we begin to develop positive qualities such as self-control, patience, and discipline.

One day a young New York housewife had a fight with her husband. Infuriated, she grabbed their small daughter, jumped into the car, and drove off. She did not care where she went; she just wanted to get away from her husband. She headed north out of New York City and into the country. As she drove aimlessly, the large highways turned into increasingly smaller country roads which wound through the Catskill Mountains.

Several hours later she found herself approaching a large resort hotel called the DeVille (now the Bel Fior), where there appeared to be a lot of activity going on. With time on her hands and with a vague sense of curiosity, she parked the car and went inside. The crowds seemed to be milling in one particular direction. She soon noticed that a long line had formed and was stretching down a corridor towards a large ballroom. She presumed that they were handing out something at the end of the line and, not having anything better to do, decided to go along and see what it was all about. When she reached the door of the ballroom she noticed, to her surprise, that the line ended before a dark man sitting in a chair. People were bowing to him and then quietly sitting down. Although it seemed strange to her, she decided that since she had gone that far, she might as well go through with it. Imitating the actions of the people ahead of her, she also bowed to the dark man when she reached the head of the line. As she rose, she looked at his face. A beam of white light from his eyes entered hers and filled her whole being with light. She stumbled to one side of the room, sank to the floor, and entered a deep state of meditation which lasted several hours. When she came out of it, she learned that the dark man was Swami Muktananda and that she had received something called Shaktipat. She later reported that within one week of this experience, all her addictions had fallen away of their own accord—she had suddenly developed a strong distate for drugs, alcohol, and cigarettes. She became more responsible and her relationship with her husband began to improve.

As the awakened Kundalini Shakti works within us, it automatically transforms our outer life as well as our inner state. Our outlook changes, and our relationships and daily activities become more positive and joyful.

Shaktipat also manifests on the mental level. As the mind is purified, we no longer have to make an effort to meditate. Instead, meditation occurs spontaneously. *Sankalpa vikalpa abhavascha*—"All thoughts and doubts vanish." *Ekagrita cha manasaha*—"The mind becomes one-pointed."

Kundalini is the source of inspiration and creativity. When a particular psychotherapist received Shaktipat at an Intensive, she did not notice any of the physical Kundalini symptoms she had expected, but she went home and wrote a three-hundred-page novel in a matter of weeks—something which would never have occurred to her before!

Kundalini improves whatever needs improvement, going to work in the areas of our life that need strengthening. Sometimes the transformation is subtle; at other times it may be dramatic.

Early in 1981, a letter appeared in a south Florida journal from an inmate of one of the toughest penitentiaries in the state. He told the story of how, several years before, he had been on his way to kill a prison dope dealer who had cheated him on a deal. The prisoner was carrying a homemade knife and, seething with anger, was walking down the corridor toward the dealer's cell, when he ran into a group of non-inmates standing around a man dressed in orange clothes. That man was Swami Muktananda who had come to the prison to give a lecture. As the prisoner passed, his eyes caught Baba's and in that moment he was seized by a strong and completely unexpected sensation of love. The desire to kill the dope dealer simply left him and he followed the group to the prison auditorium. He sat there for an hour listening to Baba talk about how a person, by his own thoughts and actions, can turn even a prison into a paradise. He took a mantra from Baba and began to meditate regularly. Over the next several years, his attitude toward himself and his life changed. Instead of feeling angry, desperate and out of control, he found himself becoming more and more in touch with a calm inner center which was unaffected by the harshness and agitation of prison life.

Ultimately the Shakti stabilizes and merges in the *sahasrara*, and the person now exists in a state of tremendously expanded consciousness. This is the state of the Siddha, the state of Self-realization or God-realization. Baba describes it by saying: "In this state there is no devotee, no God, and no world, but only oneness. Just as a river, after flowing for a long time, merges in the ocean and becomes the ocean, when Kundalini has finished her work and stabilized in the *sahasrara*, you become completely immersed in God. The veil which made you see duality drops away, and you experience the world as a blissful sport of God's energy. You see the universe as supremely blissful light, undifferentiated from yourself; and you remain unshakeable in this awareness. A being who has attained this state does not have to close his eyes and retire to a solitary place to get into *samadhi*. Whatever he sees is God, whatever he hears is God, whatever he tastes is God. In the midst of the world, he experiences the solitude of a cave and in the midst of people, he experiences the bliss of *samadhi*. This is the state which the *Shiva Sutras* describe as

Lokānanda samādhi sukham—'The bliss of the world is the ecstasy of *samadhi.*'

"It is to attain this state that we should have our Kundalini awakened. We do not meditate to attain God, because we have already attained Him. We meditate so that we can become aware of God manifest within us. This is the fruit of the inner yoga which is activated when Kundalini is awakened."

10

Jack Kornfield   The Smile of the Buddha:
Paradigms in Perspective

Some time shortly after his enlightenment, the Buddha was traveling in Northern India, as the story goes, walking down the road when some people passed him. They said he was a very handsome and charismatic man, and I am sure he exuded very good vibrations after his enlightenment. They stopped and asked, "What are you? Are you some kind of deva, an angel?" He said, "No." And they asked, "Are you some kind of a Brahma God?" He said, "No." "Well, are you some kind of a magician?" and he said, "No." And they asked, "Are you a man?" He said, "No." "Then exactly what are you?" He replied, "I am awake."

What does it mean to be awake? What does it mean to awaken in the spiritual sense? And what does it mean to awaken in the worldly sense, or as they say in Islam, to praise Allah and tie your camel to the post? To begin to awaken means to be able to see the world from more than our limited, individual perspective—that of this one human life, of who I am, what I want, my job, my country, my love life, my spiritual development. To begin to awaken is to know that it is possible to go beyond what we take to be ourselves and what we know of the world. Though there is a lot of talk about spiritual growth these days, it does not usually happen by accident. Instead, awakening comes through training, practice, and through the fruit of spiritual disciplines of different kinds. With them it becomes possible to change our habitual and limited way of seeing ourselves, where we are going, and how attached we are to the people nearest to us. We can actually learn to see the world in some greater, more universal sense.

I recently traveled to Bodh Gaya, the seat of the Buddha's enlightenment in Bihar state. At that time the Dalai Lama was there teaching under the Bodhi tree. He was surrounded by Tibetan lamas and nuns and a large number of pilgrims from Ladakh, Nepal, and Tibet. He said, "You all think you are so fortunate. Here you've come to Bodh Gaya, the holy spot of the Buddha's awakening. You're here with the great lamas and the Dalai Lama himself. You are able to hear the teachings, you get the sacred mantras. Yet it won't help. It won't really do you any good. Only if you take these words, these teachings, and apply them in a full way in your life with real commitment from your heart, with your whole being, will it help you at all. You must put them into practice." Good words will not help. They are nice, but remain a little reminder until something else distracts us. So the first point is knowing that awakening is possible, and the second is recognizing that we actually have to do it, that it is not just a theoretical good idea.

The third point is that even when we grow in compassion, love, and understanding, even when we awaken, it is still hard. People somehow have the idea that with more consciousness, things get easier. They do in some ways, but in many ways, perhaps, they become more difficult. I recently spent some time with Mother Teresa in Calcutta, partly to work on a TV and radio program on spiritual and social action for the U.S. Mother Teresa had been interviewed by another person before us who said, "Well, it's all well and good for you, you're a nun and you live a celibate and simple life, but this spiritual practice is difficult for us who are in the world, who have families and so forth." She said, "No, no. I am married too," and she showed the ring she wears, the ring of her marriage to Jesus, the symbolic marriage of a nun. Then she paused and smiled and said, "And He can be very difficult!"

It is really important to remember that if we undertake some transformation in ourselves, it requires discipline, time, and it is difficult. To awaken means to touch, to open to all the parts of ourselves, which is all the parts of the world. It means to awaken to joy, light, bliss, universal understanding, and higher consciousness—many lovely transpersonal things. And it is also to awaken to darkness, sorrow, misery, despair, and suffering. To awaken really means to see what is true: if people think that becoming conscious means somehow just joy and bliss, they are going in the wrong direction.

I was just in Calcutta where a hundred thousand people sleep on the streets and their beds are burlap bags on the concrete. It gets cold in the cold season—no shelter, rains in the monsoon. They may have a little stand where they sell bidis, Indian cigarettes, or pan, the beetlenut mixture, or shoelaces—there must be a thousand shoelace vendors on the streets in Calcutta—and they try to make enough pennies a day so they can get enough rice to eat. We interviewed a rickshaw driver, sixty years old, who is still pulling a rickshaw. He said that he supported ten people in his family, and if he got sick for more than a week as he did last year, then they ran out of money and went hungry.

There is tremendous poverty here in India, tremendous suffering. There are all kinds of diseases—leprosy, dysentery, tuberculosis—for which people cannot afford medicine. There is also much hunger. In Bihar, India's poorest state, new schools are being built for thousands of village children who have been so malnourished that they cannot learn well. Not just India, but Bangladesh, Somalia, Africa and Cambodia have tremendous poverty. I just came through Thailand and visited the refugee camps. They are still full.

So you want to awaken. It means to look at what is ugly and painful as well as what is joyful and beautiful, to open your eyes to anything in the world. It is painful for all of us, because the amount of suffering in the world is staggering. When we think about it, we start to close off. In the streets of Bombay, when beggars come up to the car window and say, "Please, money for food," it is hard to look at them. At the next traffic light another beggar comes. The Buddha looked, and he said, "I am only interested in one question, and that is the question of sorrow in the world and its end. I want to know the source of suffering and bondage and I want to know what is freedom from suffering, from sorrow."

In a letter to the *Boston Globe* last fall, George Wald, Nobel prize winning biologist from Harvard University wrote of the need for love in reply to controversy about Nobel prize winners having sperm banks. A feminist had written to say that female Nobel laureates should have egg banks as well. Wald replied, "Of course, you are absolutely right, Pauline. It takes an egg as well as a sperm to start a Nobel laureate and say all that you want of fathers, their contribution to conception is rather small." He went on, "But I hope you are not really thinking of an egg bank. . . . I am sure you are more intelligent than that because Nobel laureates aside, although there is not much difficulty in creating an egg bank, think of the trouble. Think of a man so vain as to insist on getting a superior egg from an egg bank. He fertilizes it. And when it is fertilized, where does he go with it? To his wife? 'Here dear,' you can hear him saying, 'I just got this superior egg from an egg bank and fertilized it myself. Will you take care of it?' 'I have got eggs of my own to worry about,' she says. 'You know what you can do with your superior egg, go rent a womb. And while you are at it, you better rent a room, too.' You see," Wald wrote, "it just will not work. The truth is that what one really needs is not Nobel laureates, but love. How do you think one gets to be a Nobel laureate? Wanting love, that is how. Wanting it so bad one works all the time and ends up a Nobel laureate. It is a consolation prize. What matters is love. Forget sperm banks and egg banks. Banks and love are incompatible. If you do not know that, you do not know bankers. So just practice loving. Love a Russian; you would be surprised how easy it is and how it will brighten up your morning. Love whales, love an Iranian, try a Vietnamese. Here, there, everywhere. When you get really good you could even try an American politician."

What does the world need? We must keep this inquiry very concrete because there is still the enormous question of suffering. Well, we say, we need more food, more oil, more clothing, and more shelter. Nonsense! There is enough food, and oil, but it does not get distributed because of greed, hatred, delusion, ignorance, and prejudice. It is astonishing but true: the world does not need more oil or food; it simply needs less greed, less prejudice, less fear, and more love. That is all. Do not forget about suffering and sorrow because it is right outside the door. When we look at paradigms of life and at spirituality, to be complete and honest we must remember to ask in the context of sorrow in the world and in our lives and find what is true and free in the midst of all this.

Somebody asked the Buddha, "I want you to explain to me the

world since you are the Buddha and you know." He said, "All right. The world is six things. The world is: sights, sounds, tastes, smells, perceptions of the body, and mental perceptions—thoughts and feelings." That is all it is to begin with. Let us start to look at our world and start to look at these questions. Here is a five-minute meditation to begin with. It will open with a poem by Pablo Neruda, the Nobel prize winning poet from Chile. From *Extravagavia*, it is called "Keeping Quiet."

Now we will count to twelve
and we will all keep still.

For once on the face of the earth,
let's not speak any language;
let's stop for one second,
and not move our arms so much.

It would be an exotic moment
without rush, without engines;
we would all be together
in a sudden strangeness.

Fishermen in the cold sea
would not harm whales
and the man gathering salt
would look at his hurt hands.

Those who prepare green wars,
wars with gas, wars with fire,
victories with no survivors,
would put on clean clothes
and walk about with their brothers
in the shade, doing nothing.

What I want should not be confused
with total inactivity.
Life is what it is all about; . . .

If we were not so single-minded
about keeping our lives moving,
and for once could do nothing,
perhaps a huge silence
might interrupt this sadness
of never understanding ourselves
and of threatening ourselves with death.

Perhaps the earth can teach us
as when everything seems dead in winter
and later proves to be alive.

Now I'll count up to twelve
and you keep quiet and I will go.

Pay attention first and feel your world with the eyes closed. There are
sounds, there are touch sensations. There are thoughts, there are feelings, little bits of taste and smell. Out of all these changing senses, we
construct our world. See if you can feel them without constructing anything. Pay attention to your head. Let it relax. Let your eyes
soften. Let your face soften, your mouth and jaw relax. Just be there
and feel. Pay attention to your neck and shoulders. Soften, relax. Let
your arms and hands go. Do not just relax but feel what there is—
sensations, sounds, images and thoughts. Now come down into your
body and feel the movement of the breath. Your breath is your life; it
connects you every moment to the sea of air, in which we swim like
fishes. Feel the movement, breathe in, breathe out. You are like a
plant, an animal, organic, moving. Feel that. Not fixed but changing
sensations, sounds, colors. Bring your attention further down in your
body. Let go in your belly, in your lower back. Feel what is there. If
you want to awaken, you have to start right here, with what is right
here in your six senses. Down through the body into the pelvis.
Soften, pay attention. You will start to see that there is a principle at
work. The more you hold and the more you are attached, the more
painful it is. The more you can soften and let go and allow things to
move and change, freedom and openness come by themselves. Down
into your legs, thighs, knees, slowly down, until you feel your feet
touching the floor or the ground, pulled by the earth, connected to it.
Feel it, touch it. Organic, live, moving forces, the breath, sensations.
So to learn something of our world, first we have to be here. To observe it, to feel it, to be with it, and with all the energies in the body,
the energies of every chakra, of survival, sexuality and reproduction,
power, desire, love, and of wisdom. They are all available, they are all
in here. Each one can be used with attachment and grasping or with
openness. "For once on the face of the earth, let us not speak any language. Let us stop for one second. If we were not so single-minded
about keeping our lives moving and for once could do nothing, perhaps a huge silence might interrupt the sadness of never understanding ourselves." Please allow yourself, gently, to let your eyes open,
your attention to come back to where you are.

Our learning cannot just be theoretical, it must be connected to the
truth of world suffering and to the sorrow we see in it, and it must

be connected with our bodies. Awakening is not a theory; it is something organic and whole, completely connected to ourselves.

One of the first things to learn in trying to understand paradigms, or ways of viewing, is that we create what we see by what we want. There is an Indian saying that when a pickpocket meets a saint, he sees only a saint's pockets. When you go out on the street and you are hungry, you do not see shops selling cloth or shoes, you see restaurants. You do not see people or clothing or the clouds, you see food. If you are an astrologer, you see people in terms of astrological signs. Or if you are interested in money, you see the people who are well dressed, and look rich. If you are interested in sex, what do you see? You see what you like. You do not even look at what you do not like. You might also see the competitors who are interested in the same thing you are. What you want, or are interested in blinds you, and your desire makes you see in a certain direction. Not only is that a way perspectives are created, but all kinds of systems of spiritual practice have been devised that are based on these different perspectives.

All the different kinds of yogas in India for example, offer differing perspectives. *Shabd* yoga is yoga of the inner sound meditation; *Kundalini* yoga deals with the Kundalini shakti energy; *Agni* yoga uses fire pujas; *Ati* yoga is non-dual; *Ashtanga* yoga is the eight-limb yoga of Patanjali; *Hatha*, the yoga of postures; *Raja*, the yoga of different kinds of concentrations; *jnana*, the yoga of insight or wisdom; *karma*, the yoga of service; *bhakti*, that of devotion; *nada*, that using music; as well as *Kriya*, *Laiya*, and fifty more kinds. Which yoga, which system is correct?

Each offers a new paradigm and another way to awaken. If you move your body in the right postures, if you do jnana yoga, if you get your Kundalini aroused, if you serve, or if you chant, then you will awaken. Development of consciousness itself in the Buddhist or the Vedas and Hindu traditions is similarly complicated. On one side it is said that if you develop certain qualities of love, compassion and wisdom, then gradually your consciousness becomes pure and open, and the world is wonderful. But other teachers say that you cannot develop consciousness; it is already complete. Its natural state is whole, complete and pure, and all you have to do is to stop wanting anything. There is the same question about free will and choice. On one hand, perhaps you got turned onto spiritual things because somebody gave you a book, or you took a drug; you were conditioned and did not have any choice. And on the other hand you must have choice for there is another level which you can see where it is all created by you.

Consciousness is studied in deep meditation. One way it is perceived is like the particle theory in physics. When the mind becomes very silent, you can clearly see that all that exists in the world are brief moments of consciousness arising together with the six sense objects. There is only sight and the knowing of sight, sound and the knowing of sound, smell, taste and the knowing of them, thoughts and the knowing of thoughts. If you can make the mind very focused, as you can in meditation, you see that the whole world breaks down into these small events of sight and the knowing, sound and the knowing, thought and the knowing. No longer are there houses, cars, bodies or even oneself. All you see are these particles of consciousness as experience. Yet you can go deep in meditation in another way and the mind becomes very still. You will see differently that consciousness is like waves, like a sea, an ocean. Now it is not particles but instead every sight and every sound is contained in this ocean of consciousness. From this perspective there is no sense of particles at all. Some other schools, like the *yogacarins*, the "mind-only" school, teach, as paradigms, that everything is mind. Others teach that it is all void, and that even mind is a myth, an illusion. Others teach that both of these are true. Zen master Dogen says that

> speaking of enlightenment, when we see the world from a boat on the ocean, it looks circular and nothing else. But the ocean is neither round nor square and its features are infinite in variety. It's like a palace, it's like a jewel. Only to our eyes and only for a moment does it seem circular. All things are like this. Though there are numberless aspects to all things, we see only as far as our vision can reach. And in our vision of all things, we must appreciate that although they may look round or square, the other variety, and universes lie all around us. It's like this everywhere, right here, in every tiny drop of water. (Dogen, *Meditation and Truth*. Cambridge Zen Center, 1978)

What then, is the right paradigm? Is it all one? Is it not all one? Do we develop? Do we not develop? What do we know? There is a story from the Hassid tradition of an old Hassidic master. Some of his students were wrangling, and they decided to go to the master and have him straighten it out. One student presented his case and said, "I see it this way." The master said, "You are right." The other student was upset and said, "No, it's really like this." He explained his point of view, and the master said, "You are right." And the third student sitting there said "But they can't both be right." The master said, "And you're right too." Maybe that is the beginning of the answer to the question of the paradigms; maybe all are right.

When the Buddha was awakened and walking around India in the first year of his teaching, someone asked Him, "What does it mean to be free, to be a truly realized person?" He said, "In one in whom there is not the least prejudiced idea with regard to what has been seen, or heard or thought, how could anyone in the world alter such a yogi, such a person, who does not adopt any particular stand or any point of view?" (from *Sutta Nipota*, Translated by Fausboll, Motilal Banarsidass, 1973.) As long as you believe this is how it is true, this is my way then, of course, you will get into arguments. Chuang Tzu said, "The philosopher is wedded to his opponent." We must learn not to take a stand, not to hold only this paradigm or that one, but rather learn to see them and to use them.

Let me tell you another Hassid story. An old Hassidic Rabbi in Russia used to go to the temple to pray every morning. One morning, as he walked across the town square, the Russian police chief, a Cossack, came up and accosted him. The Cossack was in a very bad mood. He said "Good morning, Rabbi, where are you going?" The Rabbi said, "Don't know." The police chief, very angry, collared him and said, "What do you mean you don't know? For twenty-five years, every single morning you've walked across this town square this way, to the temple to pray." He grabbed the Rabbi by the arm and dragged him across the town square to the police station. Just when he was about to push him in the jail, the Rabbi turned around and said, "You see, you don't know."

You think you know. You think you know what is going to happen tonight, or tomorrow, but you do not know. You could die today; you could receive a telegram that you just won—or someone left you—a million dollars. Anything could happen. There are some predictable chances, but finally you do not know. The most wonderful thing is to realize that if we want to develop some paradigm, some perspective on the world, we have to begin at this place: that we do not know.

"A human being," said Albert Einstein, "is a part of the whole called by us 'universe.' A part limited in time and space. We experience ourselves, our thoughts and feelings, as something separate from the rest—a kind of optical delusion of our consciousness. This delusion is a prison for us, restricting us to our personal desires, and to affection for a few persons nearest to us. Our task must be to free ourselves from this prison by widening our circle of understanding and compassion, to embrace all living creatures in the whole of nature and its beauty." (Einstein as quoted in J. Goldstein, *The Experience of Insight*, Unity Press, 1976.) So we really do not know much, to begin with, as our place to start. Look at all that is going on in our bodies, those extraordinary organs and amazing processes, and the fragility of life. If any one of those things stops or gets out of balance, life is gone. In the Bhagavad Gita, Arjuna asks Krishna "What is the most marvelous thing in the world?" And Krishna says, "The most marvelous thing in the world is that people can see humans die all around them and think that it will not happen to them." We must wake up and realize we know little. There is much more, and the mystery is beautiful.

The relativity of paradigms, of what Carlos Castaneda calls "controlled folly"—that in whatever direction you look, you can see something in a new way and describe it, and there you have a new paradigm—raises the question of how to put it together. The mystery of life is not a problem to solve, but rather a reality to experience, to see, to taste, to feel every day. The more that we can acknowledge that we do not know, the more we can see how incredible it is that we are here, that this building is here, that the ocean is here, that sights and sounds and smells exist at all. To touch that universal, to taste it, and yet in the opening of our spiritual life, is never to lose sight of the human side. Gandhi said that, "To see the universal and all-pervading spirit of the truth, face to face, one must be able to love even the meanest creature as oneself. Whoever aspires after that cannot keep out of any field of life. Those who say that religion has nothing to do with politics do not know what religion really means." (From T. Merton, ed., *Gandhi on Non-Violence*, New Directions, 1968.)

Somehow they have to be put together. A vision of the universal, of some capacity that we grow into—to touch ourselves, to touch the mystery, to touch the One—must be joined with compassion in the world of people, suffering, karma, and action.

When India and Pakistan were created in 1949, there was a tremendous amount of violence between the Hindus and the Moslems, the Moslems trying to run to Pakistan and the Hindu refugees fleeing into India. Into the west, in what is now Pakistan, President Nehru sent tens of thousands of Gurka soldiers to keep the peace. In the east, towards what was East Pakistan and is now Bangladesh, he sent Gandhi. The thousands of soldiers did some help, but many people were killed; the violence continued. Gandhi went to Calcutta by himself and announced that he would fast—to the death, if necessary—until people were willing to stop killing each other. Gradually the violence stopped. Gandhi was more effective as one person fasting than 50,000 soldiers. What is that power, that capacity? Westerners often think spiritual love is a weakness, but if it is really developed, it becomes not some energy that takes us away from the world, but a tremendous power, a tremendous capacity that we have to touch our world and each being in it. This is called the paradigm of love.

If the tradition of the East, or the new physics, teaches ten, twenty, a hundred, or a thousand paradigms and perspectives, we must first ask how we can work with these in our lives. Our answer comes back to the most basic principles; the first of which touches our question of suffering and its end. Suffering, personal and universal, is always caused by "I" and "me," by "I know," "I want," by our attachment. Less attachment, less "I" and "me," means less suffering. It is a very simple principle: the paradigm of non-attachment. The traditional ways of developing it are through cultivating loving thought and action. Generosity is its first foundation. Then, cultivating morality, truth in words and truth in action brings a conscious care to whatever we do. These principles, generosity and morality, are the absolute basis for the world to become freer, clearer, more harmonious: this is the paradigm of virtue. And then in inner practice, the paradigm of meditation, one can touch the divine, the exquisite emptiness, or the mystery and learn to bring that into one's life.

Above all, if you wish to awaken, pick a path. Pick Kundalini yoga or Tibetan Buddhism, or Gandhian politics, or Christian mysticism, and do it really well. It will require much time and discipline. To awaken the power of the heart is really possible, both as an inner transformation and as our manifestation in the world. But it does not happen by accident. Find a teacher, but do not just listen to the words. Take your discipline, work with it, use it over and over and over again, until it really transforms you, like fire. If you transform yourself, if you are willing to make that central in your life, everything else changes. Tremendous joy, tremendous capacity to serve, to help, all come out of it.

Here is a second meditation, a training in clear seeing that comes from the heart of all the Buddhist teachings: from the Tibetan Mahamudra, the Tibetan Book of Great Liberation, from the Zen tradition and from the Theravada Vipassana. In ten minutes, it is the essence of a month-long meditation retreat.

First, again let yourself sit comfortably, feet on the floor and allow your eyes to close gently. To begin with, just let your attention rest in your body and feel if there are any places of obvious holding or tension. Let go in the belly, lower back. Let the hands be relaxed. Now sitting quietly, first of all, just let yourself listen to the sounds. Hear whatever sounds there are. As you listen, begin to imagine that your mind is expanding in size so that it is not in your head or your body, but it gets to be as big as the space you are in. These words and the other sounds are all within the space of your mind. Now the mind opens like a sky, or like the ocean. And all sounds arise and pass and are contained within the space of mind. Look directly at the mind. The mind is open and clear. Silent. Sounds come and go but the mind is like space. Unmoving, spacious, limitless, void, empty. Sounds arise, all taking place within the serene, open space of mind. Nothing is outside. In the space of mind, also, feel the body. As you feel it, it will not be solid, it will be points and areas of sensation, floating in space, in the sea of mind. Sensations float and change, all in the space of mind. A clear awareness, unmoving, in which all things arise and the mind remains open, vast, like the sky. Notice thoughts and images; they are just like sounds, they arise and change and pass away. Be aware of them. See the true nature of thoughts, images, sensations, sounds. Feel how sensations float and change. Sounds come and go. Let thoughts and images arise and pass away. The mind remains unmoved, limitless, timeless, not composed of things, yet not separate, allowing all movement, like the open sky.

Now, in this empty, clear, silent space of mind let yourself imagine

and picture a person whom you love very much. Let the feeling of loving kindness grow in you until it begins to fill the space. Compassion
for them, how you would want to help them if they were in difficulty.
And joy for their happiness. May their heart be open and filled with
love. Picture another person you love very much. Let the feelings, experience of love grow in the space so that the sky of the mind is colored and touched everywhere by loving kindness. Let the feelings of
loving kindness grow in you to touch everyone who is near you, the
place where you are and the country, the whole planet, surrounding
the planet with love, thoughts and feeling of kindness. Then gently allow your eyes to open and your attention to come back.

There is a story in the Buddhist tradition of a Zen monk who
lived in a monastery, a very good monk who practiced his meditation and did all the things a good Zen monk should do—worked on
his koans, pounded rice, and all those things. Still he was frustrated;
his meditation was all right, but he never really got to the essence, to
the heart of awakening of who we really are, of what is the nature of
this world. You know that is the only question that really satisfies
us. We want things, but the only thing that really completes us, that
fulfills that wanting, is to know that essence, is to come to touch
that. He went to his master and he said, "Please, there is nothing
else that interests me any more in the world. I just must understand
who I am, what this is," and he asked permission to go off into the
high mountains and meditate alone. The master, knowing that this
monk was ripe, gave him permission. He packed his little bundle,
put it on his back and went. He was walking in western China, in
the high mountains. He had just left the last village behind and was
walking up a little path in the mountains, when down the path came
an old man carrying a great big bundle on his back. The old man
was really the Boddhisattva Manjushri, who they say appears to
people at the moment that they are ready for enlightenment. In some
of these traditions, he is depicted carrying the sword of discrimina-
ting wisdom that cuts through all illusion. Coming down the mountain the old man said "Hey, monk, my friend, where are you
going?" And the monk told his story. "I've been a monk and practicing. Because I know that the only thing that will ever really satisfy
my heart is to see, is to know deeply, who I am, what this is about,
I'm going on the top of the mountain to meditate or die." The old

man nodded looking very wise. The monk said, "Tell me, old man, do you know anything of this enlightenment?" The old man smiled, and let go of the bundle and it dropped to the ground. In that moment, because the monk practiced so long and was really ripe, he became enlightened. "Wow. Just let go. Don't try to do anything. Just be here." The monk stood there puzzled a minute and said, "So now, what do I do?" The old man reached down and picked up the bundle. He put it back on his back and walked off towards town.

This shows both sides of the spiritual path. First we have to touch that universal truth in our own hearts—and it does not happen by accident. Maybe it happens by grace, through our discipline, our practice, and our willingness to really inquire, to look deeply at the mystery and the sorrow in the world for its cause and the possibility in each of us for non-attachment, freedom, and liberation. If you want to help other people, you have to learn how to get out of greed and anger and prejudice and illusion yourself. If you cannot, you cannot help others. So you let go of the bundle, and then you pick it up again.

The last of the ten Zen ox-herding pictures shows a very happy monk walking into town. It is called "With bliss-bestowing hands," and is captioned, "With my wine bottle and staff I enter the market place and everyone I touch becomes enlightened." The whole path is touching that in yourself and bringing it into the world.

I called this presentation "The Smile of the Buddha." When people went to the Buddha and asked Him for the answer to the true nature of the world, sometimes He would hold up a flower, and sometimes he would say one thing and then another, contradicting himself. A few of His monks would complain, "But yesterday you said something different." Achaan Chah, with whom I studied a long time, would also say one thing and then two days later would tell someone else something different. I was at this time a new monk in the monastery and I was having a hard time in my meditation, so one day I decided, "I'm leaving, this guy's not enlightened, he is not even consistent." I went to him and said, "I am resigning. I am going to a Burmese monastery. I don't like these Thai monks and you don't seem that enlightened to me anyway." This is what a Westerner would say, of course. He thought it was very funny and said, "How come? Why don't I seem enlightened to you?" I said, "One day you say one thing, next day you say something entirely different. What kind of enlightenment is that?" He responded, "The way I teach is like this. There is a road and I know it very well. People are walking down the road. I look. It's night time, it's foggy. A man walks down, or a woman, and they get over to the right hand side and they're just about to fall into the ditch, or to go on this little side path to the right. So I yell, 'Hey there, go to the left.' A little while later I see that same person or another one about to fall off in the ditch on the left or get lost in a little side track to the left, so I yell out, 'Hey, go to the right.'" He said, "That's all I ever do. If you hold on here, let go. If you hold on there, let go." If you think this is the paradigm, fine, enjoy it, then let go and try another one. So somebody said to the Buddha, "Well, what is the real paradigm?" And He smiled.

Thomas Merton saw this when he visited Sri Lanka. Upon seeing what he called the most moving statue of Buddha in Asia, the giant rock Buddhas at Polonnaruwa, he wrote in his *Asian Journal*:

> The silence of the extraordinary faces. The great smiles. Huge and yet subtle. Filled with every possibility, questioning nothing, knowing everything, rejecting nothing, the peace not of emotional resignation but of sunyata, that has seen through every question without trying to discredit anyone or anything—without refutation—without establishing some other argument. All problems are resolved and everything is clear, simply because what matters is clear. Everything is emptiness and everything is compassion.

And Achaan Chah, who also knows this, reminds us in *A Taste of Freedom*, (Wat Nanachat Press, Thailand, 1980) that the mind

> is not really anything, it is just a phenomena, appearance in itself. And within itself, it is already peaceful. That the mind is not peaceful sometimes, these days, is because it follows its moods and its wants. The real mind does not have anything to it. It is simply an aspect of nature. It becomes peaceful or agitated because moods and wants deceive it. Sense impressions come, sights, sounds, tastes, smells and they trick it into happiness, or suffering, gladness and sorrow. But the mind's true nature is none of these things. The untrained mind gets lost and follows each of these things. It forgets itself. Then we think that it is we who are upset or at ease or whatever happens. But really this mind of ours is already unmoving and peaceful, and silent and

open, just like a leaf, which is still as long as no wind blows. If a wind comes up, the leaf flutters. The fluttering is due to the wind. The fluttering is due to the sense impressions. The mind follows them. If it does not follow them, it does not flutter. It stays still. If we know fully the true nature of our senses, of our world, we become unconcerned and free. So our practice, every practice, is to see the original or true nature of the mind. We must train the mind to know the truth of the sense impressions of the world and not get lost in them. To make it peaceful and free. And out of this comes true love. Just this is the aim of all this difficult practice we put ourselves through.*

Spiritual understanding and liberation is not just something to study, but something each person has to undertake. Choose some discipline, some way, and follow it fully. Nothing else will touch your heart as it can, nothing you can get or be, have or do. Nothing will really make a difference in our world unless you have learned in the depth of your heart about sorrow and the end of sorrow. It does not matter how you do it, but once you start, you must finish. There is no way to stop. May the Buddha smile on your journey.

*Achaan Chah, *A Taste of Freedom*, Wat Nanachat Press, Thailand, 1980.

11

Yashpal Jain   Search Within

The most important problem before mankind today is how to achieve abiding peace and happiness. This problem is not simple or easy to solve. We are surrounded by multiple temptations of the materialistic world and, willingly or unwillingly, we find ourselves often in their clutches. We are living, moreover, in an age of science, which has opened a new vista and uncovered many legendary worlds. The moon is no longer a mysterious phenomenon with an old woman plying her spinning wheel. The simile of a beautiful female face resembling the moon has lost its significance since the planet has been tread upon by human feet and everybody knows now what it actually is. New planets have been discovered, and greater wonders will follow in the future.

Despite these achievements, science has a limitation. It can create but cannot make use of its results. For example, science can create atomic energy but it cannot use it for any purpose, creative or destructive. Man is responsible for its use. We can say, therefore, that while science undoubtedly plays an important role, man is more important. That is why man has been given a higher place in the whole universe. It is said in our holy scriptures that man is the supreme being and that it is very rare to be born as man. A saint has aptly said, "Never forget, man is great, man is divine, man is perfect."

Twenty-five hundred years ago, the 24th Tirthankara of Jains, Mahavir, reiterated that the greatest victory for man is the victory over one's self. "The man who has conquered himself has conquered the whole world," he said. In order to achieve this laudable object, Mahavir not only renounced his princehood, he also left his home. He stayed in secluded places, led a hard and austere life, tried incessantly to overcome his vices—greed, anger, attachment, lust—and, after twelve and a half long years, he attained the highest place one could ever crave. He said, "Man is mortal, but the soul is immortal. Live and let live." He also said, "Love all, hate none."

In modern times we have had a similar example in Gandhi, who purified himself and was love personified. Every morning and evening he prayed:

> Oh God, lead me to truth from falsehood
> Lead me to light from darkness
> Lead me to immortality from death.

Baba Muktananda Paramahansa is a great living saint in that line. He says, "Meditate on your own self, worship your own self, kneel to your own self, understand your own self. All that you seek outside is there, Your Rama, your Krishna, your Christ, your Buddha, your Mahavir, your Mohammed are within you. Search and you will find."

I am reminded of a parable. Once a man went to a saint and said, "I want to see God. Can you help me?" The saint replied, "Yes, I can help you to meet God. Come here tomorrow morning." The man was delighted. Next morning he went to the saint who said, "Well, we have to climb to the top of that hill. Pick up this load and let us go." The man put the bundle on his head and accompanied the saint. When they went a few yards, the man felt tired on account of the load and told the saint that it was too heavy for him. The saint said, "Don't bother. The package contains five stones. Throw away one and lighten the burden." The man did accordingly. He walked a few steps and was tired again. He told the saint, who advised him to throw one more stone. By the time he reached the top of the hill, he had thrown away all the stones. At the summit he said to the saint, "O venerable sir, we are here as you desired. Now fulfill your promise." The saint said, "O ignorant fool, you could not climb the hill with five stones. You want to meet God with vices heavier than stones—anger, greed, violence, attachment, jealousy, etc."

This parable draws our attention to the fundamental fact that purity of body, heart and mind is absolutely essential for a noble life, and there is only one way to achieve this; we must search within all the time.

A poet says:

> Shun the serpent of anger,
> Elude the demon of desire.
> As long as you harbor desire
> You cannot meet Rama,
> You experience neither peace nor repose,
> Neither will you be worthy of Sanyas
> Nor will you see the inner self.

The English poet Wordsworth has rightly written in one of his poems that "The world is too much with us." The world is, really, too much with us, because we look outside and are lured by all sorts of temptations. The material forces are constantly at work, and as we are drawn towards them, we are entangled by them. We can overcome our temptation and entanglements by searching within. God dwells within all of us, but a curtain is cast, the curtain of vices. Therefore we fail to see the great treasure, and as Wordsworth wrote, "Getting and spending, we soon lay waste our powers."

The greatest handicap to the search within is that we do not know the goal of life. If we start on a journey without a clear idea of our destination, we wander aimlessly. The first essential is to have a clear perception of life and its aims. The right knowledge is followed by right faith or determination that we will not rest until the goal is reached. Our scriptures say, "ultishat, jagrai, prapya baranni bodhat," or "Get up and stop not until you have reached your destination." The chief message of all cultures, particularly Indian, is, "atmanam viddhi," which means, "Know your soul." "The true attainment," says a great saint, "is the happiness of self. . . . The true faith is to love your own self. The true worship is to see that self is within everyone." The determination to reach the goal has to be followed by firm action. This strength is possible when we look within.

Some people may say that when we look inside, we become oblivious of the outside world. This is not so. Looking inside or searching within means realizing your dormant strength and awakening it. *Samadhi* is not inert, but conscious. Once the dormant strength is awakened, our capacity is increased manifold. A person with it will not renounce the world. He will take a greater interest in it, but only in a detached way. As he will go deeper into the working inside, he will have a greater conviction that nothing is permanent in this world, and all that is perishable can never give lasting peace or happiness. This will enable him to become a *veetragi*; that is, "above attachment." Attachment and hatred are interconnected like the pendulum of a clock, which moves from side to side automatically.

By his search within, Mahavir came to the conclusion that the root cause of our unhappiness is our dogmatic attitude. We often feel that what we say is right, and come into conflict with another person who is equally dogmatic. Mahavir says that there is no such thing as absolute truth; "truth" is a relative term. The person who is your son is also a brother in relation to someone else. He is, therefore, son and brother both. To be at peace it is essential to understand the viewpoint of others.

To attain bliss or *sachidananda* is the ultimate object of every life. This has a synthesis of three fundamentals: *Sat*, or "truth," *chit*, or "soul," and *ananda*, or "happiness." Unless and until one searches inside, one can never enjoy the state of this supreme bliss. In *Shivasutra* it is said, "lokananda samadhi sukham," or "the bliss of the world is the ecstasy of the *Samadhi*."

The source for happiness is inside. Those who seek it outside never get it. I am again reminded of a parable. There was a town in which everybody was unhappy. Some had enormous work to do, some had no work at all; some had lots of money, some were penniless; some had a number of children, but some had none. One day the townspeople heard a divine voice announce that happiness was heaped on the outskirts of their town. Those who wanted it should pack their unhappiness and throw it there, and bring back happiness instead. The whole town was delighted. They ran to the particular spot to get rid of their unhappiness. When they were going they saw a saint in a hilarious mood, laughing like a child. They stopped and said to the saint, "Have you not heard the divine voice? If you have any trouble, get rid of it." The saint did not say anything. Happiness returned to the town.

But after a few days there was unhappiness again, as they all did not enjoy equal status or possessions in the society. The saint was still laughing. So some people went to him and asked him, "How is it that you were happy when everybody was miserable. When misery was gone you were in the same mood, and now when the misery has returned, you are laughing?" The saint said, "Happiness is never outside. It is within."

The most important mission of life is to march from the physical body to what is called the subtle body, which has three vital forces—mind, heart and soul. We can know and utilize them for the attainment of the highest goal in life by meditation and prayer. We witness unhappiness and violence all over the world because we rely on material prosperity. There is a great need for the synthesis of science and spirituality. For that a new search is most essential, the search not outside but within. Transformation must come from inside. It will change everything outside to the well-being of mankind. So, let us recognize our inner strength and enjoy eternal tranquility.

12

Ajit Mookerjee   Kundalini: The Awakening of the
Inner Cosmic Energy

Human experience owes to Tantra the discovery and location of the
centers of psychic energy—chakras—in the subtle or astral body.
Kundalini *Shakti*, coiled and dormant cosmic energy, is the supreme
force in the human organism as well. Every individual is a manifestation of that energy, and the universe around us is the outcome of
the same consciousness, ever revealing itself in various modes. The
passage of the awakened Kundalini through the various chakras is
the subject of a unique branch of tantric esoteric knowledge whose
goal is the merging of the Kundalini energy with cosmic consciousness.

Liberation while living is considered in Indian life to be the highest experience, a fusion of the individual with the universal. The individual manifestation is like a spark of the cosmos because the human organism, the microcosm, parallels everything in the macrocosm. Tantrikas regard the human organism as a capsule of the
whole. The adept accepts with an almost existential awareness that
"He who realizes the truth of the body," as the Ratnasara says, "can
then come to know the truth of the universe." The psychic and physical organisms are interdependent, since each makes the other possible: the forces governing the cosmos on the macro level govern the
individual on the micro level. Here, in this very body, the complete

drama of the universe is repeated. According to tantric principles, all that exists in the universe must also exist in the individual body. If we can analyze one human being, we shall be able to analyze the entire universe, because it is believed that all is built on the same plane. One's purpose is to search for the whole truth within, so that one may realize one's inner self, unfolding the basic reality of the universe.

An important tantric contribution to consciousness-expanding experience is kundalini yoga. The Sanskrit word *kundalini* means "coiled-up." The coiled Kundalini is the female energy existing in latent form, not only in every human being but in every atom of the universe. It may frequently happen that an individual's Kundalini energy lies dormant throughout his or her entire lifetime and he or she is unaware of its existence. The object of the tantric practice of kundalini yoga is to awaken this cosmic energy and cause it to unite with Shiva, the Pure Consciousness pervading the whole universe. The Kundalini Shakti or "coiled feminine energy" is the vast potential of psychic energy, the body's most powerful thermal current. The arousal of Kundalini is not unique to tantric practice; it forms the basis of all yogic disciplines. Every genuine spiritual experience may be considered a flowering of this physio-nuclear energy. Even music and dance can arouse the Kundalini's dormant force and direct it to higher planes, until its perfect unfolding and our conscious awareness of its presence within us is realized.

The static, unmanifested Kundalini is symbolized by a serpent coiled into three and a half circles and spiralling around the central axis or Svayambhu-lingam at the base of the spine. When the Kundalini Shakti (Power Consciousness) is ready to unfold, she ascends through the psychic centers—the chakras, which lie along the axis of the spine as consciousness potentials—to unite above the crown of the head with Shiva (Pure Consciousness), whose manifest energy she is. All the chakras are to be understood as situated not in the gross body, but in the subtle or etheric body. The opposites of psychic energies, they govern the whole condition of being.

Tantras commonly mention six principal holistically organized centers of consciousness, though the number varies from text to text. Starting from the base of the spine, these centers are known as *Muladhara, Svadhisthana* (around the prostatic plexus), *Manipura*

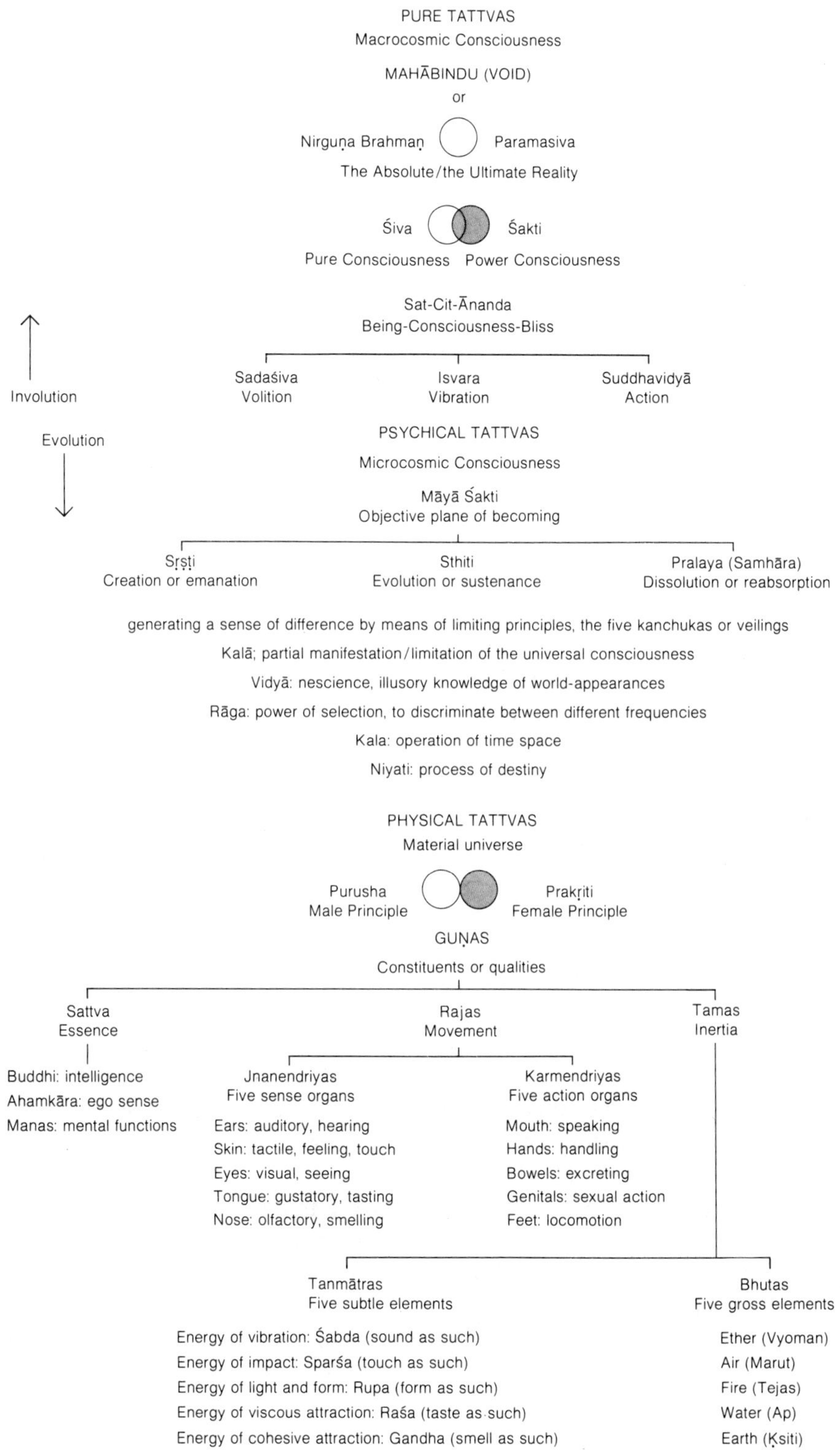

PURE TATTVAS
Macrocosmic Consciousness

MAHĀBINDU (VOID)
or

Nirguṇa Brahman ◯ Paramasiva
The Absolute/the Ultimate Reality

Śiva ◖◗ Śakti
Pure Consciousness Power Consciousness

Sat-Cit-Ānanda
Being-Consciousness-Bliss

↑
Involution

| Sadaśiva | Isvara | Suddhavidyā |
| Volition | Vibration | Action |

Evolution

PSYCHICAL TATTVAS

Microcosmic Consciousness

Māyā Śakti
Objective plane of becoming

↓

| Sṛṣṭi | Sthiti | Pralaya (Samhāra) |
| Creation or emanation | Evolution or sustenance | Dissolution or reabsorption |

generating a sense of difference by means of limiting principles, the five kanchukas or veilings

Kalā; partial manifestation/limitation of the universal consciousness

Vidyā: nescience, illusory knowledge of world-appearances

Rāga: power of selection, to discriminate between different frequencies

Kala: operation of time space

Niyati: process of destiny

PHYSICAL TATTVAS
Material universe

Purusha ◯⬤ Prakṛiti
Male Principle Female Principle

GUṆAS

Constituents or qualities

| Sattva | Rajas | Tamas |
| Essence | Movement | Inertia |

Buddhi: intelligence   Jnanendriyas   Karmendriyas
Ahamkāra: ego sense   Five sense organs   Five action organs
Manas: mental functions Ears: auditory, hearing   Mouth: speaking
                         Skin: tactile, feeling, touch   Hands: handling
                         Eyes: visual, seeing   Bowels: excreting
                         Tongue: gustatory, tasting   Genitals: sexual action
                         Nose: olfactory, smelling   Feet: locomotion

| Tanmātras | Bhutas |
| Five subtle elements | Five gross elements |

Energy of vibration: Śabda (sound as such)   Ether (Vyoman)
Energy of impact: Sparśa (touch as such)   Air (Marut)
Energy of light and form: Rupa (form as such)   Fire (Tejas)
Energy of viscous attraction: Raśa (taste as such) Water (Ap)
Energy of cohesive attraction: Gandha (smell as such) Earth (Ksiti)

FIGURE 12–1

(around the navel), *Anahata* (near the heart), *Visuddha* (behind the throat), and *Ajna* (between the eyebrows). *Sahasrara*, the seventh, transcendent chakra, is situated four fingers' breadth above the top of the head. The Sahasrara chakra is said to be the region of Shiva, Pure Consciousness, while the Muladhara chakra is the seat of Shakti, whose form here is Kundalini. Through certain prescribed disciplines the Kundalini Shakti rises through these psychic centers until it reaches its full flowering, that is, fusion with the Absolute in Sahasrara as Kula-kundalini, generating bliss-consciousness (*ananda*) from the union of Shiva-Shakti.

Each human being has an "etheric double," a subtle body. Besides the "gross" body (*sthula sarira*), there are the "subtle" body (*linga* or *suksma sarira*) and the "causal" body (*karana sarira*). In the Tantras, the human body is regarded as made up of five sheaths or *kosas*, that create layers of decreasing density. The physical metabolism is known as the *Annamaya-kosa* (food-formed sheath) of the gross body; more subtle is the sheath of circulatory vital air, the *Pranamaya-kosa*; the third and fourth sheaths, even more subtle, are the *Manomaya* and *Vijnanamaya*-kosas, mind and intelligence sheaths of the subtle body. The final sheath, *Anandamaya*, the most subtle of all, is identified with man's extraordinary capacity for joy, the bliss consciousness, and belongs to the causal body.

The physical sheath of the body, Annamaya, is connected with three of the five elements—earth, water and fire—which are represented respectively in the Muladhara, Svadhisthana and Manipura chakras. The Pranamaya sheath, bearing the universal life-force, Prana, expresses itself through the air and other elements which are represented in the Anahata and Visuddha chakras. The Manomaya and Vijnanamaya sheaths have the Ajna chakra as their center. The activation of the Ajna chakra gives the initiate inner vision, a simultaneous knowledge of things as they really are, as the cosmic consciousness opens at this center.

These subtle folds are related to the human organism at several psychic points, which are interlinked by numerous subtle channels known as *nadis*, meaning "vibration" or "motion." Though attempts have been made to identify these subtle channels with the anatomy of the physical body, they are practically untraceable by direct empirical observation. If the nadis were to be revealed to the eye, the body would appear as a highly complex network. The most important of the nadis are the central channel, *Sushumna*, and its two flanking channels: the white, "lunar" channel, *Ida*, on the left, and the red "solar" channel, *Pingala*, on the right. Within the Sushumna there are three more subtle channels, through which Kundalini moves upwards. Two currents of psychic energy flow through Ida and Pingala from the base of the spine, spiralling in opposite directions around the Sushumna, which meets them between the eyebrows. Sushumna remains closed at its lower end as long as Kundalini is not awakened.

Early scroll paintings often depict the chakras as vortices of energy, without figurative images. The chakras, however, are more frequently represented as lotuses. As Kundalini reaches each chakra, that lotus opens and lifts its flower. As soon as she leaves for a higher chakra the lotus closes its petals and hangs down, symbolizing the activation of the energies of the chakra and their assimilation to Kundalini. The increasing number of lotus petals, in ascending order, may be taken to indicate the rising energy or vibration-frequencies of the receptive chakras, each functioning as a "transformer" of energies from one potency to another. The Sanskrit letters usually inscribed on the petals indicate sound-vibrations, and also represent the varying intensities of the energies working in the different chakras. Similarly, the color which each of the chakras reflects is consonant with its vibration-frequency.

Long training and preparatory disciplines are undertaken for the arousal of Kundalini, but practices vary considerably. To activate the Kundalini energy through yogic methods, the will-power of the aspirant is directed inwards to the vital life-force (Prana) that is held in Pranayama, guiding its circulatory movement through Ida and Pingala down to the base of the spine into the space where Kundalini lies coiled. The entry of Prana produces an abrupt effect like sudden combustion in a confined space, its heat and sound combining to awaken the serpent-power from its trance-sleep. This discipline of psychosomatic regulation and breath-control is the contribution of kundalini-yoga to tantric ritual. Pranayama reinforces the power of meditative practices, and it is upon this technique that the Tantras lay the strongest emphasis.

It is to the Tantras that we owe the mature development of another system of sound equations known as *mantra*-yoga. According to the Tantras, to "awaken" a mantra is to activate vibration channels which produce certain superconscious feeling-states which aid the aspirant in his or her discipline. The very sound of a mantra, or combination of mantras, has the capacity to arouse the divine forms or their energies. The seed-sound syllable HUM is the root vibration or atomized form of sound representing the essential nature of Kundalini. In the arousal of Kundalini, the seed mantra repeated according to the rules of the doctrine serves to center and support the aspirant's auditory perception by its very continuum. In this way it contracts and intensifies the field of awareness to a single point, under pressure of which Kundalini stirs towards awakening. Since Kundalini is the origin of primordial sound, Muladhara has been called "the birth of all sounds." When Kundalini awakens, the aspirant listens to cosmic sound. When the Kundalini leaves Muladhara, he hears the chirping of a cricket, when she crosses to Svadhisthana, the tinkling of an anklet; in the Manipura, the sound of a bell; at the Anahata, the music of a flute, and finally, when Kundalini crosses to Visuddha, the cosmic sound OM, the first manifestation of Siva-Shakti as Sonic Consciousness. The proper knowledge and understanding of Sonic Consciousness leads to the attainment of Supreme Consciousness. While mantra-shakti acts to awaken and sustain a heightened plane of being-awareness, *Nyasa* and *Mudra* are also considered to be the correct ways to open the kundalini-yoga. Nyasa is the rite by which the aspirant consciously enters the sacred space. Finger-positions, or mudras, are connected with nyasa in tantric ritual. Ritual gestures create a reaction in the aspirant's mind, evoking divine powers in order to intensify concentration and infuse the aspirant with the energy to awaken Kundalini.

In the terminology of C. G. Jung, in the process of individuation the psyche becomes "whole" when a balance is achieved between four functions: thinking, feeling, sensing and intuiting. In the system of chakras we find that each phase of energy is represented by an element in ascending order: earth, water, fire, air and ether. Each of the five vortices signifies a new quality, and each is both an extension and a limitation of another. Thus, at the root center Muladhara is associated with the element earth and signifies the "quality" of cohesiveness and inertia. One may remain content at this level, experiencing no desire to change or to expand into any other state. At the same time, just as the root of a tree implies the possibility of its growth, the earth center denotes an opportunity to expand the awareness. The second chakra, Svadisthana, also has the nature of its corresponding element, water, an energy that tends to flow downward. The third chakra, Manipura, associated with the element fire, has an upward, consuming movement like flames. The fourth chakra, Anahata, associated with air, is characterized by a tendency to revolve in different directions and to relate itself to other possibilities. The name of the chakra implies that it emits a mysterious cosmic vibration, as of unstruck (anahata) sound—that is, sound beyond the realm of senses, or vibration, which in its highest, purest state is "unstruck," and therefore silent. The fifth chakra, Visuddha, associated with ether, is like a vessel within which all the elements mingle.

The process of becoming is not unilinear—that is, moving in one direction, upward or downward—but is dialectical, with pulls and pushes at every level. The Kundalini energy does not shoot up in a straight line, but at each stage of its unfolding unties the knots or psychic blockages of different energies. With each successive unlocking a transformation occurs. As Kundalini ascends through the planes of the psychic centers, the initiate experiences an interplay of visionary experiences with sensations of sound, light and color. At the level of the sixth chakra, Ajna, the center between the eyebrows, the dialectical functioning of the personality is controlled by means of a power to command that can harmonize the energies.

Just as Jung's subjects in the process of individuation transcend, with the help of a therapist, the barriers of polarities interacting within their personalities, so in kundalini-yoga the initiate learns through long apprenticeship under the guidance of a guru to balance the dialectical processes of the lower chakras. In Jung's subjects, once a balance is attained, psychic individuation results in an entirely new awareness which the adept also experiences when all functions are equilibrated at the level of the Ajna chakra. The seventh and last, Sahasrara chakra, has no associated element. As a lotus, Sahasrara has a thousand petals, but no other specific symbolism is connected with it. To attain Sahasrara is thus to attain the "world" of Brahman-Atman or Shiva-Shakti in which liberation is symbolically located.

In Jung's analysis of the animal symbols of the chakras, the black elephant at the root-supporting center of the Muladhara is equated with the tremendous urge that supports human consciousness, the power that forces us to build a conscious world. The element of the Muladhara is, of course, earth, and the force is, at this point, the earth-supporting force. Jung further observes that when Kundalini arrives at the Svadhisthana chakra it encounters the *makara*, or Leviathan. As the elephant is to earth, so Leviathan is to the waters. Jung said that it is the power that forces us into consciousness and that sustains us in the conscious world: "The greatest blessing in this conscious world is the greatest curse in the unconscious . . . so the makara becomes the dragon that devours [us]." So it must be shaken off. Passing from the Svadhisthana to the Manipura, from the makara to the ram, the animal-energy changes to the sacred beast of Agni, the god of fire. The ram is the domicilium of Mars; it is the fiery planet of passions. The ram is a sacrificial animal though, unlike the bull, it is a small sacrifice: Jung says that to sacrifice the passions is not so terribly expensive. The small black animal that is against us is not like the Leviathan of the depths of the chakra before—the danger has already diminished.

In the transition from Manipura to Anahata we leave the ram behind, for the gazelle, also a sacrificial animal, but with a difference. It is shy, elusive, and fleet of foot. There is a bird-like quality in the gazelle; it is as light as air, "gravity-defying," and a symbol of "the lightness of psychical substance, thought and feeling." The psychic substance, too, is a most elusive thing. The crossing-over from Manipura to Anahata, says Jung, is a difficult one, for in it lies the "recognition" that the "psyche is self-moving, that it is something genuine which is not yourself, is exceedingly difficult to see and admit. It means that the consciousness which you call yourself is at an end." You are no longer master in your own house. It is tantra-yoga, Jung concedes, that recognizes this psychogenic factor as the first recognition of the Purusha, the Cosmic Man.

In the Visuddha chakra, the elephant reappears, this time as the white Airavata, bearer of Indra. According to Jung, it represents the insurmountable sacred strength of the animal that now supports the volatile substance of the mind. It is the elephant that brought us to birth in the Muladhara, but we can see that transubstantiation has taken place: the black is now white, and the earth has become ether.

At the Ajna chakra, the animal symbolism fails and gives way to the linga emblem. The corolla of the chakra itself looks like a wing. The ego disappears for, as Jung remarks, "the psychical is no longer a content in us, we become a content of it." Instead of the dark germ, the linga is a "full-blazing white light, fully conscious." In Ajna chakra there is still the experience of a self apparently separate from the object of God, but in the Sahasrara chakra, it is not different. "So the next conclusion would be that there is no object, no God, there is nothing but Brahman. There is no experience because it is one, it is without a second." In tantric symbolism this state is the union of Shiva and Shakti. If it is true that this total union "knows no end," it means that the aspirant who has achieved this condition "will not return," will never again return from his free state of *jivan-mukta*, liberated while yet living.

Like the animal symbolism, each chakra has its appropriate number of petals and corresponding color: Muladhara is represented as a red lotus of four petals; Svadhisthana as a vermilion lotus of six petals; Manipura as a blue lotus of ten petals; Anahata as a lotus of twelve petals of golden color; Visuddha as a lotus of sixteen petals of smoky purple; Ajna as a lotus of two white petals; and lastly, Sahasrara is the thousand-petalled lotus of the light of a thousand suns.

In the process of self-realization, the highest goal, identified with the arousal of Kundalini, is recognized as a microcosmic version of the feminine power of Shakti. The tantrikas identify the power of Shakti with Cosmic Consciousness, since she projects the bi-unity of male and female principles. In order to realize this, the discipline of tantra-asanas, or the sexo-yogic postures, has developed into a formidable series of psychophysical practices requiring the same type of discipline as meditation.

According to tantra, the Kundalini Shakti can be aroused by the practice of tantra-yoga-asanas, as it asserts: "One must rise by that by which one may fall." What on the cosmic plane is fusion of polarities is, on the biological level, the sexual union of asana—not sexual "intercourse" as commonly and wrongly stated. Throughout the ages the sex act has been generally associated with procreation or gross physical satisfaction. Tantrikas, however, realized the immense potentiality of sex energy, and, through tantra-asanas, transferred the energy of sex and freed it to a plane of cosmic awareness. From the tantric point of view, the consummated human being is man and woman fused into a single unit. With emergence of the idea of basic unity, that the two are inseparable, the state of *ananda*, of infinite joy or perpetual bliss, is reached. Tantra thus prescribes the discipline which transforms the physical union of man and woman into a creative union of Shiva-Shakti.

How long the aspirant will have to stay at each chakra depends on his or her attachment and karmic action. The root chakra Muladhara, fourth chakra Anahata and fifth chakra Ajna are the greatest obstacles to the rising of Kundalini. These three chakras are associated with psychic blockages called lingas. A dynamization, transformation and sublimation of the physical, mental, and spiritual state is only possible with the arousal of the Kundalini Shakti and her reorientation from downward to upward movement as she rises to unite with Shiva, resulting in the flooding of the whole being with indescribable bliss. The aspirant himself rises from the grosser elements to the subtler, and realizes, in a transcendental experience, his union with Shiva-Shakti. The chakras represent a symbolic theory of the psyche. Symbols allow us to see things from the subtle aspect. It is as if, through the chakras, we viewed the psyche from the standpoint of a fourth dimension unlimited by space and time. They represent intuitions about the psyche as a whole, and symbolize the psyche from a cosmic standpoint.

Sometimes the use of psychedelic preparations is prescribed to attain the desired result, and the potential exploratory value of substances considered to be charged with pranic energies may be very striking. But for the unprepared, their use to attain altered states of consciousness is likely to give rise to many problems.

Peak experiences can occur when there is deep emotional resonance and mutual understanding during sexual intercourse, or during the delivery of a child. Under these circumstances one can transcend individual boundaries and experience feelings of oneness due to Kundalini's split-second arousal. Stanislav Grof observes, however, that "even if the sexual intercourse and the delivery of a child occur under optimal circumstances and have a cosmic quality, they seem to have a certain degree of inherent ambiguity." During sexual intercourse, Grof maintains, the partners can experience glimpses of cosmic unity and transcend their feelings of individual separateness. But at the same time, this sexual union can lead to the conception of a new individual and send him or her on the way toward isolation from cosmic consciousness and in the direction of increasing individualization and alienation. Similarly, while the mother is experiencing cosmic feelings during the delivery of her child, the newborn is confronted with the agony of birth and trauma of separation. The emotional and physical pain involved in this process then becomes the decisive factor alienating the new individual from undifferentiated cosmic consciousness that he or she experienced as a fetus.

The ascent of Kundalini as it pierces through the chakras is manifested in certain physical and psychic signs. Yogis have described the trembling of the body which precedes the arousal of Kundalini, and the explosion of heat which passes like a current through the Susumna channel. During Kundalini's ascent, inner sounds resemble a waterfall, the humming of bees, the sound of a bell, a flute, or the tinkling of ornaments. In closed-eye perception the yogi visualizes a variety of forms, such as dots of light, or geometrical shapes that in the final state of illumination dissolve into an inner radiance of intensely bright, pure light. The aspirant may experience creeping sensations in the spinal cord, tingling sensations all over the body, heaviness in the head or sometimes giddiness, automatic and involuntary laughing or crying; or he may see visions of deities or saints. Dreamscenes of all kinds may appear, from the heavenly to the demonic. Physically, the abdomen wall may become flat and be drawn towards the spine; there may be diarrhea or constipation; the anus contracts and is drawn up; the chin may press down against the neck; the eyeballs roll upwards or rotate; the body may bend forward or back, or even roll around on the floor; breathing may be constricted, (sometimes it seems to cease altogether, although in fact it does not, but merely becomes extremely slight); the mind becomes empty and there is an experience of being a witness in the body.

There may be a feeling of Prana flowing in the brain or spinal cord. Sometimes there is a spontaneous chanting of mantras or songs, or simply vocal noises. The eyes may not open in spite of one's efforts to open them. The body may revolve or twist in all directions. Sometimes it bounces up and down with crossed legs, or creeps about, snake-like, on the floor. Some perform asanas (yogic postures) both known and unknown; sometimes the hands move in classic, formal dance patterns, even though the meditator knows nothing of dance. Some speak in tongues.

Sometimes the body feels as if it is floating upwards, and sometimes as if it is being pressed down into the earth. It may feel as if it has grown enormously large, or extremely small. It may shake and tremble and become limp, or turn as rigid as stone. Some get more appetite, some feel aversion to food. Even when engaged in activities other than meditation, the aspirant who concentrates his mind, experiences movements of Prana-shakti all over the body, or slight tremors. There may be aches in the body, or a rise or drop in temperature. Some people become lethargic and averse to work. Sometimes the meditator hears buzzing sounds as of blowing conches, or bird-song or ringing bells. Questions may arise in the mind and be spontaneously answered during meditation.

Sometimes the tongue sticks to the palate or is drawn back towards the throat, or protrudes from the mouth. The throat may get dry or parched. The jaws may become clenched, but after a time they reopen. One may start yawning when one sits for meditation. There may be a feeling of the head becoming separated from the body, or "headlessness." Sometimes one may be able to see things around one even with the eyes closed. Various types of intuitive knowledge may begin. One may see one's own image. One may even see one's own body lying dead. From some or all of these signs, one may know that Kundalini Shakti has become active. The Kundalini produces whatever experiences are necessary for the aspirant's spiritual progress, according to habit-pattern formed by past action.

Swami Muktananda, initiated by his spiritual preceptor, describes in his own autobiographical account his heaviness of head, sensations of heat and of pain at the base of the spine, the involuntary movements, flows of energy through the body, unusual breathing-patterns, inner lights and sounds, visions and voices, and many other extraordinary experiences. In another recent autobiographical record, Gopi Krishna describes his experiences when Kundalini was aroused spontaneously, without spiritual preparation or the guidance of a guru.

Ramakrishna, who followed the discipline of kundalini-yoga under the guidance of a female guru, Brahmani, achieved in three days the result promised by each of the rituals. He described his experience as hopping, pushing up, moving zig-zag. He directly perceived the ascent of the Kundalini, and later described to his disciples its various movements as fishlike, birdlike, monkeylike, and so on.

Ramakrishna tried to describe the details of his Kundalini experience to his close disciples. He said: "I'll tell you everything today and will not keep anything secret." Pointing to the spot between the eyebrows, he said, "the supreme Self is directly known and the individual experiences samadhi when the mind comes here. There remains then but a thin transparent screen separating the supreme Self and the individual self. The aspirant then experiences . . ." and that moment he was plunged in samadhi. When the samadhi came to an end, he tried again to describe the realization of the supreme Self and was again in samadhi. After several fruitless attempts, he broke down in tears. "Well, I sincerely wish to tell you everything . . . without concealing anything whatsoever," but Ramakrishna was unable to speak — "Who should speak? The very distinction between 'I' and 'thou' vanishes; whenever I try to describe what kind of visions I experience when it goes beyond this place (showing the throat) and think what kinds of visions I am witnessing, the mind rushes immediately up, and speaking becomes impossible." In the final center, "the distinction between the subject of consciousness and the object of consciousness is destroyed. It is a state wherein self-identity and the field of consciousness are blended in one indissoluble whole."

Supernatural powers are one of the manifestations associated with the practice of Kundalini yoga, and they may also appear following spontaneous arousal of the Kundalini energy. Self-actualization may be manifested in such special attainments (siddhis) as living without food, duplicating one's body, gaining knowledge of the planets, stars, universe and the whole cosmos, weightlessness, levitation and travel through space, defying gravity, etc. Although they may arise in the course of Kundalini yoga, these supernatural powers are seen by tantrikas as impediments to the attainment of the higher consciousness and liberation.

There has been little systematic clinical study or scientific investigation of the Kundalini phenomena, although certain discrepancies between the classical descriptions of Kundalini experience and modern clinical findings have led Western researchers to propose a "physio-Kundalini" model to account for their observations. This concept has been derived from a model proposed by Itzak Bentov, an American researcher who approached the problem of altered states of consciousness through studies of the effects of vibration-frequencies on human physiology. All the characteristic elements of the Kundalini experience are included in the classical descriptions, yet these descriptions differ in some aspects from modern clinical observations. Researchers have found that the "energy sensation" travels up the legs to the spine to the top of the head, then down the face, through the throat, to a terminal point in the abdomen, whereas in the classical descriptions the energy awakens at the base of the spine, travels up the spinal canal, and completes its journey when it reaches the top of the head.

The classical description of Kundalini awakening at the base of the spine is similarly at variance with the experience described by Ramakrishna, that "something rises with a tingling sensation from the feet to the head." This disparity may be resolved by the traditional representations of Kundalini yoga, particularly in old scroll-paintings. The depths of the unconscious are generally depicted as the gigantic serpent *Sesha*, meaning "residue," so named because it was born from what remained after the creation. Sesha's thousand heads are expanded into a mighty hood, and it forms the couch of Vishnu who reclines on its coils in trance-sleep. An archetype of the unconscious, it rises from the depth of the primeval waters and, passing through Vishnu's early manifestations or "descents," as fish, tortoise or boar, touches human beings. Only then does it come to the Muladhara or base chakra, the controlling center which cannot be by-passed, where the Kundalini energy lies in the dormant state until its unfolding.

Classic paintings also illustrate the fact that the process does not stop when Kundalini reaches the highest chakra, Sahasrara; it becomes supra-mental as one enters the higher stages of consciousness, participating in the greatest cosmic adventure—an experiential journey of the expansion of human consciousness. Ken Wilber rightly says that "Beginning with the sixth chakra, the Ajna chakra, consciousness *starts* to go trans-personal. Consciousness is now going trans-verbal *and* trans-personal. . . . This is total and utter transcendence and release into Formless Consciousness, Boundless Radiance. There is here no self, no God, no final-God, no objects, no thingness, apart from other than Consciousness as Such. . . . Each step is an increase in consciousness and an identification of Awareness until all forms return to perfect and radical release in Formlessness."

According to Kashmir Shaivism, the highest Reality, which is nothing but *caitanya* or Pure Consciousness, is Parama-Shiva. The various planes in ascending order are: Bindu, Ardhacandra, Rodhini, Nada, Nadanta, Shakti, Vyapika, Nirvana, Unmani and finally the ultimate state of Mahabindu or the supracosmic and metacosmic Void, "a void containing everything" in Lau Tzu's phrase. An aspirant of Kundalini yoga must penetrate these stages of consciousness to reach the supraconscious levels. The realization of Mahabindu or Paramashiva is possible only after the awakening of Kundalini. One should not, however, conclude that the different stages or parts of the Kundalini process take place, as it were, externally: they are intimately connected with the broader system, and the progression is within the whole, i.e., within Sahasrara.

The symptoms of the Kundalini phenomena are of variable duration. With some individuals a specific symptom may linger for months or even years. The full symptomatic sequence may not appear immediately, or may not seem to follow connectedly. As a result, the whole process has frequently been dismissed as a psychosomatic or neurotic disturbance, and owing to the general lack of understanding of its nature, drastic and unnecessary treatment, as for schizophrenia or other mental illness, has been resorted to.

Writing of the variations in Kundalini experience, researcher, Lee Sannella, an American doctor, observes that, "if we accept the view that they are the results of the balancing action of Kundalini as it removes blocks throughout the system, then individual differences in symptom-patterns mean that separate areas are blocked. This may be due to differences in genetic make-up and past history of the persons. Also, these processes may last from a few months to several years. Such differences in time-span may be caused by variation in the intensity of meditation and in the total amount of balancing needed. . . . This arrest of the physio-kundalini cycle may occur in those who become fascinated with some particular psychic ability.

THE PLANES OF EXISTENCE

0 ● Mahābindu (the Absolute Void)

9 Unmanī (superconsciousness—beyond mind) Śiva-tattva

8 Nirvāṇa (Samanā) ⎫
⎬ Śakti-tattva
7 Vyāpikā (Vyāpinī) ⎭

6 Kalā (Śakti) ⎫
⎪
5 Nādantā ⎬ Creative pulsation of sound and light
⎪
4 Nāda ⎭

3 Rodhinī (Nirodhikā) Subtle energy of sound

2 Ardhacandra (Ardhendu) The half-moon light/subtle energy

1 Bindu (point) Compact mass of energy projecting itself/the
two poles: zero and infinity

↑

Higher Levels of Consciousness

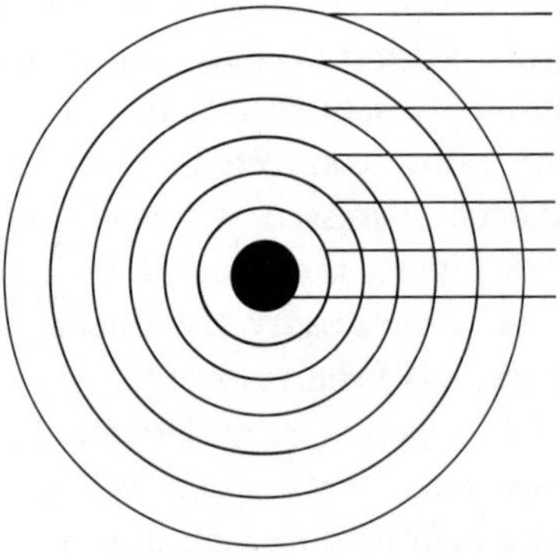

ONTOSPHERE	BODY-COSMOS
7 Satyaloka	7 Sahasrāra
6 Tapaloka	6 Ājñā
5 Jñānaloka	5 Viśuddha
4 Maharloka	4 Anāhata
3 Svarloka	3 Maṇipūra
2 Bhuvarloka	2 Svādhisthaña
1 Bhurloka (earth)	1 Mūlādhāra

↑

Emergence from the Unconscious

1 Atala

2 Vitala

3 Sutala

4 Talātala

5 Mahātala

6 Rasātala

7 Pātāla

*From below: the seven talas,
subterranean regions of the unconscious,
from which the Serpent-Power emerges
and ascends through the relative worlds,
beginning with Bhurloka (earth).*

*According to Kashmir Śaivism, the
cosmos reverts through higher levels of
consciousness to the Absolute Void, which
is the ultimate unified field, the
Mahābindu (Śiva-Śakti), the very source
and essence of all life.*

FIGURE 12–2

Such an exclusive focus may intercept the progression at that particular stage. Further variation occurs over a period of time; the signs and symptoms are not present continuously but come on at intervals, most often in meditation, during quiet time or in sleep."

Lee Sannella further observes that "Kundalini plays a much larger part in daily life than most of us have hitherto supposed; there is a far lower and gentler manifestation of it which is already awake within us all, which is not only innocuous but beneficent, which is doing its appointed work day and night while we are entirely unconscious of its presence and activity." He also suggests that the "physio-kundalini" mechanism may be a separate entity, which can be activated as a part of a full Kundalini awakening.

David Tansley, in England, recently reported on "radionic" methods of diagnosis primarily concerned with the utilization of subtle force fields and energies in the human organism. "Chakras," he writes, "can be damaged by traumatic accidents, and especially by sudden, dramatic, emotional shocks. Nagging fears or anxiety can, through constant wearing activity, disturb the functional balance. Chakras are frequently found to be blocked, either at the point where energy enters, or at the point where it exits to flow into the etheric body. If a blockage occurs at the entrance, the energy flowing in is frequently driven back to its point of origin on the astral or mental planes. This brings about psychological problems and endocrine dysfunction. If the blockage is at the exit, the energy builds up until enough pressure enables it to burst through to stimulate the appropriate endocrine gland. This causes erratic endocrine function with attendant physical and psychological problems."

There are, however, two important facts to keep in mind while research and investigation continues. One is that panic is only experienced by those individuals who are unfamiliar with meditation techniques, and who therefore have no way of understanding or of controlling these symptoms in themselves. The other is that meditation itself is no chance response to a chance stimulus. It is a systematic and willed modulation of consciousness that puts the body into harmony with itself and with the macrocosm. The importance of this initiating element is clear in all ancient texts on Kundalini and cannot be over-stressed.

A growing number of people in the West are experiencing Kundalini and new-age healing facilities are not oriented to or experienced in the handling of the Kundalini process. Many aspirants are concerned about the possibilities of dangers involved in the practice of self-taught Kundalini yoga. It is here that a competent guru will help one to progress through a systematic method, yet responsibility must finally come back to oneself. One must learn to work with and control the inner energies.

Once experienced, the awakening of the Kundalini remains a permanent element in one's life. Jung points out: "It is really a continuous development. It is not leaping up and down, for what you have arrived at is never lost. Say you have been in Muladhara and then you reach the water-center (Svadhisthana), and afterwards you return, apparently. But you do not return; it is an illusion that you return; you have left something of yourself in the unconscious." So Jung concludes that nobody touches the unconscious without leaving something of himself there. The experience may be forgotten or repressed but it cannot be lost. When the highest level is reached, the "supraconscious" state in which union is realized, one will eventually have to descend if one wants to express oneself through creativity; and when this creativity is completed, one will have the urge to return again into one's true identity, that is, to fusion with the Absolute.

REFERENCES

BENTOV, I. *Stalking the Wild Pendulum*. New York: E. P. Dutton, 1977.

GROF, S. "LSD and the Cosmic Game: Outline of Psychedelic Cosmology and Ontology." *Journal for the Study of Consciousness*, 5, (1972–3): 165.

JUNG, C. G. *Psychological Commentary on Kundalini Yoga*. New York: Spring, 1975–76.

MUKTANANDA, SWAMI. *The Play of Consciousness*. San Francisco, CA.: Shree Gurudev Siddha Yoga Ashram, 1974.

SANNELLA, L. *Kundalini: Psychosis and Transcendence*. San Francisco, CA.: H. Dakin, 1977.

TANSLEY, D. V. *Radionics and the Subtle Anatomy of Man*. Bradford, 1976.

WILBER, K. "Spectrum Psychology." *Re-Vision*, 2, (1979): 70.

Part III
NEW PARADIGMS
IN WESTERN SCIENCE

13

Fritjof Capra   The New Vision of Reality:
Toward a Synthesis of Eastern
Wisdom and Western Science

A dramatic change of concepts and ideas has occurred in physics
during the first three decades of the century. Still being elaborated in
our current theories of matter, the new concepts have profoundly
changed our world view from the mechanistic thinking of Descartes
and Newton to a holistic and ecological view.

The new view was by no means easy to accept for physicists at the
beginning of the century. Exploration of the atomic and subatomic
world brought them in contact with a strange and unexpected reality. In their struggle to grasp this new reality, scientists became pain-
fully aware that their basic concepts, their language, and their whole
way of thinking were inadequate to describe atomic phenomena.
Their problems were not merely intellectual but amounted to an intense emotional and even existential crisis. It took scientists a long
time to overcome this crisis, but in the end they were rewarded with
deep insights into the nature of matter and its relation to the human
mind.

I have come to believe that today the nations and societies around
the world find themselves in a similar crisis. We can read about its
numerous manifestations every day in the newspapers. Most of our
economies produce high inflation and unemployment, with undimin-
ishing levels of poverty and starvation; there is an energy crisis, a

crisis in health care, an environmental crisis, and a rising wave of violence and crime. I believe that these are all different facets of one and the same crisis, which is essentially a crisis of perception. Like the crisis in physics in the 1920s, it derives from the fact that we are trying to apply the concepts of an outdated world view—the mechanistic world view of Cartesian-Newtonian science—to a reality which can no longer be understood in terms of these concepts.

Although the Cartesian world view is characteristic of Western rather than Eastern culture, many of its basic principles are now also applied in the East, due to the worldwide adoption of Western science and technology. The Cartesian world view has now reached its limitations in many fields, including physics, biology, medicine, psychology, and economics. We live today in a globally interconnected world, in which biological, psychological, social and environmental phenomena are all interdependent. To describe this world appropriately we need an ecological perspective which the Cartesian world view does not offer.

What we need, then, is a new paradigm—a new vision of reality, and a fundamental change in our thoughts, perceptions and values. The beginnings of this shift from the mechanistic to the holistic conception of reality are visible in all fields and are likely to dominate the decade. The gravity and global extent of our crisis indicate that it is likely to result in a transformation of unprecedented dimensions, a turning point for the planet as a whole.

The New Vision of Reality

The new vision of reality is ecological, but it goes far beyond immediate concerns with environmental protection. It is supported by modern science, but rooted in a perception of reality that reaches beyond the scientific framework to an intuitive awareness of the oneness of all life, the interdependence of its multiple manifestations, and its cycles of change and transformation. When the concept of the human spirit is understood in the transpersonal sense, as the mode of consciousness in which the individual feels connected to the cosmos as a whole, it becomes clear that ecological awareness is truly spiritual. Indeed, the idea that the individual is linked to the cosmos is expressed in the Latin root of the word religion, *religare* ("to bind strongly"), as well as in the Sanskrit *yoga*, which means "union."

It is thus not surprising that the new vision of reality comes very close to the views of mystics of all ages and traditions and, in particular, to the views held in the spiritual traditions of India. Ten years ago, I was amazed to find the most striking parallels between modern physics and Eastern mysticism. These parallels can now be extended with equal justification to biology, psychology and other sciences. We now can say, with considerable confidence, that the ancient wisdom of the East provides the most consistent philosophical background to our modern scientific theories.

The New View of Matter

Let me begin discussion of the new vision of reality with the view of matter that has emerged from modern physics. According to contemporary physics, the material world is not a mechanical system made of separate objects, but rather appears as a complex web of relationships. Subatomic particles cannot be understood as isolated, separate entities but must be seen as interconnections, or correlations, in a network of events. The notion of separate objects is an idealization that can be useful but has no fundamental validity. In the words of Werner Heisenberg, one of the founders of quantum theory:

> The world thus appears as a complicated tissue of events, in which connections of different kinds alternate or overlap or combine and thereby determine the texture of the whole.

This is very much the way Eastern mystics experience the world. Take, for example, the following statement by Sri Aurobindo:

> The material object becomes . . . something different from what we now see, not a separate object on the background or in the environment of the rest of nature but an indivisible part and even in a subtle way an expression of the unity of all that we see.

As another example, let me quote Henry Stapp, an atomic physicist:

> An elementary particle is not an independently existing unanalyzable entity. It is, in essence, a set of relationships that reach outward to other things.

Compare this with Nagarjuna, founder of the Buddhist Madhyamika school:

> Things derive their being and nature by mutual dependence and are nothing in themselves.

The Cosmic Dance

Physicists and mystics agree that what we call "objects" are really patterns in an inseparable cosmic process, and they also agree that these patterns are intrinsically dynamic. In subatomic physics, mass is no longer associated with a material substance but is recognized as a form of energy. Energy, however, is associated with activity, with processes; it is a measure of activity. Subatomic particles are dynamic patterns, processes rather than objects. Similarly, what we call "thing" has been described by Indian mystics with the Sanskrit term *samskara*, a term that means first of all "an event," or "a happening," and only secondarily "an existing thing." As the Buddhist scholar D.T. Suzuki explains, "Buddhists have conceived an object as an event and not as a thing or substance."

The energy patterns of the subatomic world form stable atomic and molecular structures that build up matter and give it its macroscopic solid appearance, thus making us believe it is made of some material substance. At the macroscopic level, the notion of a substance is quite useful, but at the atomic level it no longer makes sense. Atoms consist of particles and these particles are not made of any material stuff. When we observe them we never see any substance; what we observe are dynamic patterns continually changing into one another—a continuous dance of energy.

The metaphor of the dance naturally comes to mind when one studies the dynamic web of relationships that constitutes the subatomic world. Since mystics have a dynamic world view similar to that of modern physicists, it is not surprising that they, too, have used the image of the dance to convey their intuition of nature. The metaphor of the cosmic dance has found its most beautiful expression in Hinduism in the image of Shiva Nataraja, the Lord of Dancers. For the modern physicist, the dance of Shiva is the dance of subatomic matter. As in Hindu mythology, it is a continual dance of creation and destruction involving the whole cosmos—the basis of all existence and of all natural phenomena.

The Systems View of Life

The holistic and ecological world view of modern physics emphasizes the fundamental interrelatedness and interdependence of all phenomena, and the intrinsically dynamic nature of the physical reality. To use this view to describe living organisms, we must go beyond physics, to a framework that seems to be a natural extension of the concepts of modern physics. This framework is known as systems theory, sometimes called general systems theory. Actually, the term "systems theory" is somewhat misleading, since it is not a well-defined theory, like relativity theory or quantum theory. It is rather a particular approach, a language, and a particular perspective.

The systems view looks at the world in terms of relationships and integration. Systems are integrated wholes whose properties cannot be reduced to those of smaller units. Instead of concentrating on basic building blocks or basic substances, the systems approach emphasizes basic principles of organization. Examples of systems abound in nature. Every organism—from the smallest bacterium, through the wide range of plants and animals, to humans—is an integrated whole and thus a living system. Cells are living systems, and so are the various tissues and organs of the body, the human brain being the most complex example. But systems are not confined to individual organisms and their parts. The same aspects of wholeness are exhibited by social systems such as a family or a community and by ecosystems that consist of a variety of organisms and inanimate matter in mutual interaction.

All these natural systems are wholes whose specific structures arise from the interactions and interdependence of their parts. Systemic properties are destroyed when a system is dissected, either physically or theoretically, into isolated elements. Although we can discern individual parts in any system, the nature of the whole is always different from the mere sum of its parts.

Systems are intrinsically dynamic. Their forms are not rigid structures but are flexible yet stable manifestations of underlying processes. Systems thinking is process thinking; form becomes associated with process, interrelation with interaction, and opposites are unified through oscillation.

Living systems tend to form multi-leveled structures of systems within systems. For example, the human body contains organ systems composed of several organs, each organ being made up of tissues, and each tissue made up of cells. All these are living organisms or living systems which consist of smaller parts and, at the same time, act as parts of larger wholes. Living systems, then, exhibit a stratified order, and there are interconnections and interdependencies between all systems levels, each level interacting and communicating with its total environment.

Self-organization

Like modern physics, the systems view is an ecological view. It emphasizes the interrelatedness and interdependence of all phenomena and the dynamic nature of living systems. All structure is seen as a manifestation of underlying processes, and living systems are described as patterns of organization.

What, then, are the patterns of organization that are characteristic of life? They include a variety of processes and phenomena which can be seen as different aspects of the same dynamic principle, the principle of self-organization. A living organism is a self-organizing system; that is, its order in structure and function is not imposed by the environment but is established by the system itself. Self-organizing systems exhibit a certain degree of autonomy; for example, independent of environmental influences, they tend to establish their size according to internal principles of organization. But living systems are not isolated from their environment; on the contrary, they interact with it continually, although this interaction does not determine their organization.

The relative autonomy of self-organizing systems sheds new light on the age-old philosophical question of free will. From the systems point of view, both determinism and freedom are relative concepts. To the extent that a system is autonomous from its environment, it is free; to the extent that it depends on it through continuous interaction, its activity will be shaped by environmental influences. The relative autonomy of organisms usually increases with their complexity, and it reaches its culmination in human beings.

This relative concept of free will seems to be perfectly consistent with the views of mystical traditions that exhort their followers to transcend the notion of an isolated self and become aware that we are inseparable parts of the cosmos in which we are embedded. The goal of these traditions is to shed all ego sensations completely and, in mystical experience, merge with the totality of the cosmos. Once such a state is reached, the question of free will seems to lose its meaning. If I *am* the universe, there can be no "outside" influences, and all my actions will be spontaneous and free. From the point of view of mystics, therefore, the notion of free will is relative, limited and illusory, like all other concepts we use in our rational descriptions of reality.

A theory of self-organizing systems has been worked out over the last decade in considerable detail by a number of researchers from various disciplines under the leadership of the Belgian Nobel Laureate Ilya Prigogine. One of the most important characteristics of self-organization is the fact that self-organizing systems are "always at work." They have to maintain a continuous exchange of energy and matter with their environment to stay alive. This exchange involves taking in ordered structures, such as food, breaking them down, and using some of the resulting components to maintain or increase the order of the organism. This process is known as metabolism.

Another important aspect of the continual activity of living systems is the process of self-renewal. Every living organism continually renews itself, as cells break down and build up structures, and tissues and organs replace their cells in continual cycles. Despite this continual change, the organism maintains its overall structure and appearance. Its components are continually renewed and recycled, but the pattern of organization remains stable. The phenomena of self-healing, regeneration, and adaptation to environmental changes are closely related to the self-renewal aspect of self organization.

The phenomenon of self-renewal, together with that of stratified order, provides us with the proper perspective on the phenomenon of death. Self-renewal—the breaking down and building up of structures in continual cycles—is an essential aspect of living systems. But the structures that are continually being replaced are themselves living organisms. From their point of view, the self-renewal of the larger system is their own cycle of birth and death. Birth and death, therefore, now appear as a central aspect of self-organization, the very essence of life. Death, then, is not the opposite of life but an essential aspect of it. This view is in perfect harmony with that of Eastern spiritual traditions which understand birth and death as stages of endless cycles that represent the continual self-renewal characteristic of the dance of life.

> Rhythmic patterns—fluctuations, oscillations, vibrations, and waves—play a central role in the dynamics of self-organization. At the same time, the notion of rhythmic patterns constitutes an important link to the views of mystics. The idea of fluctuations as the basis of order was introduced into modern science very recently by Prigogine, but it is often found in Eastern spiritual traditions. In particular, it is the very basis of the Chinese *I Ching* and of the entire tradition of Taoism. Because the Taoist sages recognized the importance of fluctuations in their observations of the living world, they also emphasized the opposite but complementary tendencies that seem to be an essential aspect of life.

The importance of rhythmic patterns in visual perception has been emphasized by Karl Pribram in connection with his holographic model of the brain. Pribram has also extended the metaphor of the hologram by suggesting that holonomy—the way that the whole is somehow contained in each of its parts—may be a universal property of nature. This is a frequent theme in the writings and teachings of mystics. Aurobindo, for example, writes:

> Nothing to the supramental sense is really finite; it is founded on a feeling of all in each and each in all.

Most extensively elaborated in the Avatamsaka school of Mahayana Buddhism, the concept of holonomy is also found in two theories of modern physics. One is Geoffrey Chew's bootstrap theory of particles, the other David Bohm's theory of the implicate order.

A New Concept of Mind

Gregory Bateson has proposed that "mind" is a systems phenomenon characteristic of living organisms, societies, and ecosystems. Bateson has listed a set of criteria that systems must satisfy for mind to occur. Any system that satisfies those criteria will be able to process information and develop various phenomena which we associate with mind, including thinking, learning, and memory. In Bateson's view, mind is a necessary and inevitable consequence of a certain complexity that begins long before organisms develop a brain and a higher nervous system.

Bateson's criteria for mind turn out to be closely related to the characteristics of self-organizing systems. Indeed, mind is an essential property of living systems. From the systems point of view, life is not some substance or force, and mind is not an entity interacting with matter. Both life and mind are manifestations of the same set of systemic properties, a set of processes which represent the dynamics of self-organization.

The new concept of mind will be of tremendous value in our attempts to overcome the Cartesian division. Mind and matter no longer appear to belong to two separate categories, but can be seen to represent merely different aspects of the same phenomenon. For example, the relationship between mind and brain, which has confused countless scientists ever since Descartes, now becomes quite clear. Mind is the dynamics of self-organization, and the brain is the biological structure through which this dynamics is carried out.

I follow Bateson completely in his concept of mind, but use a slightly different language. I reserve the term "mind" for organisms of high complexity and use "mentation," a term meaning mental activity, to describe the dynamics of self-organization at lower levels. Every living system—a cell, a tissue, an organ, etc.—is engaged in the process of mentation, but in higher organisms the unfolding of an "inner world" is characteristic of mind. It includes self-awareness, conscious experience, conceptual thought, and symbolic language. Most of these characteristics exist in rudimentary form in various animals, but they unfold fully in human beings.

The fact that the living world is organized in multi-leveled structures means that levels of mind also exist. In the human organism, for example, various levels of "metabolic" mentation occur in cells, tissues, and organs, and neural mentation occurs in the brain, which consists of multiple levels corresponding to different stages of human evolution. The totality of these mentations constitutes what I would call the human mind, or psyche. In the stratified order of nature, individual human minds are embedded in the larger minds of social and ecological systems, and these are integrated into the planetary mental system which in turn must participate in some kind of universal, or cosmic mind.

It is evident that such a view of mind comes very close to the views in spiritual traditions. The concept of stratified order plays a prominent role in many traditions. In modern science, it involves the notion of multiple levels of reality which differ in their complexities and are mutually interacting and interdependent. These include levels of mind which are seen as different manifestations of cosmic consciousness.

Views of Consciousness

This brings me to my last topic, the nature of consciousness—a fundamental existential question that has fascinated men and women throughout the ages. To facilitate discussion of this important subject, let me first clarify my terms. I use the term "consciousness" to mean self-awareness. Awareness is a property of mentation at any level, from single cells to human beings, but self-awareness emerges only at high levels of complexity and unfolds fully in human beings. We are not only aware of our sensations, but also of ourselves as thinking and experiencing individuals. It is this property of mind, which emerges together with the "inner world," that I call consciousness.

Most theories about the nature of consciousness seem to be variations on either of two opposing views that may nevertheless be complementary and reconcilable in the systems approach. One of these views, the Western scientific view, considers matter as primary and consciousness as a property of complex material patterns that emerge at a certain stage of biological evolution. The other view of consciousness, the mystical view, regards consciousness as the primary reality and ground of all being. According to this view, consciousness in its purest form is nonmaterial, formless, and void of all content; it is often described as "pure consciousness," "ultimate reality," "suchness," and the like. This manifestation of consciousness is associated with the Divine in many spiritual traditions. It is said to be the essence of the universe and to manifest itself in all things. All forms of matter and all living beings are seen as patterns of divine consciousness.

The mystical view of consciousness is based on the experience of reality in non-ordinary modes of awareness, which are traditionally achieved through meditation. Psychologists have come to call non-ordinary experiences of this kind "transpersonal" because they seem to allow the individual mind to make contact with collective and even cosmic mental patterns. Transpersonal psychology is concerned with the recognition, understanding, and realization of non-ordinary states of consciousness, and with the psychological conditions that represent barriers to such transpersonal realizations. Its concerns are thus very close to those of spiritual traditions and, indeed, a number of transpersonal psychologists are working on conceptual systems intended to bridge and integrate psychology and the spiritual quest.

According to numerous testimonies, transpersonal experiences involve a strong, personal, and conscious relation to reality that goes far beyond the present scientific framework. We should therefore not expect science, at its present stage, to confirm or contradict the mystical view of consciousness. Nevertheless, the systems view of mind seems perfectly consistent with both the scientific and the mystical views of consciousness, and thus it provides the ideal framework for unifying the two.

The systems view agrees with the conventional scientific view that consciousness is a manifestation of complex material patterns. To be more precise, it is a manifestation of living systems of a certain complexity. On the other hand, the biological structures of these systems are expressions of underlying processes that represent the system's self-organization, and hence its mind. In this sense, material structures are no longer considered the primary reality. Extending this way of thinking to the universe as a whole, it is not too far-fetched to assume that all its structures—from subatomic particles to galaxies and from bacteria to human beings—are manifestations of the universe's self-organizing dynamics, which we have identified with the cosmic mind. But this is almost the mystical view, the only difference being that mystics emphasize the direct experience of cosmic consciousness that goes beyond the scientific approach. Still, the two approaches seem to be quite compatible. The systems view of nature at last seems to provide a meaningful scientific framework for approaching age-old questions about the nature of life, mind, consciousness, and matter.

The new vision of reality has many important implications not only for science, philosophy, and religion, but also for society and everyday living. The new paradigm consists not only of new concepts, but also of a new value system that is reflected in new forms of social organization and institutions. The paradigm shift is not something that will happen some time in the future; it is happening right now. In many countries around the world, the 1960's and 1970's generated a series of philosophical, spiritual and political movements that all seem to go in the same direction; they all emphasize different aspects of the new paradigm.

A rising concern with ecology is being expressed by citizen movements that are forming around social and environmental issues. These movements are often the sources of emerging counter-economies based on decentralized, cooperative and ecologically harmonious life styles. In the political arena, the anti-nuclear movement is fighting the most extreme outgrowth of our aggressive technology and, in doing so, is likely to become one of the most powerful political forces of this decade.

At the same time, values are beginning to shift from the admiration of large-scale enterprises and institutions to the notion of "small is beautiful," from material consumption to voluntary simplicity, from economic and technological growth to inner growth and development. These new values are being promoted by the human-potential movement, the holistic health movement, and by spiritual movements that re-emphasize the quest for meaning and the spiritual dimension of life. Lastly, but perhaps most importantly, the old value system is being challenged and profoundly changed by the rise of feminist awareness, originating in the women's movement, which may well become a catalyst for the coalescence of many other movements.

One of the most interesting cultural phenomena in the United

States is the recent confluence of three powerful trends: ecology, spirituality, and feminism. The spiritual essence of the ecological vision has found an ideal expression in the feminist spirituality advocated by the women's movement, and based on the age-old identification of women and nature. Feminist spirituality is based on awareness of the oneness of all living forms and of their cyclical rhythms of birth and death, thus reflecting an attitude toward life that is profoundly ecological. As feminist authors have pointed out, the image of a female deity seems to embody this kind of spirituality more accurately than the image of a male god does. Indeed, worship of the Goddess predated worship of male deities in many cultures, East and West. With the renaissance of the Goddess image, the feminist movement is also creating a new female self-image, new models of thinking, and a new system of values. Thus feminist spirituality will have a profound influence not only on religion and philosophy but also on social and political life.

Most of these new movements still operate separately and have not yet recognized how their purposes interrelate. The human potential movement and the holistic health movement often lack a social perspective, and spiritual movements tend to lack ecological and feminist awareness, as Eastern gurus display Western capitalist status symbols and spend considerable time building their economic empires. However, some movements have recently begun to form coalitions: the ecology and feminist movements are joining forces on several issues; and environmental groups, consumer groups, and ethnic liberation movements are beginning to make contacts. We can anticipate that, once they have recognized the communality of their aims, these movements will flow together and form a powerful force of cultural transformation.

I have called this force the rising culture, following Toynbee's persuasive model of cultural dynamics. Toynbee and other cultural historians have often pointed out that the evolution of cultures is characterized by a regular pattern of rise, culmination, decline, and disintegration. The decline will occur when a culture has become too rigid in its technology or social organizations to meet the challenge of changing conditions. During this process of decline and disintegration, while the cultural mainstream becomes petrified by clinging to fixed ideas and rigid patterns of behavior, creative minorities appear on the scene and transform some of the old elements into new configurations which become part of the new rising culture.

This pattern is now quite apparent in Europe and North America. The traditional political parties, the large multi-national corporations, and most of our academic institutions are all part of the declining culture. They are in the process of disintegration. The social movements of the 1960s and 1970s represent the rising culture. While the transformation is taking place, the declining culture refuses to change, clinging ever more rigidly to its outdated ideas; nor will the dominant social institutions hand over their leading roles to the new cultural forces. But they will inevitably go on to decline and disintegrate while the rising culture will continue to rise and, eventually, assume its leading role. As the turning point approaches, realization that evolutionary changes of this magnitude cannot be prevented by short-term political activities provides our greatest hope for the future.

14

Rupert Sheldrake   Morphic Resonance

Since the time of the ancient Greeks, Western thinking has been
based on the idea that the phenomenal world—the world we see
and experience, and the world with which science deals—is the reflection of a timeless or eternal world of order. This idea, rooted in
the Platonic tradition, has deeply influenced modern science. Modern mechanists claim to be hard-nosed empiricists concerned only
with facts and with their experience of the senses, but underlying the
hard-nosed mechanist is a Platonic metaphysician who believes that
the world reflects eternal laws. Even though science may never know
them in full, underlying the regularities of nature are the eternal
mathematically formulated laws of physics.

I suggest that the regularity and order we experience in nature—
the kind of order that is reflected in the form of animals and plants
and the patterns we experience with our senses—do not so much reflect eternal laws that are somehow outside nature as they depend
on what has happened before in the world. What has happened in
the past influences what is happening now through patterns in nature that are more like habits than fixed laws. The connection between the past and the present is such that the past is as if leaning
upon the present, conditioning everything that happens. What has
happened in time feeds back to influence what happens in the present, which is conditioned both by the eternal and by the past.

149

To clarify this hypothesis, I start with the scientific problems from which it emerges. It is based in the tradition of attempts to understand the nature of biological form. All living organisms, animals and plants, have shapes and forms; it is on the basis of shapes and forms that we recognize species. The classification of plants and animals, taxonomy, is based on morphology; namely, the shape or form. Morphology is thus the basis of biological classification and the basis of our understanding of species and of life.

How does the form come into being? All biological forms develop from simpler forms. Each plant or animal develops from an egg, a cutting or a part of a previous organism which grows into a whole organism. The process of coming into being of form, or *morphogenesis* (from the Greek *morphe*, or form, and *genesis*, or "coming into being"), brings more form from less. Beginning as the small circular fertilized egg, a little blob of protoplasmic jelly, the embryo develops through various stages, and organs appear until it becomes a complete animal or plant with its characteristic form. The problem is, how does this form arise? We can understand scientifically how it develops, but the cause of that development is one of the central problems of biology. The mechanistic answer—the current scientific answer—explains form in terms of chemistry.

The hereditary chemical DNA is central to this explanation. Although DNA is undoubtedly an important factor in heredity, and although genetics tells us much about the way in which hereditary differences work, DNA does not itself explain form and the coming into being of form. All the cells of our own bodies contain the same DNA. We inherit from our parents' genes and chromosomes the particular DNA that is reproduced exactly in all our cells. Yet the form of the arm or the leg is completely different from that of the ear and the eye: if the DNA is the same and the form is different, then DNA alone cannot account for the difference in form. Something else must interact with the DNA to cause these differences.

In the vitalist tradition of biology it was believed that what interacted with the material basis of life was a formative agent, or *entelechy* that is inherent in living organisms and directs their vital processes, but is not discoverable through scientific investigation. This was rejected in the mechanistic tradition partly on the grounds that it was dualistic, psychic, and not purely chemical, and reductionist.

But the concept of entelechy, this purposive, controlling agent, has been reintroduced into biology in the concept of the genetic program. Since DNA alone cannot explain the coming into being of form and the purposive way in which organisms develop and behave, it is believed that a genetic program, like a computer program directs development and behavior. But the genetic program hypothesis cannot explain why, if all the cells have the same program, they develop differently. It is a dualistic concept that implies the idea of a conscious intelligent design—a programmer. But, when mechanists are asked who the genetic programmer is, they deny that there is any such thing and say chance is responsible. This is unsatisfactory; the genetic program theory is in effect a form of crypto-vitalism, a concept that explains everything and therefore nothing. It does not help us if we are trying to understand the basis of form.

The mechanistic attempt to explain the coming into being of form assumes, in the end, that everything depends upon chemical and physical interactions structured in space. The genetic program is vaguely supposed to account for the structuring, but if a living organism is nothing more than the sum of its interacting parts, it is difficult to account for the holistic properties of organisms, for the fact that they remain wholes when we take parts away.

In experimental embryology the mechanistic approach to morphogenesis is challenged by the fact that when we cut a bit off an embryo, very often the embryo manages to grow and to form a complete organism. If a young sea urchin embryo is cut in half, the result is not half a sea urchin, but a complete sea urchin which is about half the normal size. The rest of the cells adjust; although part of the embryo has been removed, the remaining part somehow remains a whole and gives rise to a whole organism.

A similar phenomenon occurs in regeneration when the cut off part of an organism develops into a complete organism. For example, we can cut a bit off a plant, when propagating by cuttings, and this part will grow into a whole plant. We can cut up a flat worm into small pieces and each small piece can grow into a complete worm. We cut the leg off a newt and the newt can form a new leg. This process of regeneration involves quite different processes from the ones involved in the normal formation of the leg and the embryo. A newt leg and an embryo grow in one way, but when the leg

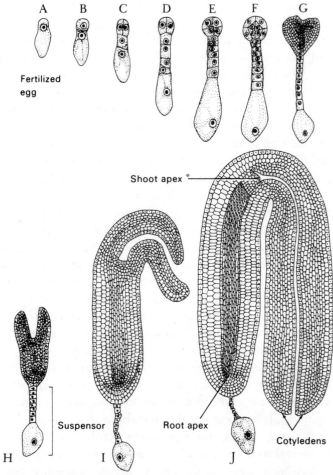

A B C D E F G

Fertilized
egg

Shoot apex

Suspensor   Root apex

H   I   J   Cotyledens

FIGURE 14–1   Stages in the development of the embryo of the
shepherd's purse plant, *Capsella bursa-pastoris*. (After Maheshwari,
1950).

is cut off an adult newt, it is regenerated in a new way. It is not a
mere replay of the embryonic process of leg formation.

Figure 14-1 shows the early stages of the Shepard's purse plant
embryo, and illustrates the general principle of embryology. The
process begins with the fertilized egg, which has very little form. As
the embryo develops, gradually more and more form and order
come into being. The number of cells increases and they take on a

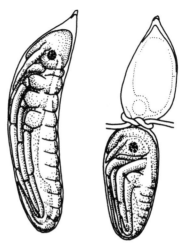

FIGURE 14–2 An example of regulation. On the left is a normal embryo of the dragonfly *Platycnemis pennipes*. On the right is a small but complete embryo formed from the posterior half of an egg ligated around the middle soon after laying. (After Weiss, 1939).

definite pattern, until in the last stage (right hand bottom corner), the embryonic root and shoot, and the two cotyledons, or seedling leaves develop. When the seed germinates, even more form appears. The mature leaves, the stem, the branches, the branches of the roots, and finally the flowers and the seeds with their characteristic forms come into being. The coming into being of form is so commonplace that we tend to forget how extraordinary it is that such order and complexity arise from something that seems so simple.

Figure 14-2 illustrates the process of embryonic regulation. On the left is a normally developed dragon fly egg containing a dragon fly embryo. On the right, the egg has been tied in half with a cotton thread and the top half destroyed. The bottom half of the egg would normally form the back part of the embryo, as shown on the left hand side, but instead it has "regulated" to form a small but complete embryo. If each of the parts was mechanically programmed to develop in only one way, this kind of regulation would be difficult to understand. The processes involved in regeneration pose similar problems.

Figure 14-3 shows the regeneration of lens in the eye of the newt, a type of regeneration discovered in the late nineteenth century by German embryologist Wolff. At that time, Darwinians tended to say that natural selection was responsible for regeneration: those newts able to regenerate legs would naturally be favored over newts whose legs, if removed, would not regenerate. Wolff, therefore, chose quite

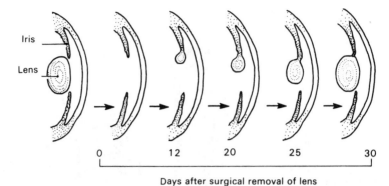

Days after surgical removal of lens

FIGURE   14–3   Regeneration of a lens from the margin of the iris in a newt's eye after the surgical removal of the original lens. (Cf. Needham, 1942).

deliberately a kind of damage which could never have occurred in nature; and which, therefore, natural selection could not account for. He surgically removed the lens from the eye of the newt, causing no other damage. In nature it is almost impossible to conceive of accidental damage that would specifically just remove the lens from the eye. As illustrated here, the eye regenerates a new lens created by the infolding of outside skin. In this regenerative process, the lens forms from the edge of the iris—a completely different tissue—in a completely different way than lens tissue normally forms. This kind of regenerative process suggests that if the normal pathway of development is disrupted, something in the organism adjusts to guide it towards its final form in a different way. There is a purposive or goal-seeking aspect of this process which makes it difficult to understand simply in terms of mechanical or physico-chemical interactions.

This is a brief summary of morphogenesis research in biology. For the last 50 years or so, the mechanistic school has assumed that further research in the chemical and physical interactions involved in the generation and regeneration processes will clarify what is not now understood. This view is thus an article of faith rather than a testable hypothesis. Other embryologists have called for a completely new way of thinking about regeneration. The concept which has found most favor among these embryologists is the concept of morphogenetic fields.

Introduced in 1922, by Russian scientist Alexander Gurwitsch, the morphogenetic field is a field that gives rise to form, or a form field that governs regeneration or regulation. These form fields, Gurwitsch thought, directed tissues and cells so that they developed their characteristic shape or form in the embryo.

If part of an embryo is cut away, the remaining part still has the morphogenetic field associated with it. This field has a holistic property, because fields are continuous; they are not atomistic, one cannot cut bits out of fields. The complete form is restored because the field remains a whole. It is not simply a product of the system it is associated with; rather, the field is a causal structure that guides the development of form and remains associated with the form, maintaining and restoring it, if damaged.

Embryologists understand morphogenetic fields as analogous with magnetic fields. If an ordinary iron bar magnet is cut into two pieces, the result is not two half magnets, but two small whole magnets, each of which has a complete field. Fields are spatial dispositions and not material structures. They are physical, in the sense that physics can explain them but they are not material in the sense that they can be seen or touched. That invisible, spatial structures of a physical nature guide the developing form is implicit in the idea of morphogenetic fields, but as soon as this concept is introduced as explanation for the cause of form, various questions arise: Where do the fields come from? What are they? How do they fit in with the known fields of physics?

For 60 years these questions have not been satisfactorily answered. Some biologists claim the morphogenetic fields must just be a way of talking about such known fields of physics as electrical fields, magnetic fields, chemical interactions, gradients of chemicals, or complicated kinds of statistical interactions between large assemblies of molecules. When pressed hard, such biologists say that the field is a "heuristic device," that is, something that aids the solution to a problem but which cannot itself be specified. So morphogenetic fields are understood as a concept or way of clarifying rather than as physical, empirically discoverable entities. Most biologists still regard morphogenetic fields simply as a way of thinking about morphogenesis rather than something that really exists. The philosophical question of what is real and what really exists is beyond the scope of this discussion, but in the traditional scientific understanding of reality, these fields are not usually considered to have any kind of physical existence.

Some biologists in this tradition think that these fields really do exist but explain their nature and origin with what amounts to a modern form of Platonic metaphysics. According to Brian Goodwin, a biologist who writes on morphogenetic fields, they are none other than archetypal Platonic forms. From the eternal realm of forms or archetypes, they somehow come into time and, acting as morphogenetic fields, bring about the production of forms in space and time. To this view, morphogenetic fields are considered as eternally given; they belong to the timeless, metaphysical realm of Ideas or Forms.

The Platonic view and mechanistic explanation are two ways of thinking about morphogenetic fields. I suggest a third way, which is to regard morphogenetic fields as having a cause. If the field has a structure which determines the form and pattern of the system it is associated with, then the field has a cause, and that cause is the form or organization of previous similar things.

The cause of the morphogenetic field that guides the development of a cat embryo for example, would be the form of previous cats. The growing cat embryo would "tune in" to the forms of previous cats, and their forms would influence its morphogenetic fields. Forms would be determined, guided and maintained by morphogenetic fields, and the actual forms that systems develop would return into the morphogenetic field of that characteristic of that species to influence and modify it. Existing across time, from the past to the present, morphogenetic fields would be determined by what has happened before in that species. Form would influence form, past forms and patterns of organization becoming present to similar systems, so that a species would be influenced by and connected with all of its past members.

This process I call *morphic resonance.* The word "morphic" simply means form; and resonance compares with physical resonance, which works by a sort of self-selection process. Tuning a radio set to a particular transmitter involves a kind of resonance. When we pick the right wave length, we adjust the oscillating circuits within the radio set so that they are oscillating at the same frequency, the same number of kilohertz, as the transmitting station, and that resonance puts the radio in tune with transmissions from that station. Of all possible transmissions, only those in tune will be picked up. In the same way, cat embryos are tuned to the characteristic DNA and proteins of the cat and not to the influence of past dogs, giraffes or oak trees.

One way of thinking about this is in terms of an analogy with the television set. On the television screen we see pictures—forms of people and images of various kinds. If we were trying to understand the nature of these images on the screen, a simple hypothesis—one that children often adopt—is that the television set contains lots of little people whose shadows are cast upon the screen. However, if we look inside the television set, we do not see lots of little people, so that idea must be dropped. A more sophisticated version of the same idea would then be that the people are so little, they are beneath detection by the naked eye or even a microscope inside the wires and transistors. An even more sophisticated idea is that the little people arise through complicated interactions among the parts of the television set such as the wires, transistors, or condensers.

That the picture arises from these interactions and that it is dependent on energy would seem easy to demonstrate: the picture disappears when the TV plug is pulled out; it reappears when the plug is put back in. Likewise, when parts of the circuitry, transistors, or wires are removed, the picture becomes distorted or it disappears; when the parts are replaced, the picture reappears. This would seem to be persuasive evidence that what gives rise to the picture is inside the transistors and the wires. Or, these facts might suggest the more sophisticated explanation that the images depend on complicated interactions between these parts and the rest of the set.

The idea that these little TV people are actually real people who are somewhere else, perhaps hundreds of miles away, and that an invisible influence is traveling from them to the set and interacting with it to produce these images, could be rejected as a sort of occult notion, or a gratuitous mystification. It would seem to be disproven by the fact that the TV weighs no more when it is switched on than it does when it is switched off. If this hypothesis were right, the set should be heavier when it is on because anything coming in from the outside, to exist, must be material, and to be material, must weigh something.

One could then claim that since nothing is entering into the set from outside, what happens there depends on ordinary energy, on wires and transistors, and chemically all these are composed of substances we can easily understand—copper, silicon and other chemicals which can be studied in the laboratory. One might say that although we do not understand the way these complicated interactions give rise to the pictures, we have already found out a great deal—the chemistry of the wires, the nature of the silicon crystals, for example—and in time we will understand much more; in maybe 50 years' time we will probably be able to give a complete explanation of how these images arise just from interactions among the parts of the sets. I think this is exactly the position of current mechanistic biology.

A further argument that nothing enters the set from the outside is the fact that an exact, working duplicate of the set can be created, a replica which is identical in every way. This creation would seem to prove we understand the TV fully—just as the creation of life in a test tube could be thought the ultimate proof that we understood it in terms of chemicals and mechanistic concepts.

The mechanistic picture of the genesis of form is a sort of half truth. It is all right as far as it goes but it really does not take us very far. It is true that we know much about the proteins and DNA of living organisms thanks to the very detailed and intelligent work being done in biochemistry and molecular biology.

But the trouble with the mechanistic view is that it takes a part for the whole. The DNA is indeed involved in heredity, but in my view the DNA is something that sets up the tuning. Like the transistor wires in the TV set, the DNA is necessary for the tuning; it sets up the right proteins and chemicals; it enables the organism to make the characteristic proteins of the species. These proteins and DNA put the organism in tune with past members of the same species because they have the same proteins; this similarity enables morphic resonance to occur. As the organism develops and takes up more order, the tuning becomes more specific. The more order there is, the more it relates to specific past organisms.

I suggest that there is a new kind of connection between similar things that physics, at present, does not take into account. Since the seventeenth century, from Newton onwards, we have been familiar with the idea of action at a distance in space, or, rather, action through fields. This was difficult for people to grasp at first—Newton himself had problems with it—because the idea that the moon and the earth could act reciprocally on each other through what Newton himself describes as an occult, hidden force countered the belief that causation can only work through contact. When we want to cause something in the physical world, we ultimately push or pull something. Even a modern automated machine has push-buttons. The idea of an action at a distance which does not involve pushing or pulling or a medium through which it could work, was difficult. In the context of electromagnetism, the ether was introduced as a medium through which influences could travel. In modern physics the concept of the field serves that role. It has an important psychological function by providing a continuous medium through which causation in space can work.

Although we accept the idea of action at a distance in space, modern science still retains its original presupposition that there is no such thing as action at a distance in time. The present is supposed to be caused by the immediate past—milliseconds before—and so the immediate pushing of the past on the present through a very small space of time is usually understood as contact between past and present. I suggest that things in what we normally think of as the distant past actually influence the present directly. This causation across time, like action at a distance in time, questions our understanding of time as being extended in a quasi-spatial manner. It suggests, instead, that the whole of the past is simply present everywhere, always. Instead of stretching out as if a hundred years were a hundred units away and two hundred years, two hundred units away, the whole of the past may be as it were *concertinoed* into the present so that the past is present always.

This concept is testable experimentally. We can illustrate that if animals and plants are influenced by other members of the species, then this influence will depend on the numbers of past organisms that are influencing them. There is a cumulative effect of the past and, since not all past organisms are the same, you get a sort of averaging of past organisms.

Figure 14-4 illustrates the influence I mean. Given systems that are similar but existing at different times, the first such system will have

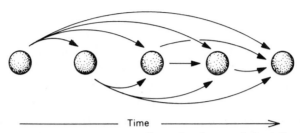

Time ————————→

FIGURE   14–4   Diagram illustrating the cumulative influence of past systems on subsequent similar systems by morphic resonance.

no influence from the past acting on its characteristic type. But the second one will be influenced by the first; the third one will be influenced by the first and the second; the fourth one by the first, second and third; the fifth one by the first, second, third and fourth, and so on. The influence will have a cumulative character: the more often things happen, the greater the influence will become. Since this kind of influence through morphogenetic fields is not energetic in the normal sense of physical energy, I do not think it is attenuated or reduced by distance in space or time. In fact, I think that, in a sense, it abolishes distance in space or time; these influences, once there, continue indefinitely. The more systems brought into being, the greater the influence piling up through this kind of process becomes.

Morphogenetic fields are not sharply defined; they are probability structures, because they depend upon a sort of statistical aggregate of past systems. Since no two systems—human faces or cats, for example—are identical, the morphogenetic field is not sharply defined. Species are not sharply defined but they do have a common form. We recognize individuals because of the way they deviate from a similar type, but there is something similar in all the members of a species.

Figure 14-5 illustrates how morphogenetic fields are hierarchically ordered. Hierarchies are usually represented with the tree diagram (on the left), but exactly the same hierarchical organization can be represented with a "Chinese box" diagram (on the right) that shows, I think, how morphogenetic fields work. The morphogenetic field of the organism, represented by the outside ring, governs and controls the probabilistic processes within the morphogenetic fields of the organs, the circles next in. Those control the morphogenetic field of

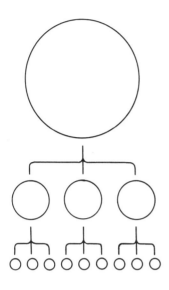

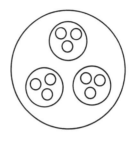

'Tree' diagram of hierarchical   'Chinese box' diagram of

system   hierarchical system

FIGURE   14–5   Alternative ways of representing a simple hierarchical system.

the tissues, which control those of the cells, which control those of the subcellular parts, and so on.

Morphogenetic fields could be responsible for the forms of chemical systems as well as those of biological life. The outer circle could be the form of a crystal, the inner ones the forms of molecules, those inside them the forms of the atoms, and those, in turn, would have within them forms of subatomic particles, and so on. In nature there are hierarchies of the morphogenetic fields which are probabilistic and work upon other morphogenetic fields, ordering and fashioning them.

This, then, is the basic structure of the hypothesis. Although this hypothesis was primarily developed to explain the organization of form and pattern and shape, many who have worked in this area of biology believe the organization of behavior, and movement, in animals is similarly directed. Because movements involve changes in shape, the control of movement and action through the nervous system could also be determined by fields of the same kind, organizing and patterning behavior. Behavior is, in fact, a kind of morphogenesis which involves change of form often in cyclical patterns, like running or walking. As we run or walk, the body form changes, but it keeps returning to where it was before and the net result is movement.

This hypothesis can be tested in chemistry, plant and animal genetics, as well as in the realm of behavior. In the chemical realm, the form of crystals, for example, is determined by characteristic morphogenetic fields which organize the way in which the molecules crystalize. It is usually assumed that ordinary chemistry can predict the forms of crystals, but this is not the case. Quantum theory, which is assumed to provide the theoretical basis of chemistry, cannot be extrapolated to predict definitely the form of a complicated molecule or a crystal. Chemists simply use approximate methods that enable them to calculate sometimes hundreds of different structures, which, as far as they can see, have an equally low potential energy and are equally probable. But they cannot determine exactly which of these will be realized. I believe the morphogenetic field is responsible for these unique forms, giving, of all the possible forms, a particular one. The lattice molecular structure of the crystals is, for example, determined by morphogenetic fields.

Given a type of crystal that has existed for a long time, like sodium chloride—ordinary salt—the numbers of past crystals acting upon each new salt crystal that appears are countless; crystals have been forming for so many millions of years that the habit of crystallizing is well established, and it appears governed by changeless laws.

But a new compound that has never existed before should be very difficult to crystallize, because it would lack a morphogenetic field and past influences to channel it into a particular form. However, once it had crystallized a first time, it should do so more easily the second time because of the influence of the first crystal. It should get easier and easier to crystallize particular compounds as time goes on. In fact, it does. Of several conventional explanations for this phenomenon, the most popular is that fragments of previous crystals get carried from laboratory to laboratory on the clothing or beards of migrant scientists, and then infect subsequent crystallizations. We know that when compounds are seeded with crystal fragments crystallization speeds up, but that the process can be explained in terms of migrant scientists seems rather implausible.

A second conventional explanation is that people learn and use increasingly better methods to make crystals. But this cannot be the whole answer, because unwanted crystals often spontaneously turn up as contaminants in industrial processes and appear in factories all over the world.

A third explanation is that fragments of previous crystals, as microscopic particles of dust, are blown through the air and settle in laboratories all over the world, accelerating crystallization. This is a testable hypothesis, but it has never been tested.

The explanation I propose can be tested with the following experiment. Take a new compound, see how fast it crystallizes under standard conditions, and then test the rate at which it crystallizes somewhere else in the world; during the experiment, air should be filtered to keep out dust, and bearded scientists should be carefully excluded. Increase in the rate of crystallization as these crystals are made elsewhere in the world would be evidence in favor of the morphogenetic field hypothesis.

This hypothesis applies to the inheritance of behavior as well as the inheritance, so to speak, of form in chemistry. It has been observed, amazingly enough, that learned behavior spreads among members of a species without any known kind of physical connection. It has been found that if rats are trained to do a new trick, rats of the same breed all over the world learn the same trick more quickly.

In an attempt to prove the Lamarckian theory of inheritance, in 1920 William MacDougall of Harvard trained rats to escape from a water maze by swimming out of a tank of water and climbing out by one of two exits. If they got the wrong one, he gave them an electric shock. The number of errors—the number of shocks they received before learning—gave a measure of the rate of learning. The first generation made over 200 errors. MacDougall then bred from those, choosing the parents at random. The next generation made about 180 errors. He bred from them the next generation, which made about 160. After 25 generations the rats averaged 20 errors: they were learning about ten times faster than the first generation.

This amazing result seemed to prove the Lamarckian theory, that

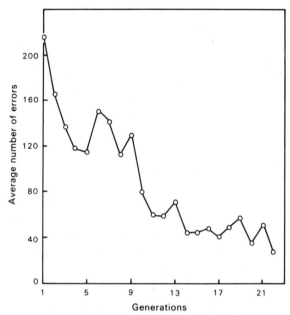

FIGURE   14–6   The average number of errors in successive generations of rats selected in each generation for
slowness of learing. (Data from McDougall, 1938).

acquired characteristics can be inherited through changes in genes.
But Lamarckism is a heresy in biology, and MacDougall was criticized for not selecting the rats at random before breeding them so as
to avoid any bias. It was objected that the stupid rats got so many
electric shocks that their fertility was reduced and therefore, by natural selection, they were giving fewer progeny; as a result, an inbuilt
natural selection in favor of smarter rats occured. MacDougall
started a new series of experiments, in which he selected the parents
on the basis of their learning performance: he selected only the most
stupid rats as the parents of each generation. According to genetic
theory, their offspring should have become stupider and stupider.

Figure 14-6 shows the results of that experiment. The left hand
axis shows the number of errors, and the bottom axis, the number
of generations, so a decrease in the number of errors means an increase in the rate of learning. The number of errors decreased from
230 to 25 over twenty-two generations. In this series of experiments
MacDougall was breeding only from the most stupid parents; according to conventional theory the number of errors should have in-

creased as time went on. Instead it decreased. MacDougall regarded this as even better proof of the Lamarckian theory, and his opponents had no alternative but to repeat his work.

Exactly duplicating MacDougall's experimental design, Crew, in Edinburgh, found that in the first generation, his rats made an average of about 20 errors. Some of them got the task right the first time. Crew could not detect much improvement after that, because if the rate of learning is fast, the rate of improvement decreases. Neither Crew nor MacDougall could explain why Crew's rats learned so fast, and Crew gave up.

Then Agar in Australia repeated the experiment. He slightly changed the breed of rats and the design of the experiment. His rats started off with about 60 errors and he found as MacDougall had, that they got better and better. Agar had a control line of rats; in each generation, they were bred from untrained parents, and some were kept for breeding while others were tested for the rate of learning. Agar found that there was exactly the same rate of improvement in these untrained control rats as in the trained rats. Whatever this effect was, it could not be due to Lamarckian inheritance, because that could only be passed on from parent to offspring. The improvement seemed to be happening independently of direct descent; not only the rats descended from trained parents, but *all* the rats were getting better in the same way. People concluded that Agar had refuted MacDougall's work. But in fact Agar had confirmed MacDougall's results and had showed that something far more mysterious was going on. There appeared to be a kind of influence which could not be explained in genetic terms. This is just the kind of phenomenon which my hypothesis would lead one to expect; it in fact provides circumstantial evidence for it.

Another piece of circumstantial evidence comes from the work of the dreaded behaviorist B. F. Skinner, who developed standard pigeon training experiments using operant conditioning. Repeating Skinner's experiment, Brown and Jenkins found in 1961 that pigeons learned far more quickly than they had in Skinner's original work. The whole of the operant conditioning procedure—putting pigeons in a Skinner box and gradually training them to peck a panel to get grain—was quite unnecessary. The pigeons would peck at the panel more or less straight off. I think that Skinner's training protocol may have become unnecessary, because he and his students had been training pigeons for years, with the result that subsequent pigeons were learning much more quickly. This result is like that of many other experiments, none of them in themselves conclusive, but all of them suggestive.

The morphic resonance hypothesis suggests the way patterns and forms are repeated in nature. It obviously does not explain where the first form, the first pattern, or the first creative idea comes from. It explains how once it has happened, it can be repeated. The question of creativity cannot be answered by this hypothesis, because it deals only with repetition. The nature of creativity is really a philosophical question which does not lie within the realm of natural science, because science deals only with regularities. To this hypothesis, a creative act is unrepeatable because by the very fact of having happened, it influences everything that happens thereafter. A particular thing can never be done for the first time again, because it has already happened for the first time, and that first occasion will influence subsequent occasions.

Thinking about the creative process is beyond the scope of this discussion, but this hypothesis is quite open to ideas of creativity of an entirely non-mechanistic kind. By this I mean that creativity need not have to do with chance—that is merely a materialistic prejudice.

The hypothesis of formative causation obviously has many implications for understanding human behavior. For example, it leads to a completely new way of thinking about memory. If morphic resonance enables the past to act directly in the present, it is no longer necessary to think of memory as having traces stored inside the brain. The memory-trace concept, even the sophisticated holographic theory of memory, is based on the idea that for things to persist through time, they must have an enduring material basis. If the past connects directly to the present, we can have a completely new theory of memory. Our brains may tune in to our memories, but the memories need not be stored inside the brain. If they are not stored inside the brain, other people might be able to tune in to our memories, or we might tune in to other people's memories.

I would like to conclude by emphasizing that so far this is only a hypothesis. It is a guess about the way things may be; but it should be possible to test it by means of various experiments. I very much hope that within the next few years these experiments will be done.

15

Karl Pribram   The Holographic Hypothesis
of Brain Function: A Meeting
of Minds

The holographic principles which have emerged from science in
the last twenty years, represent the first instance since the time of
Galileo that a scientific discovery, in and of itself, has led to a closer
relationship with man's spiritual nature. In the past, science was
seen as something entirely separate from the spiritual nature of man,
which was taken care of by the esoteric traditions—by religion and
not science. Now, with a paradigm shift in our understanding, scientists are face to face with the same traditions that have motivated the
peoples of the East, and that have influenced Western philosophy as
well. As Fritjof Capra has pointed out, in the last fifty years many
scientists, especially physical scientists, have become aware of a convergence between these theories and ideas expressed in the Vedas,
and other Eastern sources.

Consciousness

What do we mean by consciousness? There are three rather different interpretations of the concept. The first refers to *states* of consciousness. If suddenly a cat walked in front of you, and I asked you,
"Is the cat conscious?" you would say, "Of course, why do you
ask?" Or if a surgeon comes into an examining room, finds a patient

lying down, and pokes that person, who says, "Look, I am trying to get a little bit of sleep here. I have been up all night," you do not say that person is unconscious. You know he has been in a state of consciousness which we call an ordinary state of sleep. If, however, the doctor pokes and the patient just groans a few times and turns over, or if he pokes harder and nothing happens, the patient is in a stupor. If he does not respond at all, he is in a coma. The cat's awareness, or sleep, coma, or stupor are among the states of consciousness.

A second definition, in the Eastern tradition, is that mind and consciousness are extended. Consciousness is everywhere, and we happen to be particular instantiations, or precipitations out of this consciousness.

A third definition refers to the difference there may be between what people do or how they behave, and what they are aware, or conscious of doing. Someone who is hypnotized, for example, may be conscious of doing one thing while he or she is actually doing something else. This way of understanding consciousness is used in Western philosophy almost exclusively to mean a reflexive sort of consciousness, self consciousness, or the distinction between self and other. This distinction is called "intentionality" in philosophy and is based on the idea that we can tell our own awareness from that which we are aware of. It reflects the fact that we can know the difference between our intentions and our actions. In *The Origin of Consciousness in the Breakdown of the Bicameral Mind*, when author Julian Jaynes describes the change in consciousness which presumably took place between the *Iliad* and the *Odyssey*, he is referring to this kind of self-reflective consciousness. It is what we mean when we say we want to widen our consciousness, and include within our field of attention things that we have not been attending to.

These three ways of understanding consciousness are related. The first definition essentially determines what state we are in; the concept of extended consciousness found in Eastern philosophy involves the content of consciousness, or that which we are conscious of; and a third meaning, called attention or what we pay attention to, relates state to content. Attention is the process of consciousness which gives rise to self-reflection.

Holonomy

From these three definitions, I will turn to the notion of extended consciousness, the content of that consciousness which is not the ordinary one. This is related to our perception of reality—what is real, how we go about finding out what is real, and how we construct our realities in general. As you all know, we construct not one, but several realities for ourselves. Our perceptions may differ from our cognitions. For example, when the Copernican revolution took place, many people wondered if they had to hang on because the earth was round. They had, up to that time, perceived the earth as flat. Suddenly it was round and spinning, posing to people a danger of falling off. Christopher Columbus faced this problem with his crew, who were afraid that over the horizon, somewhere, they might drop off. One of my colleagues, James Gibson, who died last year, used to say, "You know, I really do not believe the world is round because I see it is flat." He was joking but, in a way, it is true that what we see and know can be quite different.

In the last twenty years we have discovered another reality, which is as slippery and strange as the idea that the earth is round, but which will eventually prove to be just as important. Mystics have been telling us we can experience from time to time a reality that has strange properties we do not appreciate in our ordinary, everyday perceptual state. I call this strange reality a *holonomic state*, a concept based on the invention of holography.

Implemented in the early 1960's, the hologram is an engineering device based on a mathematical invention by Dennis Gabor, who wanted to improve the resolution of electron microscopy. For this purpose, he developed a new technique of storing on film what was not the intensity of reflected light or transmitted light, but actually the square of the intensity and the relationship of a particular beam with its neighbors. It is called the complex conjugate of the intensity. If I drop a pebble into a pond, ripples emanate out from the place where the pebble was dropped. If I drop two pebbles, two sets of ripples form and these ripples interfere with each other. If I throw in a whole handful, there are many such ripples, and the pond is perturbed in a complex way that appears quite irregular. If I take a

movie of someone throwing pebbles into a pond, and then play the
movie backwards, I would find that I could reconstruct from this set
of ripples the location and the actual image of the pebbles as they
entered the water.

Gabor's invention, for which he received the Nobel prize, was to
show mathematically how such a movie could be made. If I take a
mathematical transform, and play it forward, I get the ripples in the
pond. If I store these, I can, by doing the inverse of exactly the same
transform, play it all backwards and the image reappears. That discovery was based on a theorem formulated by Fourier, a Frenchman
who lived from the end of the 18th century to the beginning of the
19th century. Fourier's theorem states that any pattern, no matter
how complex, can be analyzed into regular wave forms which are
called sine-waves. A pattern that has been decomposed can be re-
composed when sine-waves are synthesized or "convolved" with
each other: this is the act of superpositioning, or essentially adding
them, one on top of the other. To Fourier's theorem Gabor added
the ripple phenomenon, that each pebble in the pond leaves its own
signature in the wave form.

Holograms were developed from Gabor's original work with light
photography. His technique never worked very well in electron-
microscopy, the purpose for which it was built, but led to optical
holography, three-dimensional photography without the use of a
camera.

Holonomic Brain Functions

A major problem in the brain sciences until about the mid-1960's
was how it is that we can see and feel away from our own body
surfaces, away from our eyes. If I see this young lady who just
walked in, I do not feel her walking across my retina. Basically it is
at the sensory surface that I am being tickled, as it were, by the stimulus, but I project out into the world that which is stimulating my
senses. With this is the related problem of where vision occurs. Do I
see Al Huang, who is sitting over there in my cortex? Vision cannot
occur only in the eye, because if someone took out my occipital
lobes I would not see Al. Does that mean I see *in* my senses and
brain? When you sit on a tack, where do you feel it? You think you

feel it in the buttocks. But if I cut out the correct portion of your brain you would not be feeling it.

Another problem that was even more severe for brain scientists was that people who have strokes or head injuries of any kind never lose a particular memory trace. Memory is all of a piece; it seems to be distributed in the brain so that even huge destructions do not remove a particular piece of a memory.

This is where holography is of great interest. If I cover up half of a hologram, the whole image is still there. At the same time (around 1964) that I suggested holography might provide a useful way of looking at brain physiology, Fergus Campbell and John Robson at Cambridge University discovered, while investigating visual resolution, what is called hyperactivity, a phenomenon in which one can see detail that is finer than the grain of the retina.

They also discovered that seeing the same thing repeatedly causes habituation or adaptation to it. It is the same with your clothes. You know that you have got clothes on, you wiggle a little bit and you realize that you have got clothes on, but most of the time you do not notice them at all. The way scientists study this process is by presenting the same stimulus over and over again and calling that the adapting stimulus or background stimulus; then, they present a new stimulus which is different. Fergus Campbell was very surprised to find that his background stimulus influenced the test stimulus in a very peculiar but regular way. The adapting stimulus also influenced the test stimuli that were *harmonics*, or simple ratios, of the number of stripes in the pattern. This suggested that the eye responds to patterns in very much the same way that the ear responds to patterns, in terms of frequencies. Essentially, Fergus Campbell's work, conducted about 1967 and first published around 1968, provided the first evidence that the brain might indeed function very much like a hologram.

Campbell's work was largely on humans, and it involved inserting very fine wires into the brains of people during surgery, or in animals. In Figure 15-1, the wire is represented by line "a" going into the computer. The computer moves a white spot on a black background to a monkey, in this case—and since the computer knows where the spot is, it can record what the response of a neuron in the brain is doing. It is as if I could ask you, "Do you see my hand

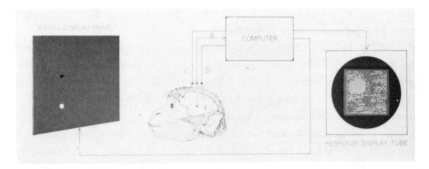

FIGURE   15–1

wiggling?" and you would say without moving your eyes, "yes" or "no," depending on where my hand is. Similarly, a cell in the visual system responds yes or no when it sees my hand waving, or the spot moving about. An electrode attached to a loud speaker allows us to hear the cell going along at a resting level emitting sounds at a slow frequency. When it sees something that it is responsive to, the cell develops a much faster rate of response. Since the computer knows where the spot is, it can correlate very simply what the spot is doing with what the cell is doing. In this way, it is possible to plot the receptive field.

When a spot is in one location, the cell responds a great deal: when the spot is in another place, the cell does not respond so much. This, as illustrated in Figure 15-2 is called a Mexican hat function: When we cut the Mexican hat function across, parallel to the brim, we get this picture on its side. You see here what is called a "center-surround field."

In the late 1950's, Hubel and Wiesel discovered that these receptive fields (which in the retina and halfway to the cortex were round) became elongated in the visual cortex. This discovery suggested that we perceive things because cells in the brain actually make stick figures. Obviously, the stick figures have to be embellished, and texture has to be added, but basically the idea was that each cell responds to lines of a certain orientation which the brain adds together.

But in 1966, we mapped receptive fields like this and found (Figure 15-3) that the receptive field is more complex than just a simple line. It has an inhibitory flank and then another excitatory flank be-

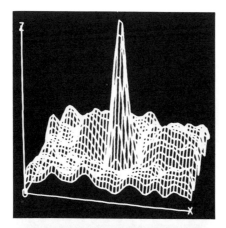

FIGURE   15–2

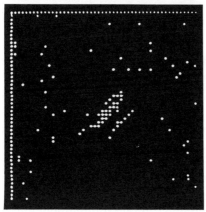

FIGURE   15–3

yond that. A group in Leningrad found several such "side bands," as they are called, and Dan Pollen at Harvard University showed that every cell had at least three or four such side bands.

Finally the idea penetrated in the early 1970's that maybe these were not line detectors as they had originally been called, but that they were like Fergus Campbell's spatial-frequency sensitive cells. They were sensitive to several lines or *stripes*, lines with certain frequencies across space. I can illustrate this by walking in front of what is called a low spatial frequency system of vertical black and white bars projected on the screen behind me. (Figure 15-4) You see me flickering. Figure 15-5 shows a set of lines that is finer, a high spatial frequency. Each of these tuning curves represents one cell;

FIGURE   15–4

FIGURE   15–5

they illustrate that individual cells are tuned to approximately an octave of spatial frequency. It is possible to think of the brain cortex as being like a piano sounding board where each cell, when stimulated, resonates maximally to a particular frequency with its broad band tuning at approximately one octave as can be seen in Figure 15-6.

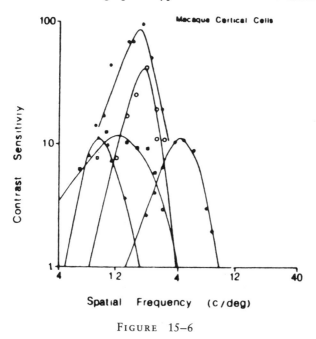

Spatial   Frequency   (c/deg)

FIGURE   15-6

The only difference is that in vision the frequencies are spatial. This is a very important discovery. If the brain is made not to construct stick figures, but to resonate with particular frequencies there is a much richer perception that is like the richness of sound a pianist can produce from a piano.

These ideas, of course, are not new. Around the turn of the century, Jacques Loeb and others were thinking of the brain as resonating to an input and Helmholtz performed experiments to show that the ear worked this way. But excepting its implications for the auditory domain the general theory got lost during the 20th century and we forgot that the brain does in fact resonate. We do respond to vibrations in our environment, whether these vibrations are the "vibes" of other people or the vibrations that are set up by electric lights.

More recently, Russell and Karen de Valois have greatly refined our understanding of how brain cells function. Figure 15-7 shows the tuning curve of the cells suggesting that a cell cannot tell the difference between a very fine line and a rectangle; it is not very sensitive to the width of a single line. However, the tuning curve for spatial frequency is *very* highly specific. In another experiment

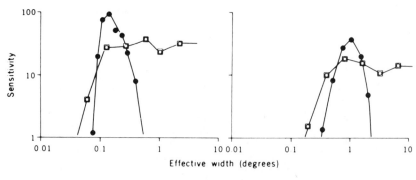

FIGURE 15–7

de Valois showed that the cell is responsive to the orientation of pattern as in a shirt plaid, for instance. De Valois scanned a plaid with a computer, did a Fourier transform on it, and showed how the axes of the transform were oriented. Then she measured whether the cell responded to the pattern as a whole or to the single lines in the pattern.

Figure 15-8 shows various patterns and their Fourier transforms. By testing, it was possible to discover that each cell was responding not to a set of lines but to their Fourier transform. De Valois found that every one of 224 cells was responding to the exact degree and minute of visual arc predicted by the Fourier transform—a convincing proof.

Holonomic Reality

In another experiment, instead of taking a spot and moving it about on an oscilloscope screen or television screen—as in all of the previous kinds of experiments—we took a television set displaying a lot of spots appearing simultaneously. This snow or "noise" on the television screen is called visual white noise. From the noise, which contains all possible patterns, the cell should pick out that which it is responsive to.

Figures 15-9 and 15-10 show how one cell responds to visual white noise, when its responses for about 30 milliseconds are added together. When the cell was responding to a dot in a particular place on the television screen we intensified dots in that area. When the

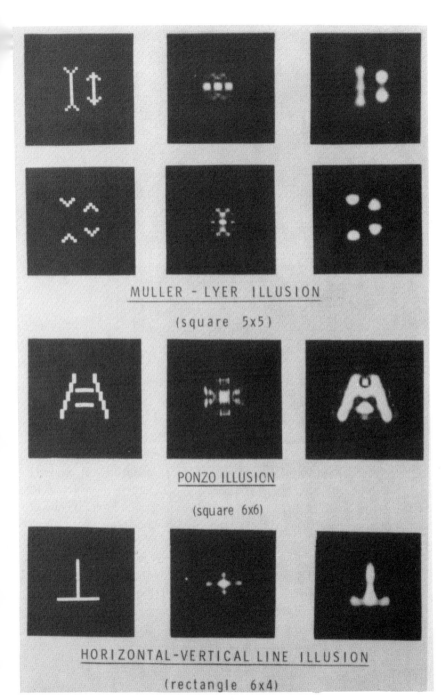

MULLER - LYER ILLUSION

(square 5x5)

PONZO ILLUSION

(square 6x6)

HORIZONTAL-VERTICAL LINE ILLUSION

(rectangle 6x4)

FIGURE 15–8

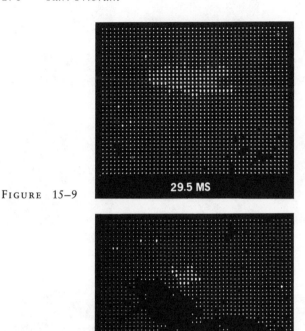

FIGURE 15–9

29.5 MS

FIGURE 15–10

40.0 MS

cell fired less than normal, we removed it and detensified it, making a black hole. This pattern produces a cigar-shaped receptive field with an inhibitory flank coming on 10 milliseconds later. If, out of random noise, our brain cells are picking up what they are sensitive to, what is it that we are perceiving? If our cells are set to create this pattern out of noise, how do we know what is really out there? We do not know because we are always constructing our own reality out of a great deal of what ordinarily seems like noise. But it is a structured noise: We have ears like radio tuners, and eyes like television tuners that pick out particular programs. With other tuners, we could be listening to other programs.

Conclusion

The importance of holonomic reality is that it constitutes what David Bohm calls an "enfolded" or "implicate order," which, as we have seen, is also a distributed order. Everything is enfolded into everything else and distributed all over the system. What we do with our sense organs and telescopes—lenses in general—is to explicate, to unfold that enfolded order. Our telescopes and microscopes are even called "objectives." That is how we explicate things: we make objects out of them with the lenses in our senses. Not only the eye, but also the skin and the ear are lens-like structures. We owe to David Bohm the conceptualization that there is an order in the universe—the enfolded order—which is spaceless and timeless in the sense that both space and time are enfolded in it. We now find that an important aspect of brain function is also accomplished in the holonomic domain. This aspect of brain function operates much as do those who perform statistical operations using the FFT—fast Fourier transform—in order to speed the computation of correlations. In medicine, computerized tomography uses a similar operation for image processing and image reconstruction.

Critical to such operations is the fact that the ordinary Euclidean and Newtonian dimensions of space and time become enfolded. Synchronicities and correlations characterize the operations occurring in this domain. There is no here, no there. There is no-thing. But this holonomic order is not empty; it is a boundariless plenum filling and flowing. Discovery of these characteristics of the holonomic order in physics and in the brain sciences has intrigued mystics and scholars steeped in the esoteric traditions of East and West: for is not this just what they have been experiencing all along?

16

Joseph Chilton Pearce   Role Models and
Human Development

When a baby is born in this world, it has no teeth. Baby teeth grow
in by the end of the first year; in the sixth year, six-year molars grow
in; in the twelfth year, twelve-year molars; and sometime around
eighteen wisdom teeth grow in. Spin that organism so many times
around the sun and those teeth will pop into view. They will appear
whether or not the infant or the child is nurtured properly; nurturing only affects the quality of the teeth and whether the baby will
keep them awhile.

Observing children for over fifty years in one of the most monu-
mental studies ever done in the history of science, the great Swiss
psychologist Jean Piaget found that the growth of intelligence in the
child is on the same neat periodicity. The intellectual development of
the child is marked by specific stages that seem to fall every three
and one-half to four years, and that are preceded by or simultaneous
with the beginnings of each stage of physical development. Connections among these stages, yogic psychology, and recent discoveries in
physics point to a profound understanding that is shaped by Eastern
and recently some Western students of consciousness and self development.

Each of the Piagetian stages of development begins with brain
growth spurts that get the brain ready for massive new learning.

Each of the stages is marked by a specific intent, a non-volitional, non-willful movement on the part of the child. Intent moves the child's body to interract selectively with his environment for certain specific needs, each changing according to his stages of development. The intent that moves that child's body is like a blueprint, or a form that is filled in with content from the child's environment, which determines the nature of the final expression. The internal intent and the external content given by modeling from outside determines what Piaget calls "a construction of knowledge in the brain system": a conceptual ability of the mind-brain-body to collect and interpret information in meaningful whole experiences, and to make a meaningful response to that experience.

The intent-content-ability model is seen easily in language. In the seventh month in utero, the child begins movements of his body every time the mother speaks. Studies published by Condon and Sanders in 1974 show that when the newborn infant comes into the world, he has a complete repertoire of physical movements to make in response to all the parts of speech. For every part of speech used around him, the child moves a specific muscle.

Through this sensory-motor activity, the child starts construction of language in his brain system. This internal intent moves him on a sensory-motor level to interact with the language content given from without. With a Chinese mother, he speaks Chinese; with a French mother he will speak French. It makes no difference to the biological plan; that intent is only looking for some model to match its inner needs. But development of overall ability is determined entirely by the nature of the content or the model given that child. For each stage of intelligence to develop, the child needs an appropriate model.

Developmentalists agree that intelligence growth is from concreteness toward abstraction, from the child's sensory-motor physical interaction with the living material world into increasingly less material and more mental experience, until finally intelligence reaches pure abstraction, or pure mental operation. Not only is the child's development of each specific stage entirely contingent on the kind of modeling he is given, but if he is not given modeling appropriate to that stage, its stage-specific effect breaks down and does not develop.

But the process goes right on; nature cannot program for failure. If modeling of the stage is missed or faulty and the stage is incomplete, the next stage will nevertheless flip right in, on time, as a new intent takes over. While the timing is universal and not much affected by nutrition or nurturing of the system, if the system does not develop in each stage, intelligence will not develop as it should.

Piaget calls birth to age seven the pre-logical stage, seven to age eleven the operational-logic stage, and thereafter, the logic of reversibility develops. The first stage after the child is born is the period of world-view construction, during which he constructs knowledge in his brain about the world itself—the world of physical objects. He sees the world and its objects as extensions of himself, and his intent drives him to want to taste, touch, feel, smell, or cuddle every conceivable object he can get his hands on or move into contact with. His world, at this time, is a floating world of objects without stability or fixed pattern; out of sight is out of mind. Language at this stage is the child's muscular movements in response to the parts of speech, and his experiments with what we call lalling sounds as he begins to match the sounds he hears with the sounds he makes.

Somewhere around the first year, according to Piaget, a wonderful thing happens; brain processing takes a quantum leap. All of a sudden object constancy happens, and that shifting world of objects stabilizes into a fixed, patterned world, marking the first great logical leap in the whole brain system. World-view construction then continues on up to about age seven.

After object constancy, a brain-growth spurt prepares the brain for construction of knowledge of one's own person. Intent drives the child to interact with events and form his relationship to objects. He begins to distinguish the difference between objects out there and his own body and to sense the feeling tone of his world. This is the time in which the child's emotional center in relation to the world is developed.

Throughout this time he takes all cues for construction of his own self in relation to the world from his models, his parents. He reads their emotional responses without having to be told about them, and he makes a corresponding emotional response. Patterns of aversion and attraction are built as the child filters out what will not be retained within a world-view that is in keeping with his parents' world-view. His knowledge of himself is likewise in keeping with his parents' knowledge of themselves in their relation with him.

During this period the child has a passionate drive for a name for every object and event in his world. Luria, the great Russian child developmentalist, points out that the word is not just a communication device for the child: it is also the way by which the mind-brain-body and sensory-motor systems are coordinated and unified in the child's body. The word—a name for a thing—and the concreteness of that thing or event form a single entrainment in the child's mind. The word evokes its thingness in that child's mind; the thing evokes its word.

Concrete language use is unchanged through age seven, and through age eleven, with certain modifications, naming is extraordinarily important. At the end of this four-year period, about eighty percent of the child's language, world-view, and self structures are completed. He will be filling in the gaps for the rest of his life.

The child as subject and his world as object are still in single entrainment in the brain, a single rapport, but at age seven world and child begin to separate into a beautiful balance between subject and object. At this period of the child's history, he is convinced that the entire world is conscious. He believes the trees and rocks are alive, he talks with flowers, and he has an uncanny relationship with animals. The child's intent drives him at this period to establish a level of communion and communication with this world that is difficult for westerners to understand.

The best possible example I have of it is the communion between self and world that the Australian aborigine develops, a communion that exists through what Lévi-Strauss calls dream time. By bouncing back and forth between dream time and now, the Australian aborigine can tell you, for instance, where his kinsman tribes are, even if they are fifty miles away; he can tell you where the animals he is allowed to hunt are, even though they are miles away; he can tell you where the water is under the desert sands; he can follow a trail that is a year old. He and the person leaving the trail become a synonymous unit; he simply leaves that trail himself. His relationship with dream time results from his communion with his world, established, between the ages of four and seven, because proper models for and positive social response to that communion are available, and because the aborigine's survival depends on it.

Eloise Shield, Gerald Jampolsky and others have found that sometime between the late third and early fourth year, these communication capacities open for development in the western child as well. However, in our culture there is no modeling for what we call by misnomer "extra-sensory perception." The sensing which could unfold at this period rarely develops because society and parents respond to it negatively.

During the period from age four to eleven, the child also has a passionate desire and biological need to play with parents and peers, and he needs an enormous amount of fantasy imagination input. He plays that the entire world is conscious and animated. As David Bohm says, deadness is the greatest abstraction of all; the concrete thinking and playing child cannot yet grasp abstractions. Representing this another way, we can say that the egocentricity of the newborn child, simply a point of awareness, moves out to the construction of objects, and then to the construction of knowledge of events and the person. As he begins to distinguish between the object of self and the subject of self, object and subject move into a balance in which the world and self are still a synonymous and yet separate unit. In what we call magical thinking, the child is convinced of a direct interrelation between what he thinks and what happens out there in the world.

Then, as world becomes an object out there, and self becomes a subject in here, the child is moved into the next stage of development, which is preceded by a growth spurt in the brain. Because subject self and an object world are separate, the child is able to respond to high level logical processes, if exposed to them as models. Piaget refers to this as concrete operational thinking, the stage at which the child's mind can manipulate information from his concrete world, according to an abstract idea. The child cannot furnish himself with his own ideas; if they are not modeled for him, concrete operations will eventually fade out as new operations take over.

Piaget uses academic examples of concrete operational thinking, but its non-academic uses are demonstrated in Indonesia, Sri Lanka, India, and remote parts of Greece, and Africa, where many thousands of people walk across beds of fire coals every year and are not burned. The alteration of ordinary consciousness this walk requires is concrete operational thinking, available to children between age six and seven, but only when it is modeled for them.

Ten years ago, when Uri Geller was on television doing such things as bending metal without touching it, there were thousands of children all over the world—Japan, France, Germany, England, United States—who, as a result of seeing him, could then immediately do these tricks themselves. Brian Josephson, 1973 Nobel Laureate in physics, observed one of these children at the University of London and concluded the laws of physics should be completely reorganized, but the children's magical abilities to bend metal or tie into knots metal encased in sealed glass simply illustrates what Piaget defined as operating on concrete information with an abstract idea.

For formal operational thinking, which occurs next, Piaget supposes that the brain is able to operate on its own mechanisms and change its own conceptual systems. But this is no more likely than a TV set changing its own interior workings. Current research and the overall thrust of development suggests that formal operational thinking is taking an objective standpoint from which we can look back over our entire development to that point. From an objective viewpoint of our physical process and the workings of our own mind, we can make creative abstractions that are no longer directly related to concreteness. With a model for this thinking, the child develops the ability to create from the imagination of the mind, which has separated fully from brain.

Formal operational thinking is exemplified in music and mathematics, which are pure, abstract forms of art expressed in concrete media. (Children can start these activities long before age eleven, but around eleven they can begin to create fully and openly in them.) Formal operational thinking can also create states of reality. When intelligence must express itself through a concrete medium, it is not moving forward toward a final abstraction. Because the whole system is pushing for autonomy of the self, and freedom from dependence upon anything other than the self, the push is always towards abstraction, because that is where our autonomy lies. Charles Tart discovered that in mutual hypnosis, people were using formal operational thinking to create stable reality states that were available to all five senses. They remained as permanent reality states, but were not in the physical world at all—they were in what Northrop Frye might call the eternal world of the human mind.

Carlos Castaneda has also described reality states which, brought about by consensus between a sorcerer and his apprentice, are not drawn from the concrete world. The Sufis use formal operational thinking in their work, creating reality spaces as ways for teaching their disciples, and followers of Swami Muktananda experience states of reality which come from some source entirely outside the system, purely created states. Although formal operational thinking is necessary to science, the overall push of development is toward true formal operations, which are beyond reference to any physical process whatsoever.

The final stage is reversibility thinking, which, according to Piaget, is the ability to reverse our thinking and trace it back to its source in a process that leads outside the brain system entirely. This riddle to western academic process is exemplified in Einstein's ten years' passionate search for an answer to certain universal problems. Suddenly, in what he calls "a moment out of mind," Einstein felt a bolt of lightning hit his brain with a highly symbolic imagery of the answer. Then he had the hard job of translating this insight into the language of mathematics, so that it could be shared. Had he had reversibility thinking, when that answer arrived in his brain, he could have traced it back to its source. To do so, he would have become one *with* that source, and could then have answered easily questions that took ten years of hard work.

This final Piagetian stage leads inevitably to something we will have to call the Self, and to a conception of mental operations that corresponds with discoveries made by University of London theoretical physicist David Bohm, a protege of Einstein's in his early years. In 1940, it was estimated that only a handful of people on earth understood Einstein's proposal that energy and matter were equivalent. I remember my eighth grade science teacher holding up a lump of coal, and saying: "In this lump of coal, according to Einstein's theories, there's enough energy to run a steamship for a year." We all snickered, because we came from the coal fields and we knew it took tons of coal to make one of those old Malley steam engines run. Counter to our practical intelligence that more energy required more fuel, more matter, Einstein was saying that the most energy exists in the least matter. Today every school boy knows that energy and matter are equivalent.

In 1950 Bohm computed the zero quantum energy in a single cubic centimeter of empty space and came up with 10^{38} ergs, which translates as twelve billion tons of TNT explosion.

It is accepted that underneath all physical matter is energy which exists simply as waves. The longer the energy waves, the weaker they are: the shorter they are, the more powerful. The larger waves resonate out of the shorter waves. Recently, Bohm has laboratory evidence of waves of energy as short as 10^{-17} centimeters. The zero quantum energy of this kind of wave length, in a cubic centimeter of empty space, is greater than the energy in the entire conceivable physical universe. Extrapolating from this finding, Bohm claims there are wave lengths as small as 10^{-34} centimeters, which is twice the power of all conceivable physical universes. Where energy is so reduced in its wave length that it is in a state of no movement whatsoever, it is infinite energy. Out of that point of infinite energy each of these modes of energy resonates. Bohm says that by mathematical interactions, these final slow and weak wave lengths create three-dimensional forms and a physical universe.

A single flow from this state of total energy is what Bohm calls *holomovement,* or the holonomic process of creation. That is exactly what the ancient yogis have always called the *spanda,* energy moving out of that point. No matter how much it mathematically interacts with itself, it is always a whole movement that never divides against itself, even though it can represent itself through infinite kinds of explicate forms.

According to Bohm, this holomovement can be expressed as four orders of energy existing not as a mechanism, but in a vital, functional, organic process. The first is the *explicate order energy,* the weakest of all energy systems. It is made explicit as a manifest product of any material reality. Bohm believes that this explicate order resonates out of and is an expression of an order of energy which is infinitely more powerful. It is the *implicate order of energy,* because it has implied within it the presage of what is to come. It is the precursor of the explicate, the dream-like vision or the ideal presentation of that which is to become manifest as a physical object. The implicate order implies within it all the physical universes. The implicate order, Bohm says, resonates from an energy field which is yet greater, *the realm of pure potential.* It is pure potential because nothing is implied within it: implications form in the implicate order, and then express themselves in the explicate order.

Had David Bohm stopped at this point, he could have remained within the brotherhood of regular academic science, but he is pushed with the integrity and honesty Einstein had. He goes on to find a final state of infinite energy which he calls the *realm of insight-intelligence.* The creative process springs from this realm. Energy is generated there, gathers its pure potential, and implies within its eventual expression as the explicate order, in a single fluid movement, all enfolded within itself.

David Bohm claims that all time is enfolded within any single second of time (as in the aborigine's dream time); all space enfolded within any single cubic centimeter of space; all physical matter within any grain of sand; the whole enfolded within itself. Thus the holomovement in its entirety is enfolded within every human brain. "Thou art that," in effect. Furthermore, the entire process is a simple pulse of consciousness; energy and consciousness are equivalent; consciousness can express itself as energy or as matter.

Bohm has described something that ancient Yogic psychology speaks of as the four states of consciousness, the four worlds and the four bodies. Bohm's explicate order is what the East calls the physical body, or the physical world, and the waking state. For the yogis, the implicate order of energy is the subtle body, the subtle world, or the dream state, which is infinitely more powerful than the physical state. The realm of pure potential energy is the causal body, the causal state, or the state of deep sleep, vastly more powerful than any of the others.

Bohm's insight-intelligence realm, the fourth state, is the super-causal, the "silent witness" or *Turiya* state. All realms express the Self, which operates as a single unit of energy, or spanda, expressing itself in pulsation. The holomovement is thus what the great yogis have called the Self, and they call the orders of energy "bodies" because we are those bodies. The entire movement is enfolded within us; "Thou art that," means thou art that Self.

Bohm's realms, Piaget's stages, and the ancient yogic states are related to what Paul McLean, brain researcher at the National Institute of Mental Health, has found about the structures within our brains. We actually have three unique brains, each one separate and operating differently. Each of these brains has its own use of language, communication level, imagery and way of viewing the world, its own chemistry connections with the body and its own brain waves. McLean finds that each of these brain systems represents our entire heritage from this earth.

He calls the oldest one the reptilian brain, the way by which we inherit hundreds of millions of years of genetic development on this earth. The whole world, the universe, our bodies and brains, all register through this reptilian brain, the system for representing all objects, materials, and the human body itself; and the source of sexuality. Next is the old mammalian brain, the source of all feeling-tone, our emotions, the nurturing of infants, and our social sense; the center of our feeling of being an individual self. This represents an additional millions of years of mammalian development. The third, or new brain receives information or content from the other two brains, and acts on, or manipulates, that content. The locus of our consciousness moves back and forth through these three brain systems. The first stage of sleep stops all sensory messages from the world and all muscles relax as our conscious awareness shifts out of the reptilian system and into the old mammalian brain. Then we begin dreaming in the emotional, feeling tone state arising from this brain.

When the dream cycle is over, we move into the new brain system, and enter a state of deep sleep. Brain waves are extremely slow, body tonus begins dropping off; rapid eye movements stop, and body movement stills until finally there is little brain activity. As we go deeper into sleep, at the end of this forty-five minute cycle, all muscle tonus drops from our body; our heartbeat and breath are very slow and sluggish, and there is no brain activity at all. During this stage occur bursts of brain activity which are similar to our ordinary wake state, a composite of all three systems.

The reptilian brain is clearly the modus operandi of David Bohm's explicate order energy, the physical body, or the wake state of the yogis. The old mammalian brain is clearly the implicate order of energy, the dream state, or the subtle body state of the yogis. What

David Bohm calls pure potential and the yogis call the causal body, the deep sleep state, is the new brain. When all these states are finally turned off entirely, and the system is on pure automatic pilot, we get bursts of extremely active consciousness which may be the fourth state. We move into this state about every forty-five minutes and then back down through dreaming into the wake state. This cycle occurs during the day as well. During our daylight hours we never lose consciousness connections, but part of our consciousness continues the sleep cycle in miniature.

During the child's first period in the Piagetian stages, when he is first out of the womb, the locus of awareness and intent driving his body to interact with this world is centered in the reptilian brain system. For about a year his "reptilian centered" discoveries feed into the old mammalian brain and the new brain. When he achieves object constancy, this reptilian activity continues to feed construction and knowledge of the world into the other two brain systems, but the locus of awareness and intent move to that implicate order, that subtle system, which is a vastly greater energy system than the explicate order. The child begins to explore his personal system in all of its ramifications, and information he feeds into the new brain is simultaneously fed into the reptilian brain.

In that period of perfect balance between the child and his world, when he thinks the world is all animated consciousness and wants to play in highly imaginative ways with that world, the child begins to develop the lines of communion and communication among these unique and separate brain processes. He establishes communications between them before separating from his identification with the reptilian when, at age seven, his locus of awareness shifts into the new brain system. All early learning feeds into the new brain, which keeps the system in its integral whole.

What happens then at the separation from the world system, the fall of maya? The original meaning of the Sanskrit word *maya* was the "capacity for measurement," which is precisely what Jean Piaget says happens at age seven. The capacity for measurement, or maya, has come to mean illusion. But in Latin the word "illusion" means "inner play." The child's inner play—a play within his mind-brain system—is the holonomic movement itself. From the causal framework, the locus of awareness and the new brain system act through the supportive system of the midbrain. Using the great energy that can act on reptilian systems, or the explicate order, the child, if given a model for it, can change concrete information according to an abstract idea.

Thus the child can walk across hot beds of coals when this power of the causal order moves into the power of the subtle system or the implicate order, which can change the weak energy physical system of the reptilian order. Neither the fire nor the child's body changes; what changes is the relationship within his own brain system. Beyond fire walking or metal bending, other possibilities for this power are limited only by the kinds of models available to the child at this period.

The next period, formal operational thinking, represents not only movement in the new brain causal system, but also a further specialization of the left hemisphere, which develops the ability to analyze the rest of the system. The corresponding specialization of the right brain, if developed, is to maintain its ongoing unity and awareness. This specialization, rarely established, would maintain unity among the three systems while the fourth system moves out to its position of total objectivity. Awareness would move into *mind* outside the brain, and finally into the Self system and reversibility thinking. The whole thrust of human development, maturity, lies beyond the mind-brain-body process in an awareness where one can range freely throughout the entire system.

Western science, however, accepts as real within its paradigm only those activities which fit within the explicate order modes of energy, which are developed during the first four years of a child's life. Expressions of the brain and mind which unfold for development after age four all employ the implicate mode of energy or the subtle system. But we call pathological the concrete operational thinking that uses this system and is expressed beautifully among the Australian aborigine, or in our children.

Playing with the world implies moving or interfering with concreteness through implicate and causal order energies, which are denied by the scientific paradigm. Because science admits only the purely physical orders which are formed in the first four years, the child is locked into a material form of development. All further processes can only unfold as they find models available, and allowable models within the scientific paradigm must generate from material process. This means not only that the child's development stops at this point, but also that when he reaches age eleven, when formal operations open up, his developmental system is so crippled that he can follow only the scientific model of thinking.

Evolution pushes for the development of formal operational thinking, but there is a certain terror, a certain failure of nerve, at the idea of leaving concrete processes and moving into purely abstract realms—a failure of nerve that sends us careening back into material process, holding onto this early matrix and refusing to move. When development stops, anxiety begins. Anxiety is simply nature's cue that progress towards autonomy has stopped. Our system cannot help but feel anxiety because we have no place to go except back into material process.

We are locked into this material state despite tremendous energies trying to open up. The Kundalini is the only energy that can take us over into the final stage of insight intelligence, but this energy, which comes between eleven and fifteen, cannot open up because it is not part of our cultural heritage. Our culture finds itself with not only a massive anxiety, but also a massive obsessive-compulsive consumption of material goods, and an obsessive-compulsive attachment to the physical body. Our sexuality is overdeveloped, but we lack development of social instincts and the instincts for nurturing infants that unfold with development of the old mammalian brain.

Paradigms are not made by man's intellect, but are given by the realm of insight intelligence. We find this realm in Rupert Sheldrake's morphogenetic field theory, which posits a causative state lying across or outside the ordinary time-space dimension—a causative state with which our brain resonates and from which our whole species springs. Sheldrake's speculation that learning and memory take place not in the brain at all, but through the brain's resonance with a morphogenetic field, corresponds perfectly with yogic psychology, and with David Bohm's energy order theory.

Sheldrake also is trying to figure out a way by which evolution changes a species. His theory of evolutionary process depends on what Bohm calls the realm of insight intelligence. If a member of a species achieves a new behavior, Sheldrake postulates, and if enough members of that species pick up the new behavior and repeat it long enough, it becomes highly probable that the new behavior will become a genetic, inherited characteristic of the whole species. Throughout history, evolutionary processes have occurred, with these great leaps.

Biologist Lyall Watson has conducted research that confirms Sheldrake's hypothesis. During long-term studies of a species of macaque monkey living on islands off the Japanese coast, a new food, sweet potatoes, was introduced. Because the sweet potatoes were covered with grit and sand, the monkeys could not eat them. One day, after mulling this over for a long time, an 18-month-old female monkey took sweet potatoes, rushed down to the ocean, washed them, and ate them. Watson points out that this was a light-year leap of brain system processing in that species, nothing less than Einstein's receiving his great flash of lightning after ten years of work. It is also an example of insight intelligence, which, according to David Bohm, can move into and reorganize a brain system to instill a new form of intelligence.

The monkey immediately taught her mother how to wash potatoes. Then she began teaching the other young monkeys, each of which began to teach his mother. More and more monkeys were washing potatoes, but the monkeys without children to teach them could not learn the activity. Suddenly what Sheldrake might call the "critical mass" was hit in what is now called the "hundredth monkey" syndrome. Without any warning, overnight, every member of that species began to dig up potatoes, wash them in the ocean and eat them without going through any learning process. Amazingly, all of the members of that species on the other islands, simultaneously began to exhibit the new behavior, demonstrating Sheldrake's hypothesis. According to the Gospels, "what you loose on earth is loosed in heaven, and what is loosed in heaven is loosed on earth." The creative process out of which we are resonating mirrors our actions.

Ancient Hindu yogic psychologists have always had a word for this principle, the guru principle, which leads from ignorance to knowledge. For the last 2,500 years certain great beings—the Buddhas, and the Jesuses—have somehow, through intense internal discipline and meditation, prepared themselves to enter the highest realm of intelligence: the state of Self.

These great beings, among them my guru, Swami Muktananda, range through the whole spectrum; they are here as a model for us. Transformations occur when one is in Muktananda's presence. People who are taken grudgingly and embarrassed to meet Muktananda are deeply affected. They shake Baba's hand and all of a sudden, when they turn to move away, they burst into tears that they cannot control at all. Tremendously embarrassed, they do not know what has happened. But their bodies know. Built into them is that lodged, blocked-up intent looking for its outer model so it can start development. The body gives a great burst of energy, generally in tears.

Let me mention a very personal thing. My first son was a brilliant boy when he was young, and in his early teens he had many serious mystical experiences which stopped when he was about fifteen years old. When he was eighteen he was out on his own and got into drugs, as many young people do. When he took some drugs, he immediately had a replay of one of the mystical experiences he had had at fifteen. He thought, "Wow, this is it! Why didn't they tell me it came in a bottle?" So he began to take more drugs, but he could not quite get it back again. He took heavier and heavier ones.

When he was nineteen, he went down to my brother's country place on a lake, where he could be all by himself. After fasting for several days, he took massive doses of LSD three consecutive days in a row. On the second day, he had the ultimate, final, complete, and total breakthrough into the great realm out there. All was explained to him. But on the third day he fell from that great paradise of heaven down to the blackest pits of hell, and he did not come out. Four years later his sensory system was still poor. He could not hold his world together, one thing melted into another, and voices came from all parts. In order to maneuver, he had to concentrate hard, and he lived in a constant state of panic. He could still function, more or less, but he was in a state of sheer anxiety, and had become pretty emaciated. It was concluded that he was permanently neurologically damaged. He thought his life was over at nineteen and there, at twenty-three, after four years of it, he was a sad sight.

I talked him into meeting Muktananda, although he resisted, saying this was a bag of worms and he would have nothing of it. "He's a friend of mine," I said, "and I want him to meet my son." Finally, he went down and Baba touched him with the peacock feathers, patted him on the head, held his hand, looked at him, laughed, and then motioned him on his way. In some kind of a meditative state, my son fell into a heap. When he came out of it, I asked him what had happened, and he began saying, over and over again, "He knows! He is there! He is in that place!" He was ecstatic. It took me a long time to find out what he meant. Here was a man who was in that place my son had been trying to get back to. Simply coming into the presence of Muktananda, he had experienced it. The long and short of it was that my son got the first job of his life as a carpenter's helper and he held onto it, so he could live near the ashram. Finally, he was taken on as a crew member of the ashram and within a year he was not recognizable as the same person. He was my fifteen-year-old given back to me, in an adult form.

What can happen around a great being is limitless. He meets the needs of each as they come to him; he does not do anything, but much happens as a result. He is in that fourth state, radiating up into our weak state. He can lend us his energy from that point so we can experience that fourth state ourselves. Because we can only learn from the concrete toward the abstract, as all the developmentalists tell us, the guru goes to the concrete experience, and then he sets us on our way to learn, and to get there permanently. This is the awakening of the Kundalini energy, that bond which takes us over into that fourth state. Then the guru guides: from 10,000 miles away he can keep that developmental system going. When Kundalini is awakened it starts repairing all the breaks in the developmental system, and anxiety drops away because development has started again. The teacher points only toward the final goal.

He also demands that you meditate, taking some time each day to open in willingness to that insight intelligence realm within you. And the teacher demands discipline. You have to take yourself, your body, and your mind in hand, and strengthen them for the moment when that great insight intelligence *does* move in to restructure and transform.

It is a race against time. The guru is working for nothing less than the critical mass effect. If that critical mass effect can jump across islands to teach monkeys how to wash potatoes, could it not work for the human race, jumping a few continents to heal a ruptured brain system? That is the only hope we have.

I will close with two sayings of the great being Muktananda: "Thou art that," he says. He also says, "See God through meditation, see that Self within your own heart. See that God within your own heart first, and then see him in every single human being you ever meet." Could we ask for any greater paradigm than that?

17

June Singer   The Yoga of Androgyny

To understand our role in the emerging new paradigm and in the "rising culture," we have travelled many different routes—some of us from the halls of science in the universities, some from ashrams where we sat at the feet of gurus, some from work as therapists in search of a clearer knowledge of human conditions, some as seekers of wisdom, and some to find more personal integrity in our lives. But all of us are united in a transpersonal context. We have learned that we do not exist as individual entities in this world, that we do not control our lives with our own egos, but that what is beyond ego carries far greater weight. We want to know in our own experience the union within ourselves and union of ourselves with the rest of the universe.

I have titled my presentation, *The Yoga of Androgyny.* Androgyny means, essentially, union within ourselves—union of the inner opposites. Yoga is derived from the Sanskrit word that means "to join" or "bind together," and it implies a union of the personal with the transpersonal. Yoga means uniting the lower levels of consciousness—which include the personal unconscious, the repressed parts of our individual personality and pre-personal, archaic aspects of the collective unconscious—with the higher levels of consciousness—the transpersonal aspects of the collective unconscious and the collective consciousness.

I came to the transpersonal movement from the professional context of Jungian analysis. My becoming a Jungian analyst would be a kind of a fluke, an accident—were it not that in this universe of interconnecting and interrelating events, there are no accidents. I went to Zurich not to become a Jungian analyst, but as a traditional wife accompanying her husband, who was to study at the Jung Institute. As a visitor there, I attended a course entitled "Anima and Animus." This course split open my view of myself as a woman and offered me an alternative view of the relationships between our conscious sexual image of ourselves and the unconscious contrasexual image. This unconscious, contra-sexual image in woman, which Jung called the "animus," represents all those probing, thrusting, seeding, creating, activating dynamics which in the process of acculturation are somehow caged in. We are taught these impulses are not socially acceptable, not exactly what the woman should be like.

When I first heard about animus I knew what tiger had been locked up in my cage, waiting to spring out when the door was opened. My own Jungian analysis unlocked that door and led me into the frightening and fascinating possibility of integrating my own inner opposites.

Jung observed a yoga of his own, in linking his considerable knowledge of contemporary physics (he was a friend of Einstein's) with his interest in Eastern thought. His commentary on the *I Ching* shows that he understood—or at least appreciated—the interrelationships of cosmic and human dimensions. From research based on his collaboration with physicist Wolfgang Pauli, he worked on a theory of synchronicity, in which he viewed acausal relationships in matter and psyche. The issue of transpersonal psychology was one of the major reasons for Jung's break with Freud, with whom he had been closely associated between 1907 and 1913. Jung early saw the spiritual implications of a science of consciousness, while Freud staunchly refused to acknowledge them. Because Jung was probably the first psychologist to refer to his world view as "transpersonal" —he used the term *überpersonliche Unbewusste*, "transpersonal unconscious," in writing as early as 1917—I feel justified saying Jung was the father of transpersonal psychology.

Jung's concept of the animus as the unconscious, contrasexual or masculine aspect of woman had its counterpart in his concept of the anima as the unconscious, contra-sexual or feminine aspect in man. Anima and animus are among the archetypes. Archetypes, according to Jung, are those tendencies in the unconscious part of the psyche which give form and structure to the contents of consciousness. Thus the animus conditions woman's expectations of masculine functioning in the world and raises some questions about certain qualities in herself which may seem out of context with her feminine nature. Similarly, the anima archetype gives rise to man's images and expectations of the feminine, in himself and in the world.

For Jung, the archetypes were not only structural forms, they also functioned as dynamic patterning-processes. This means that the archetypes belong to the self-renewing function of the psyche. The archetypes may produce inner images: for example the anima appeared in the early matriarchal civilizations between 4000 and 2000 BC as Great Mother or fertility-goddesses; later under a patriarchy the anima was more likely to appear as frivolous, seductive, trivial. Today again her appearance has shifted. She becomes stronger. The Valkyrie and the Amazon frequently appear in men's and women's dreams.

When I first heard of biologist Rupert Sheldrake's new "hypothesis of formative causation" I was struck by its implicit resemblance to Jung's theory of the archetypes. Sheldrake posits "morphogenetic fields" which, built up from the influence of previous similar forms, affect all subsequent forms of the same species, no matter where they may be located. He suggests that the tendency of organisms toward repetition of forms works across time and space, owing to the continuing influence of similar past systems. These morphogenetic fields, like the unconscious mind, are endowed with properties unlike those of any known mechanical or physical system.

Sheldrake points out that "In C. G. Jung's development of this concept, it is not even confined to individual minds, but provides a common substratum shared by all human minds, the collective unconscious" (Sheldrake, 1981, p. 27). And he quotes Jung:

> In addition to our immediate consciousness, which is of a thoroughly personal nature and which we believe to be the only empirical psyche (even if we tack on the personal unconscious as an appendix) there exists a second psychic system of a collective, universal and imper-

sonal nature which is identical in all individuals. This collective unconscious does not develop individually but is inherited. It consists of
pre-existent forms, the archetypes, which can only become conscious
secondarily and which give definite form to certain psychic contents
(Jung, 1959, p. 43).

Sheldrake suggests that psychological theories need not be confined
within the framework of a mechanistic theory. "If memories
[learned behaviors] are not stored physically within the brain, then
certain types of memory need not necessarily be confined to individual minds; Jung's notion of an inherited collective unconscious containing archetypal forms could be interpreted as a kind of collective
memory." (Sheldrake, 1981, p. 28). If "collective memory" is organized as archetypal patterns, we may ask whether these archetypal
patterns are eternally fixed and unchangeable. It may be that while
archetypes are functioning in us to give form to our images, thoughts
and behavior, another process is also taking place. Our interaction
as individuals with the rest of the universe produces effects upon
us to which we, in turn, react. Insofar as our reactions are assimi-
lated, they affect the archetypal background of consciousness. We
renew our consciousness, and this is due in part to the eternally
renewing nature of the archetype. This implies that the maturing,
self-renewing unconscious aspects of the psyche produce an ever-
changing background upon which attitudes and behavior rest.

Among the evolving archetypes which, according to this theory,
supply the background of conscious experience, is the archetype of
androgyny—the archetype of male/female coexistence, of union and
separation. We can trace the history of this and other archetypes
through the language of the collective psyche, which is mythology.

One of the first Western myths of androgyny is of Greek origin,
belonging to that early matriarchal period before the age of Zeus. At
that time, so the story goes, Eurynome, the Great Mother Goddess,
was all alone dancing on the face of chaos. She danced and danced
upon the waves, feeling very cold, for there was no sun yet. A wind
began to move around her, produced by the energy that her dance
had created. This energy became the North Wind. Eurynome, feeling
her loneliness, reached out to the North Wind and molded it in her
hands until it took form. That form became the great World Serpent, Ophion. As Ophion danced with her the dance grew wilder

and wilder and they coupled together; and after a while Eurynome gave birth to the world egg. In due course of time, after Eurynome had brooded upon it, the egg cracked open and out of it tumbled all the ten thousand things of this earth, all the beings, the creatures and everything that lives. Eurynome and Ophion lived together in perfect harmony until one day when Ophion raised his head and said, "You know, I had quite a part in this creation." Eurynome was furious and stamped on him with her heel and consigned him to Tartarus under the earth. So much for the matriarchal myth.

A later myth appears in Plato's *Symposium*. Here too is a myth of an androgyne, but this one comes from a patriarchal perspective, as you will surely see. In those days, there was on the earth, in addition to the races of men and the races of women, a race of strange creatures that were androgynous. Their bodies were spherical in shape and they had four arms, four legs, two heads, and two sets of genitals, pointed in opposite directions. As you can imagine, these creatures had a lot of energy; so they began turning cartwheels, and with their four legs and four arms they became very adept at it. They began to think, "With all this energy and power, why don't we climb up on Mt. Olympus and take over?" So they began to cartwheel up the lower slopes of Mt. Olympus. Zeus looked down upon this race and became quite concerned: "Those androgynes with all their energy are threatening the gods." So he grasped his lightning bolts and, flinging them down upon the Earth, split the androgynes in half so that there were men on one side and women on the other. Since then, men and women have been using up their energy seeking one another, and the gods are safe.

When I visited the ancient cave Temple of Shiva at Elephanta, I was particularly fascinated by a certain image of Shiva, as Ardhanarisvara, in which the god is shown with one half being a strong, sinuous male body and the other half the body of a graceful, curving, voluptuous female. Our guide told us the old myth that when humanity was created, there were only males. Shiva was quite unhappy, as one might expect to be in a world that is entirely male. So that the creative powers would create another kind of person, he manifested himself in an image which showed, at least on one side, what a female should look like. What we see at Elephanta is not an image of what a person should look like, but it is an inner image

—an image of that inner, androgynous being which contains both male and female and which is lived out in both men and women.

It appears to me that the Indians learned long ago a truth that we are only now beginning to appreciate in the West: Shiva without Shakti is a corpse; Shakti empowers Shiva. Together they form the androgynous nature of humanity. Unless they are united, Shiva and Shakti, male and female, man and woman, they cannot regenerate themselves. Human life would end, were it not for the equal value and importance of male and female. Neither one alone can renew or reproduce itself. The image at Elephanta suggests that if we are to participate in an ongoing renewal of human life, male and female must join as absolute equals, each participating in the purpose for which I believe we were placed on this Earth—to carry forward the process of evolution.

But of course there is nothing new about this. The human animal has always mated and produced offspring. What is new, is the renewing of the archetype of androgyny through evolving forms of its archetypal images. In Sheldrake's terminology a certain morphic resonance is taking place. All over the world, Eastern wisdom, modern science and the recognition of the masculine and feminine within each individual is becoming manifest. The androgynous image of the human organism is re-emerging into consciousness in new ways that have evolved from past experience. We are learning to recognize and to differentiate the opposites in our nature. It makes no difference whether we call these opposites masculine and feminine, creative and receptive, knowledge and wisdom, competition and cooperation, explosion and implosion, or logos and eros. What is important, is that while these opposites become differentiated in form, they continue to be experienced in union as aspects of our own inner self. They are the self-renewing possibilities of our own individuality. Yoked together, they can fertilize each other to generate the creativity which is the potential of human beings.

How do we experience this in our own lives? We begin life in a pre-personal or pre-ego stage. At conception and possibly for the first five or six weeks thereafter, our future sex has been determined, but there is no apparent difference between the male and female embryo. Then differentiation begins to take place. As the characteristic forms of the child's reproductive system begin to take shape, the contra-sexual elements are suppressed. From birth onward the differentiation continues. While the biological difference—with all its psychological implications—is recognized, all too often we go on suppressing the contra-sexual in the psychological realm of our lives. As little girls and boys are taught that they cannot do certain things because of their biological sex, the contra-sexual becomes needlessly suppressed, and the human being becomes needlessly limited. There are only a few things that a man cannot do because he is male: he cannot menstruate, bear children or nurse them. But he can, if he chooses, cook, sew, rear children, as well as aspire to the presidency of a corporation. And a woman cannot do only one thing because of her biological sex: she cannot impregnate another person. It is of course true that on an average men are larger and stronger than women and women live longer, but this is only statistical. There is more variation from person to person than from one sex to the other. After recognizing these basic differences, it seems to me that our view of androgyny requires that we recognize, and teach our young to recognize, that biological sex is no barrier to living out one's fullest creative potential. By yoking the opposites in our nature and seeking to harmonize diverse tendencies in ourselves, we can set up a model of creativity within open systems, for our children and for the children of the world.

To see androgyny now in its transpersonal dimension means to recognize and to bring together—to yoke together—the opposites in the rising culture. The rising of feminism returns the goddess to our midst. This is what Shiva of Elephanta longed for. The return of such female values as cooperation and forbearance is longed for in a world torn by war and threatened by nuclear disaster, poverty, disease and the rape of the land. When the goddess of fertility is reunited with the god of consciousness, the renewed culture will have its conception. To bring it to birth and nurture it is a task to which we can commit our energy, our devotion and our daily practice.

The yoga of androgyny, like all yoga, is not only a philosophy. It is a way of life—an endless resource of spiritual discipline that enables us, step by step, to transcend the limits of successive levels of consciousness and to extend the boundaries of the soul.

It may be that modern science made its closest approach to Eastern wisdom on that day when millions of men, women and children sat before their television sets and saw through the eyes of the human beings who stepped upon the moon for the first time in history. What they saw as they looked back to the distant earth was beamed to us, and we saw it on our television sets and were astonished. We saw our Earth for the first time, and we saw that it was whole and perfect. Deep blue oceans the color of lapis lazuli circled the globe; patches of emerald green showed where the continents lay, and streaks of yellow marked the great deserts; and all around, girdling this beautiful earth, were swirling, crystalline clouds. And God saw his creation, that it was good. And we human beings saw that it was perfect, just as it was, half-lit by the sun, revolving slowly on its axis. We had transcended the context of what was then ordinary reality. A mystical vision took form and appeared to us through the agency of modern science. It was a glimpse of a possible reality, a united world.

This glimpse of wholeness is one of the many transpersonal visions that spur us onward toward conscious cooperation with the evolutionary process.

Carl Jung was one of the first of the Western psychologists to give form and shape to the vision of wholeness in the individual as well as in the entire cosmos. He was a sort of Moses figure—he ascended to the height of the holy mountain. There, far above the clamor of separate individual strivings, he saw the Promised Land, the land of wholeness, but he did not go over. It was to the next generation that the charge to cross over was given. I believe that this crossing over to a new order of consciousness is what the transpersonal perspective is all about. And further, I believe that what I have called the "Yoga of Androgyny" may provide us with some practical helps for the crossing over. First and foremost of these is the ability to withstand the tension of the opposites. Next is the acceptance of what Jung had called the shadow—the dark unconscious aspects within an individual and within a culture.

When we live in tension, we do so because of our inner divisions. When we forget the practice of yoga, the meditation that brings about the union of opposites, we ourselves become identified with one polarity or the other. When we forget our needs for the opposite, the opposite within and between individuals, masculinity and femininity fall apart. Body is seen as separate from mind; good is seen as static and opposed to irreconcilable evil. There is a shadow tendency in the West to embrace Eastern thought and to discard scientific material as a whole cloth. There is a tendency in the shadow side of the feminist movement to depreciate the contributions men have made to civilization. There is a shadow tendency among people suffering from a one-sided rationalism to embrace its opposite.

Jung often liked to tell the old Taoist legend of the rainmaker: In a certain village in ancient China there was a severe drought. Crops dried up and the people were threatened with starvation. After much fear and worry they decided to call upon a certain sage and bring him to the village. This sage was a rainmaker. He came with his small bag of belongings hanging on his little staff. He sniffed the air in this village and looked about him. The townsfolk said, "We hear that you have a marvelous talent, that you are sometimes able to produce rain."

He replied, "Just get me out of here and get me to the little hut outside of your village. And I don't want anyone to disturb me. Just put a little bowl of rice outside of my hut each day, and we'll see what happens." So the people went and took him to the hut. Every day they brought him his bowl of rice. After a few days the rain began to fall, and the man came out of the hut.

There was much rejoicing in the village, and the villagers said to him, "How is it that this has come about? What did you do?"

He answered, "I did nothing. When I came to your village I smelled the disorder and the dissension. I picked up your vibrations. So I quickly had to leave. When I turned inward and healed the disturbance within myself, naturally the outer conditions would also change."

When we students of Jung in Zurich heard this Chinese Taoist story, we would be greatly reassured. We were learning that we had only to work on ourselves for everything to turn out all right. But today, I reflect that in China Taoists or rainmakers are not so clearly in evidence as they were in those fabled days. The Taoist monasteries have been destroyed by a different kind of government and the monks have fled away. Only the gentle spirit of that ancient wisdom remains, for example, in the beautiful movements of the t'ai chi which is regularly performed by young and old alike, harmonizing within their bodies the forces of heaven and earth and wind and water. The spirit did not die.

I believe that the non-action of the rainmaker is absolutely essential; and the quiet, centering meditation of yoga which the gurus have so movingly taught us is a condition from which we need to come, and to move from, as we go about our days. Inner self knowledge is not yet integrated into Western culture. It represents the deep, basic source of all of our actions. It is a spirit of total acceptance of that which life brings, and willingness to commit ourselves to the nurturance of this acceptance. If we tune ourselves to this source, the patterns of nature will unfold within us. They will become manifest to our own consciousness, transcending much of the received knowledge with which typical western modes of intellectual training has filled our heads. The rational disciplines are not in themselves dangerous or destructive; the danger comes from how their tools are employed in society. Nuclear power, for example, is neutral in and of itself. It can be harnessed to destruction when employed in weaponry. It can be directed toward increasing productivity and making more energy available, or it can be employed in medical research to better health.

When Jung traveled to India some fifty years ago and sat at the feet of some of the gurus and teachers of yoga, he was filled with profound respect. He understood how deeply rooted is yoga in the soil of India. All of us who have come to India from distant lands have experienced the profound impact of the silences between the words, the spaces for reflection between the moments of action, and the commitments made to inwardness. Yet we also hear Jung's warning to the people of the West not to try to take Eastern wisdom into ourselves whole and undigested. People in the West are not innately different from those born in the East, but our experience has directed our attention to different aspects of being—toward the interpersonal, toward material objects and problem-solving, and toward what we like to call scientific progress. It is possible that Westerners, becoming disillusioned with some of the failures of the Western world to bring about spiritual redemption, will want to turn their backs upon the ways of the West and put on the spiritual garments of the East. But we have been warned by Jung that this will be insufficient. Appropriating the wisdom of others will not solve our problems. For Westerners, the ego tends to be one-sided. It is trained to accept a rational perspective, to be outer-directed. But the Self—the totality of consciousness and unconsciousness, manifest and latent, the explicate order and the implicate order—this Self also embodies the spiritual side of life which is compensatory to the ego.

Jung taught the necessity for allowing that inwardness, that spiritual life, to unfold from within ourselves and infuse the totality of our being with the inner light that was always present in us. There is a strange paradox here. We of the West do not need to come to India in order to find our own souls; we need only to make space in our own lives for the soul to emerge. We need to step back from our accustomed stance to make space for the influx, the flowing-in of the Other. It is as close to us as our own hearts. And yet, in a very real sense, we do need to come to India. For in coming here, we make the symbolic statement. We acknowledge, with respect, that there is another way. We place ourselves in a position to reflect on that other way; and when we do, we find our inner resonance.

We grow as boys into manhood, and as girls into womanhood. The differences can be limiting or, when properly understood, they can become facilitating and empowering. The differences between the sexes can be used for excuses for discrimination, or they can be used to show us how to expand our possibilities by utilizing together the special attributes of masculinity and femininity, of mothering and fathering, of inwardness and worldliness. Androgyny is sometimes described in sexual terms, and sexuality is important to it. Through sexuality we renew ourselves, producing the next generation which, we hope, will preserve human life and enable it to further evolve. Androgyny is a metaphor for bringing together the opposites in our own nature in whatever ways they show themselves. It does not allow us, when we become deflated, to identify with the "right" position and to project sin or error upon the others, the opposing position. Nor does androgyny allow us, when we lose heart or become disappointed, to blame ourselves and to project everything of value on somebody else or on another way of life.

We have it all. We have the potentials within us for healing ourselves of our inner divisions, and for healing that part of the universe which we personally can affect. Everyone of us can be a seminal vessel, spreading the seeds we have taken from each other to all the corners of the earth. And we can, at the same time, nurture those seeds within our own body, mind, and spirit, living so that they mature and grow strong. Whether we are male or female we carry within us the potentials of both kinds of energy. Harmonizing them within ourselves and out in the world is the practical task we have before us. It is a special yoga which I have called the "Yoga of Androgyny."

REFERENCES

JUNG, C.G. *The Archetypes and the Collective Unconscious, Coll. Works. Vol. 9,i.* Princeton: Princeton University Press, 1959.

SHELDRAKE, RUPERT. *A New Science of Life.* Los Angeles: J. P. Tarcher, 1982.

SINGER, JUNE. *Androgyny: Toward a New Theory of Sexuality.* New York: Doubleday/Anchor, 1976.

———. *Energies of Love: Sexuality Re-Visioned.* New York: Doubleday/Anchor, (in press) 1983.

18

Cecil E. Burney   Jung's Active Imagination:
A Technique of Western
Meditation

One of the most significant and useful techniques of western psychotherapy is *active imagination*, developed by the Swiss psychiatrist
C. G. Jung. I believe this technique constitutes a way of "western"
meditation which parallels many of the schools of meditation in the
east. But in its essentially *active* approach it also differs from eastern
approaches and may be better suited for many in the west.

Theoretical Considerations

For C. G. Jung the center of consciousness, or *ego*, is a relatively
small aspect of the totality of the psyche. Beyond the ego lies the
personal unconscious, comprising those experiences during one's
lifetime which condition future experiences. Certain childhood experiences, for example, may affect the way a person preceives a situation or acts in it. Such influences are generally unconscious and remain so until they are examined and integrated into consciousness.
But beyond the personal unconscious lies the realm of the *collective*
or, we might say, the *transpersonal unconscious*. The collective unconscious is a repository of all human experience from the dawn of
mankind to the present. From this perspective there are ancient patterns which arise to affect the formation of the personal uncon-

scious, and therefore, the daily actions of a person. Jung observed that there are certain primordial patterns of experience in the collective unconscious which he termed the *archetypes*. Archetypes are the templates from which individual variations of experience are drawn. Although, for example, each of three different women experiencing what it is like to be a mother of a child has an individually different experience of her role and her children, all three share certain characteristic patterns of mothering which are true for all women who ever had children. In other words, there is a *transpersonal* backdrop to personal experience.

Since something seems to be working from behind the scenes of our personal awareness, it seems that any attempt by the individual to strive toward wholeness—a goal of Jungian analysis—must take into account the role and influence of the archetypes.

One way to see the influence of the archetypes in one's life is to look at experiences which appear to be repetitive. Often such experiences are troublesome in that they seem to bring one to the same difficulty over and over again. Jung felt that the repetitive nature of such experiences was an indication of a *complex*, which repeats itself endlessly unless one can examine its presence and somehow get to the center of what is bringing it about. Jung felt that each complex had a nucleus which was archetypal. If one can get to the center of the complex, one can dissolve its deleterious effects. Archetypes express themselves in feelings and images. John Weir Perry, M.D., an analyst in San Francisco, has described archetypes as *affect-images*. This accounts for the interest of many analysts in the imagery of their analysands and for the often volatile emotions which are aroused as such imagery is contemplated. When the effect of an archetype on one's experience is repetitive, the process of changing it is stormy and difficult. This process involves an *active* role, which is the essential ingredient of active imagination.

The archetypal source of repetitive experiences was observed by the American poet Robert Frost in his poem *Snow*, from which I quote:

> One of the lies would make it out that nothing
> Ever presents itself before us twice.
> Where would we be at last if that were so?

Our very life depends on everything's
Recurring 'til we answer from within.
The thousandth time may prove the charm.

There is an old story from Greece about this repetitiveness of human experience. The gods, looking down on mortal humans, could see things that the humans could not see. After all, humans were imperfect and not omniscient. So, from time to time the gods would decide to send useful information to the poor mortals to help them in their lives. They did this by utilizing the services of a woman called "The Mother of Dreams." Now the task of the Mother of Dreams was to take the messages from the gods, wrap them each night in the skins of animals and send these animals into the dreams of the mortals for whom they were intended. If the mortals were observant, they would remember the dreams they had of these animals, and symbolically, remove the skins of the animals—in a form of dream interpretation—and see what the gods had to say. If a dream was not remembered, an animal would return to the Mother of Dreams. Perhaps the next night, or a few nights later, she would send the animal back into another dream with the hope that it would be seen and the message would get through. If, after some attempts, the message was not heard, she would wrap the message in the skin of another kind of animal and try again. Her task was to send the message over and over again until it got through.

In modern psychological terms we could see repetitive dreams and experiences in the same way. Something from a source in the psyche which is essentially unconscious tries to get through. And it persists until we take the action necessary to hear what it is trying to say.

A Personal/Transpersonal Example

I first encountered Jung's technique of active imagination on a kind of pilgrimage to the east in which I traveled to Zürich for the purpose of undertaking a Jungian analysis in 1976. I arrived in Zürich prepared, as I thought any good Jungian analysand should be, with a big stack of dreams under my arm. I thought that good analysands took their dreams, sought out a good analyst, and then, in the confidentiality of the analytic relationship, pondered them in a deeply introverted way, seeking their great meanings and messages.

The analyst I had sought out in Zürich was Jung's close collaborator and secretary, Frau Aniela Jaffé. I never knew Jung when he was alive, so wanting to get as close to his spirit as I could, I sought out Frau Jaffé.

For the first four sessions, everything went as I had expected. I brought in a dream, I was asked what my associations were and what I thought it meant, and then Frau Jaffé provided insightful amplifications (ideas about the symbolic aspects of the dream contents). I left each dream and each of those sessions carrying a "pearl of wisdom." I was in Jungian heaven.

But at the end of the fourth session, Frau Jaffé turned to me and said, "You know, you are making a terrible mistake." I gulped and cowered a bit, for this was a shock to my view of things, and I couldn't imagine what was going wrong. Cautiously, I asked, "Oh, what's that?" She said, "You're making the mistake that a lot of 'Jungians' make. That is, they think that Jung thought the psyche was only in the inner world, in the world of dreams and images. But that wasn't so, Jung also thought the 'outer' world was the psyche. All of what is, is psyche. So, you bring me your dreams, and that is fine, but you never tell me about your outer life. You don't tell me about your friends, your relationships, what you do in your free time, and your work."

I began the next session to change the course of our work together so that my "outer" life would be as important as my "inner" life. As we talked I began to see that there was a troublesome aspect of my relationships with certain people which bothered me very much. There appeared to be a repetitive pattern in my life of feeling smothered by women who seemed to want to demand all of my time and energies. I often felt helpless to untangle myself from situations in which such women would appear.

Frau Jaffé suggested that the use of active imagination might help. I remember her great caution as we proceeded to work with active imagination. She said, "I always have to ask myself in good conscience whether I can recommend this to those I work with." It seemed that she felt that active imagination was powerful and must be treated with reverence in its application. I soon found out that she was right.

Frau Jaffé suggested to me that perhaps an image would come

to mind which reminded me essentially of the women with whom I had been having this problem. She said it might be an animal or a person or something else, but it was clearly to be something of the imagination and not an image of a living person I knew in my life. Immediately the image of an octopus came to my mind. Its arms surrounded me, suffocating me, and restricting my movements.

The next suggestion was that I go to a quiet place where I could write and begin to write out a dialogue with this octopus. Frau Jaffé said that active imagination works best when writing is involved, as it requires more of the body and concentrates the mind. She suggested that I might begin by asking the octopus its name. I should write down each question and each answer the octopus gave.

I returned to my house near Zürich and began to work. I asked the octopus its name, and the answer quickly came: "Esther." As I began to write more questions to Esther and receive answers, I found I was afraid. In fact, as I heard that she wanted to control me completely, I began to feel extremely terrified. She grew in strength and power as I talked to her. I began to tremble and shake. I continued this rather difficult dialogue for several days, aided by daily sessions with Frau Jaffé in which we would discuss what was happening in these dialogues. Frau Jaffé was supportive and encouraging, urging me to go on with the writings.

After a few days I reached such a point of desperation that I finally gave up my battle with Esther and simply cried out into the universe and in my writings for help. I wrote, "Can't somebody help me? I'm really losing control and I can't handle this monster Esther."

Suddenly, a second figure appeared as I wrote. I could almost see it when my eyes were closed or as I was writing. I heard its voice, "Don't be afraid. I am here and I will help you." "Who are you?" I asked. The figure replied, "My name is Glenda. I am the Good Witch of the North." Glenda began to talk to me. She began to describe Esther as a being who had many problems. Until this point I had only seen Esther as a monster, and as Glenda talked I began to notice that my feelings about Esther were changing. Glenda told me that she would help me with Esther. For the first time, I began to have some feeling of compassion for Esther's rather miserable lot in life. It struck me that someone had to be pretty unfulfilled to need to control someone else entirely. I felt much stronger knowing that Glenda had arrived on the scene.

At that time there also arrived a little frog. This frog walked into the writings and introduced himself as "Hermes." Hermes told me that he was my friend and that Glenda was my friend, too. They said they were going to help me do something with Esther.

As I began to feel more compassion for Esther's plight, I wished less than I had earlier in my writings to kill her, but I wished that I could kill off her suffocating, controlling part. With the help of Glenda and Hermes, I realized that this destructive aspect of Esther would not disappear on its own. I had to do something. I took some colored pens, drew a cross, and I stabbed the cross into Esther's heart, killing off what had begun to appear as her vampire-like quality. (I remembered that driving something in the heart of a vampire was the only way to kill it.) This act allowed Esther to live, but with the vampire quality gone. I was able to have further dialogues with the part of Esther which remained, and it seemed that we came to a good understanding.

At this point an image of the Biblical King David appeared. In a very poetic way David said that I had found a certain amount of strength and that there was much more to find throughout my life. He said that my entire life should be dedicated to honoring the strength that I had found. I was very moved. These words seemed to me as real as any I had ever heard.

The active imagination I was using thus seemed to come to an end. And with it, remarkably, there were for a long time no more of the kind of suffocating encounters with women I had previously experienced. Several years later there was one such encounter that seemed to repeat itself, but when I got out my notebook and began to write to Esther again, she admitted that she had tried to catch me unawares and fool me. In a matter of a few minutes, I once again worked things out with her, and I was no longer bothered by such recurring experiences.

Some Clinical Examples

A woman who consulted me in my clinical psychology practice some time ago described initially a great number of problems. She said she had been losing weight dramatically and that she was tremendously depressed. She had had rotten luck with all the relationships she had ever had in her life. Her self-confidence was blown apart. She had had dreams about being sick in a hospital, which gave her the feeling that there must be something wrong with her. She was feeling that she was in the midst of deep despair.

After some initial sessions I suggested that active imagination might be a useful way for her to come to grips with her problem. After we talked about this possibility, she decided to try it. At first, two figures came to her mind. One was described as the "white robe." It was a long, cloth robe, somewhat in the shape of a body, but it had no face and was essentially undifferentiated. This robe seemed quite positive to her. The second image she could only describe as "the black." The black was a hazy, dark image with no form, and it threatened and frightened her.

This woman began her active imagination process by asking the white robe if it had some things to say. She said, "I feel there are many things you wish to tell me, so please come and talk to me." The white robe responded, "I've been waiting a long time to talk to you. I followed you around last weekend until you finally turned around and saw me." The robe said that it wanted to tell its story and that there was a certain sense of urgency about the story being told. At first general in its comments, the white robe later became more and more specific.

The black, on the other hand, was at first vindictive, an angry figure when it began to speak. It criticized the white robe for being a "weakling." It tried to tell the woman that she shouldn't listen to the white robe at all. The black said that it was going to be in charge of things and that she had nothing to say about it.

In the dialogues which this woman was writing out, she found over time that the white robe became a good friend. The robe offered to help her to understand the black. After awhile the white robe began to take more form, filling out with flesh and blood, and it developed the face and a body of a beautiful woman. As this woman appeared she became an even closer friend and ally of my patient.

The beautiful woman helped my patient understand something about how the black was the way it was. As my patient understood the black, it became less threatening and terrifying. The black began to change into a black cloud as it told its story. The black cloud began to tell the tragedies and disappointments of its own life, and as it did, it began to cry tears of rain. After some time, my patient found that she liked the black cloud as much as the beautiful woman in the white robe. And she felt, as the tears were shed from the black cloud, that the earth was being watered by those tears and new life was coming to the earth and to herself. It was not long before this woman began to feel very much better about her life. She changed her job and for the first time found a relationship with a man about whom she cared a great deal. From active imagination she apparently learned a way of relating to inner figures that enhanced her ability to maintain satisfying relationship with others.

Another woman, also depressed on initial consultation, began active imagination and discovered a black and threatening eagle named "Igor." The initial contact she had with Igor was terrifying, reminding her of her brother-in-law, a religious cult leader who had seduced and later abandoned her. After some time, Igor became very friendly. He explained that he had become threatening because he was lonely and could only get her attention by frightening her. He said that he was afraid and needed companionship. My patient became his friend, and he began to help her. Later, other helpful figures appeared and became both my patient's and Igor's friends. It was as though Igor had been a caged-up animal who became more insistent on attention the more isolated he was. Slowly, the beast in him became personified and friendly, ultimately becoming a friend and helpmate. Igor and my patient pledged loyalty to each other and promised always to help one another. This woman's depression lifted, and she began to participate more fully in the activity of life she had feared. She was able to turn something of little value into something of great value.

A third woman who came to consult me was a devout Christian who always wore a heavy metal cross around her neck. She was in her sixties, having spent many years going to Christian study groups and church services. But something was not working. It seemed that the forms of the church could no longer contain her deep feelings about her life. She felt that only the Christian tradition could give her meaning, but she had somehow not found there the meaning she needed. She was terribly depressed and lost. Her sad face belied her statements of certainty.

In active imagination, after some time, this woman discovered the presence of an "inner guide." Wanting typically, to make sure that everything she trusted was Christian, she asked, "Are you divine?" The answer came: "I don't like the word divine. It separates." Then she asked, "Is there no source?" The guide said, "The source is within each atom. You are struggling with 'good and bad,' and 'divine and other than' controversies. All is. If you must separate, then all is divine, or all is evil. The point of consciousness that carries both is divine. I am aware, and I would hope that your own awareness could let go of the 'divine' concept. You're coming into a focus where you are consciously carrying the whole." The woman asked, "The whole?" The guide answered, "Yes, but not the conscious whole, for the whole will always be much unconscious. A conscious person is always aware, honors the unknown. Like the galaxies it is without boundaries. When you can say 'I don't know' my heart is warmed."

This dialogue was very meaningful for this woman, who always thought she knew the truth. Somehow she began to recover a sense of the numinous and the mysterious in her experience of her life. She made fewer judgments about other people's points of view, and she started making some new friends. She began to arrive for our sessions without wearing her heavy cross. Her countenance lifted. She wore jewelry for the first time in her life, often jewelry from many different cultures and countries. Somehow she began to feel more a part of the world. And she was happier.

Practical Considerations

The decision to begin active imagination must be the patient's; it is not something to be imposed. It should be undertaken only when the patient is willing and when there is an adequate place for the sharing of what is produced with another person. Active imagination often needs the confidentiality and protection of the analytical or therapeutic relationship to be fully contained. Because this process can release strong forces of psychic energy that can overwhelm the patient, the therapist must always ask himself or herself in good conscience whether the time is right to begin.

Active imagination begins when the therapist suggests that the patient contact an image which exemplifies the general situation of the patient's life or a particularly repetitive situation. Often the image can appear as an animal or a person either familiar or unfamiliar to the patient. At times the image can be vague and unformed. It is important that the patient be dissuaded from working with an image of an actual person who is alive. There are hazards in using a living person as a focus for active imagaination, for if something bad happens to that person during the active imagination process, the patient may bear a feeling of deep guilt for having caused it to happen.

In general, active imagaination proceeds in the direction of *personification*. The patient is asked to ask the images contacted their names, or at least to seek clearer mental pictures of who and what they are. The search in this process of contacting the image is for some kind of *relationship* with the image. This does not mean that the relationship must be a positive, loving one. Indeed, many relationships, at some point in active imagaination, are marked by intense struggle.

It is advisable for the patient to embark on sessions of active imagination in a quiet place, away from other people, telephones, and other distractions. One needs significant time away from other concerns to see and hear the figures which appear. It also seems vital for the patient to give the dialogues which appear some kind of concrete expression. Recording them in writing, without censorship of any kind, is often a satisfactory way of proceeding. Because writing incorporates more of the senses, active imagination becomes a psychophysical process rather than just pure imagination.

Sometimes a ritual of preparing the place where one is to work is useful. Lighting a candle, delimiting a sacred space, or other such activity may be helpful. Active imagination may lead to avenues of creative expression other than writing. Often one may feel the urge to paint the inner figures one sees or try to mold them in clay. It seems terribly useful to follow such urges on their natural course, gently allowing for such expression. I have consistently observed that *ex*pression may be the activity needed to counterbalance *de*pression.

It also seems important to delimit the amount of time set aside for work with active imagination. It appears that "inner" figures do not live in a world of time and space and often do not understand, unless they are told, that living in the world often demands such practical considerations as doing the laundry, cooking dinner, and sleeping. I often suggest that patients work for a delimited amount of time and "make appointments" for future sessions with the figures which appear in active imagination. The patient might say "I would like to continue talking with you now, but I must go to pick up my laundry at the cleaners. I shall spend an hour talking with you again tomorrow from 5 to 6 P.M., if that is o.k. with you." This setting of limits helps to avoid the possibility that one will become overwhelmed by a demanding inner figure who takes over one's conscious focus and does not allow for attention to practical matters.

It is very important that one have someone with whom to share his or her experiences in the process of working with active imagination. The telling of the story about one's inner journey helps make a further bridge between the inner and the outer realities. Since active imagination is primarily concerned with relationship, the relating of a deep personal experience helps bring one more in touch with interpersonal and transpersonal perspectives.

Eventually active imagination comes to a stopping point. When this happens it is clear to the patient, and an experienced therapist can often sense that it is coming. At this point it is not enough that the images have just appeared. One must live the imaginal experience onward into one's life, into the world of flesh and blood and bones, into the arena of human activity and into nature. By the time active imagination has ended the patient should have had a real encounter with inner figures and an experience of working things out with them to a point of conclusion. A German word which best describes this is *Auseinandersetzung*, which implies an ethical confrontation that leads the patient and the inner figures to an eventual agreement about their relationship with each other.

Implications for Transpersonal Psychotherapy

The transpersonal perspective holds that there is an essential unity underlying all of humanity and the material world. This position is essentially non-dualistic, and it allows us to break down the barriers between what has classically been seen as the "inner" and the "outer." Active imagination is a vital tool for achieving this non-dualistic integration.

As a civilization has developed, powerful instinctive forces have been buried like caged animals within the depths of the psyche. As much as modern man has tried to suppress such instinctive forces, they have built up an intense reactive strength which often erupts with great force, aggression, and destruction. A proper relationship with such forces is essential for peace within the individual and in the world.

In seeking to master matter, modern man has also been trying to conquer his own soul, but it has rebelled and demanded attention. Active imagination can bring one into renewed contact with the soul, and from the new relationship which is thereby formed, wholeness is possible again.

We have begun to believe that there is nothing in the darkness worth integrating into our modern life. And yet, following the lead of the alchemists, we find that even the basest of components of our experience can provide the *prima materia* for a transformation into something of great value, or gold. Paracelsus provides the clue: *au rum nostrum non est aurum vulgi.* (Our gold is not the common gold.) The gold of the alchemists is not money but that golden experience of unity and totality.

Transpersonal psychology and psychotherapy may find that active imagination is an invaluable vehicle for traveling the *via regia* to totality.

19

Alyce M. Green   Psychophysiology and Health:
Personal and Transpersonal

A number of years ago Elmer Green and I became dissatisfied with
the image of humanity portrayed in our literature, art, theater, science, and especially our psychology. Humans were portrayed as
helpless victims of their genes, their conditioning, their environment,
and fate, or chance.

We could not accept such a picture. From our reading and experience, we knew of people who could do "impossible" things. We
wanted to study the human potential for choice, self-direction, and
self-regulation. In order to do this we needed more information, so
we went to the University of Chicago, Elmer, a physicist, to study
psychophysiology (the brain, nervous system, perception, etc.) and I,
with a background in speech and drama, to study psychology, counseling, client-centered therapy, and creativity.

When we came from the University of Chicago to the Research
Department of the Menninger Foundation in 1964, the world was
rather a different place than it is today. Such things as meditation,
yoga, and the ability of some yogis to control various autonomic
functions (to say nothing of parapsychology), were not to be mentioned in polite academic or medical circles. Neither was the possibility of the average person's using the mind to intentionally influence or direct "involuntary" processes of the body—in fact, in the

Department of Psychology at the University of Chicago, talk about the mind, imagery, or consciousness, was definitely discouraged, since their existence could not be "proved." About that time a noted psychologist said of psychology, "First it lost its soul, then it lost its mind, and now it has lost consciousness."

So when we wanted to conduct research at the Menninger Foundation on human potential to voluntarily influence or regulate "nonvoluntary" aspects of physiology and psychology the question was, "How to begin?" We knew about autogenic training, a system of therapy that taught people to heal themselves with self-suggestive phrases and visualization, originated by Dr. Johannes Schultz, a German psychiatrist, in the early part of this century (Schultz and Luthe, 1959). Since autogenic training was developed by a westerner, and a German doctor, and since one of the Menninger doctors had heard it discussed at an international conference it was thought respectable.

The first research project was a brief two-week study of autogenic training, testing the ability of people to warm their hands through the use of our adaptation of Schultz's phrases. Thirty-two women from the community were subjects. We had hoped to combine temperature biofeedback with the use of the autogenic phrases, believing that feedback would greatly accelerate learning, but since the machines (designed by Elmer Green and built by our Bio-medical Engineering Laboratory) were not ready in time, we used twice-daily practice of the relaxation and warmth phrases alone. Nevertheless, several women were able to learn to intentionally raise their hand temperatures two to three degrees Fahrenheit and two of the women raised theirs ten degrees in the two weeks' practice of phrases and accompanying visualizations. When temperature machines finally became available we found that nine out of ten average healthy people could learn to raise their hand temperature ten degrees Fahrenheit in two or three days. From this first study came the serendipitous finding that intentionally raising the temperature of the hands (which means increasing blood flow to the hands, which in turn means "turning off" the stress response in the sympathetic nervous system), can alleviate and often eliminate migraine headache (Green and Green, 1983). Dr. Joseph Sargent, head of Internal Medicine at The Menninger Foundation, was interested in pursuing that particular finding in headache research and treatment. Elmer and I, however, were primarily interested in studying states of consciousness. The main biofeedback technique for the study of consciousness is training in control of the electrical rhythms of the brain, commonly called "brainwaves." Since brainwaves are not known to have any sensory representation by which a person can detect them, their control is gained by self-elicitation of the subjective states of consciousness with which particular brain rhythms are associated. The feedback signal (usually a tone) tells when the desired state has been achieved by signalling the presence of the brain rhythm associated with that state.

There are four major rhythms. BETA, 13 to 26 cycles per second (cps), is usually associated with "active thinking," as when focusing on the outside world, or meeting a stressful situation, or solving a concrete mental problem. ALPHA, 8 to 13 cps, is associated with a more relaxed state. The mind is alert but engaged in internal experience (e.g. daydreaming), rather than focused on the outside world or on organized, logical thought. THETA, 4 to 8 cps, is usually associated with deeply internalized near-unconscious states. It appears as consciousness slips toward unawareness in drowsiness or in deep reverie and is often accompanied by imagery not associated with conscious thought. DELTA, 0 to 4 cps, is primarily associated with deep sleep. As the psychological state changes from active concrete mind toward reverie or sleep. The brain rhythm slows down, as do other physiological rhythms of the body.

We carried out several brainwave research projects with college sophomores as subjects. One finding from these studies was especially interesting. With the slower brain waves, theta and low-frequency alpha, (which signify a quiet body, quiet emotions and quiet mind), some subjects experienced hypnagogic imagery. The term "hypnagogic" comes from the Greek, *hypnos*, or sleep, and *gogic* or leading to. It was formerly thought that such imagery came only in the state just preceding deep sleep, but the term "hypnagogic imagery" no longer pertains only to pre-sleep states. We know now that such imagery can occur in deep relaxation, deep meditation, or deep internal quiet, coming suddenly into consciousness from some unconscious source. As one student phrased it, "It just popped into my mind." It is not necessarily visual, but can be auditory, or related to touch, fragrance or taste—any sensation that would ordinarily come through one of the five senses.

The research seemed to indicate that there was a relationship between hypnagogic imagery, low-frequency alpha or theta brain-waves, and a deeply quiet subjective state that we called "reverie." I knew from my study of the creativity literature while at the University of Chicago, that there was also a relation between the deeply quiet state, hypnagogic imagery, and creativity. Some of the most highly creative "intuitive" ideas and solutions have come to creative people during states of reverie and near-dream.

Usually such imagery has come spontaneously in unplanned ways at unplanned times, when the mind was not engaged in active thinking or striving for a solution. But some people have been able to use this image-making faculty intentionally, putting themselves into the state of consciousness in which it can occur.

For instance, Robert Lewis Stevenson was able to command the "brownies" of his mind to produce stories while he slept. He would awaken with plot and characters fully developed and ready to be put down on paper. Jean Cocteau, as he awoke from a fitful sleep, "witnessed as from a seat in a theater" scenes which became the basis for his play "The Knights of the Round Table." Poincaré described mathematical symbols rising in clouds, dancing before him, as he lay in bed awaiting sleep, and colliding and combining into the first set of Fuchsian functions, mathematical functions that his reasoning, logical mind had thought could not exist.

The chemist Kekule had repeated "visions" of this kind and was proficient in the use of the image-making state. At a dinner in his honor he told of a series of deep reveries in which the atoms "gamboled" before his eyes, leading to the development of his theory of molecular structure. And he told of a night when, working late, he turned his chair to the fire and dozed. Again the atoms gamboled before his eyes, this time forming structures in long rows that turned and twisted like snakes. Suddenly one of the snakes took hold of its own tail and whirled "mockingly" before him. From this image Kekule worked out the molecular concept he is most famous for, that many organic compounds come in closed chains or rings such as the benzene ring. It was the solution of a longstanding problem in organic chemistry.

Elmer Green had been interested in the "image-making faculty" for a long time. Such imagery was natural to him and he had often used it to solve problems in physics and mathematics. So, putting together his experiences, my information from the creativity research, and the experiences of our student subjects, we considered the possibility of biofeedback-aided brainwave training as a way of releasing or enhancing creativity. First we ran a pilot study with psychologically-sophisticated subjects, members of a yogic meditation class. The resulting imagery was interesting and promising, so we designed a research project (funded by the National Institute of Mental Health) titled "Alpha-Theta Training, Reverie, and Imagery" to test whether students could, through alpha-theta training, achieve a state of deep reverie and become aware of, and report, hypnagogic imagery. Subjects were 26 college men, juniors and seniors from Washburn University of Topeka. (Green and Green, 1977).

Feedback of brainwaves was from the occipital area at the back of the head, where the visual faculty is located. We used auditory feedback, a low tone to signify the presence of the theta rhythm, and a slightly higher tone to signify alpha. We did not mention imagery or creativity to the students at the beginning of the project. We merely explained that we were studying the possibility of building a bridge between conscious and unconscious processes, and gaining some control over that bridge.

Each student came to the laboratory once every two weeks for alpha-theta biofeedback practice during which brain waves were recorded. Each lab session was followed by a tape-recorded interview in which the subject reported his subjective experiences during the session. (Becoming aware of and being able to report such experiences is part of the task in biofeedback training.) In addition, each student practiced daily with portable biofeedback machines and kept a notebook in which he recorded physical, emotional and mental experiences. He came to the laboratory to report and discuss this material on alternate weeks.

There were ten weeks of training, divided into two five-week periods. During the first period all subjects significantly increased alpha production and many were able to produce some theta, which is more difficult because it requires deeper physical, emotional and mental quietness. Although there were great individual differences, subjects were becoming more able to be aware of, and describe their subjective experiences.

At the beginning of the second five-week period we explained hypnagogic imagery and expressed our interest in increased theta production, and increased awareness of imagery. During this period there was a significant decrease in alpha production, an increase in theta, and an increase in number, variety, and complexity of imagery reported.

Briefly summarized, the results of this brainwave-and-reverie research were:

1. Early in the training, many subjects reported increased recall and vividness of dreams, and some of them reported the recall of forgotten early childhood experiences through hypnagogic imagery during their sessions.
2. There were reports of what Jung termed "archetypal" imagery, a universal imagery, common to people of all cultures. Sometimes the same kind of imagery was reported by two or more students. For example, there were several images of going through a tunnel; climbing up or down a mountain or a staircase; experiencing a vast expanse, or the sea or prairie; floating out in space; meeting a "wise old man"; being given or shown a "Book of Knowledge"; seeing a pair of eyes, or the "single eye."
3. There were experiences related to creativity: everything for a school paper falling into place during a training session; a photography student being shown pictures from an artist's portfolio; an art student experiencing greater freedom in drawing; the occasional use of a training session in creatively solving an interpersonal problem.
4. There were several psychic or ESP experiences. The state of deep quietness of body, emotions, and mind achieved in theta training sometimes allowed usually "unheard" and "unseen" things to come to consciousness.
5. We had not anticipated the relatively high frequency of subject reports implying that integrative experiences are associated with extended alpha-theta practice: students reported having more energy, improved concentration, greater ease in taking

tests and writing papers, improved interpersonal relations, greater awareness of self and others, and greater sensitivity to, and appreciation of, nature. Some students expressed their feeling in such phrases as "I feel so put together," "so with it," "whatever I have to do, I can do."

Because of these results, we hypothesized that the creative potential of the hypnagogic image, the different ways of experiencing things associated with a quiet body, quiet emotions and quiet mind, and the ability to creatively visualize when in such a state, need not be limited to literary, artistic, or scientific insights. In our student subjects it applied to their daily lives, their school work and their interpersonal associations. These were the things that concerned them. They were not yet scientists or artists, but they realized and took with them the value of deep internal quietness for creative thinking, for finding solutions, and for integration.

These kinds of research results led us to broaden our concept of creativity to include creative visualization for physical, emotional, mental and spiritual health. Most importantly these ideas apply to all of us, not only for restoring and maintaining good health from day to day, but in creating and recreating our very lives. For it appears that what we vividly visualize, or creatively imagine, tends to come into being—in our bodies, and in our lives.

While we were engaged in research, Menninger psychiatrists asked, from time to time, if we might be able to help one or another of their patients. When we agreed to try, patients were referred for a variety of syndromes including muscle tension, anxiety tension, bleeding stomach ulcer, tachycardia and high blood pressure. Fortunately, in these early cases we were able to be helpful and in 1975 with our colleagues we established, for clinical purposes, the Menninger Biofeedback and Psychophysiology Center.

When a person comes to the Center for biofeedback-aided psychophysiologic therapy, we explain that "biofeedback" means the feedback of biological information (by a needle on a meter, a light, or tone) about ongoing internal physiologic process, such as heart behavior, blood pressure, muscle tension, temperature, or brain rhythms', and that biofeedback training means using that information to extend voluntary control over that physiological process. We explain that self-regulation of an automatic process is accomplished through (1) learning to quiet the body, emotions and mind, (2) imagining and visualizing the change wanted, (3) "feeling" it happen, and (4) in a detached way, "letting it happen," allowing the body to carry out the visualization. The biofeedback meter acts as a guide, indicating the degree of success.

We show the patient how our thoughts and emotions get into the nervous system to effect our health (through the limbic system, hypothalamus, and pituitary) and we emphasize that this process is happening all the time with either helpful or harmful results. We stress the fact that it is natural for the body to heal and to be well, and that our minds can play an important part in creating and maintaining health.

We discuss the importance of choice—that we can choose to hold one thought or one emotion rather than another. It is the long-held anxiety, anger, frustration or despair that leads to psychosomatic illness. To be of good cheer, to love and to laugh leads to psychosomatic health. By our choice we move toward disease or well-being.

When the patient understands the rationale and the process of biofeedback training, we discuss goals. This discussion includes, for example, what is to be achieved in control of temperature and muscle tension, and in the amelioration of the problem for which the client has been referred. Additional goals often include gaining the ability to deal more successfully with interpersonal problems (at home or at work), gaining in self-confidence and self-assertiveness, and developing a better sense of self-worth. Clear goals stimulate motivation, an important element in learning self-regulation skills.

During the first session we teach the patient the use of the temperature feedback machine and demonstrate how, by the use of autogenic (self-suggestion) phrases for relaxation of the body, and visualization of warmth in the hands (Schultz and Luthe, 1959), one can increase hand temperature and "turn off" the sympathetic fight-or-flight reaction we inherited from our cavemen ancestors, the "stress response" responsible for much modern disease.

Having learned how to use the temperature feedback instrument and the hand-warming technique, the patient takes the machine home for twice-daily fifteen-minute practice sessions. This begins the transfer of self-regulation training to the life situation at the very start of training.

The patient comes to the Center once a week for electromyographic (EMG) training—training in muscle tension control, and other self-regulation procedures. Most frequently we place the EMG electrodes on the forehead; relaxation usually extends to the jaw and neck muscles, and often it generalizes to the whole body. In the same way that EMG feedback may be used later for relaxation of tense muscles in other parts of the body such as the neck, shoulders, or back, so temperature control, once learned, can be used to bring warmth and increased blood flow not only to hands, but also to the throat, to an arthritic knee or back, or to the feet (as in the treatment of high blood pressure, Green, Green, and Norris, 1980).

Depending on the needs of the patient, other biofeedback modalities may be introduced: feedback of brain rhythms for insomnia or pain control, heart rate for tachycardia and arrhythmias, or galvanic skin response (GSR) for control of emotional response. After completing a biofeedback session, at home or at the Center, the patient fills out a questionnaire describing physical feelings, emotions, thoughts, and fantasies which occurred during the session. This is an "awareness increasing" procedure. We often call biofeedback practice "awareness training." The answers to the questionnaire add to the understanding of problems and progress by both patient and therapist.

In addition to biofeedback, we teach other psychophysiologic procedures, including diaphragmatic breathing for tension reduction, specific breathing exercises for stilling the mind, guided and unguided imagery, and internal dialogue with the body. We encourage physical exercises (active ones like walking, running, swimming, tennis, and stretching ones like yoga), and give information and suggestions about nutrition. Visualizing what is to be accomplished plays an important part in all our techniques: it helps to make change happen.

Techniques of self-regulation not only teach patients ways of managing stress, but begin to re-establish healthy homeostatic balance, preparing the body for self-healing. These techniques have proven useful in the treatment of many psychosomatic or psychophysiologic disorders such as headache (migraine and tension), gastro-intestinal problems (stomach ulcers, colitis, irritable bowel syndrome, esophageal dysfunction), cardiovascular disorders (tachycardia, arrhythmia, hypertension), and various forms of cancer. They are also useful in relief of chronic pain, in neuromuscular re-education of paralyzed limbs, and in the treatment of epilepsy.

I would like to briefly describe self-regulation training for control of high blood pressure as an example of biofeedback-aided psychophysiologic therapy. The most common form of high blood pressure is "essential hypertension," which means abnormally high pressure with no known physical cause. It is a stress-related disorder, and as a precursor of stroke, heart attack, or kidney failure, it kills more people than any other disease. In the words of Dr. James Hunt, Chairman of the Department of Medicine of the Mayo Clinic in the U.S.A., hypertension is the "silent killer" because normally there is no warning that blood pressure is building up. This should alert us to the necessity of preventive measures and the need for drugless treatment.

Stress activates the sympathetic nervous system, that section of the autonomic nervous system that prepares us for emergencies. It increases activity in the cardiovascular and respiratory systems, it curtails gastro-intestinal activity, causes the release of glucose in the blood stream, and changes the distribution of blood and various chemicals throughout the body. The sympathetic nervous system prepares us for fight-or-flight, just as it prepared our cave ancestors when a bear came into the cave at night. In modern humans, however, with highly developed emotional natures, emotional problems are the most frequent and important stressors, and throwing stones, picking up a club, or fleeing the "cave" are not appropriate responses, even if our bodies behave as if they were.

We accepted our first hypertensive patient before we had established the Biofeedback and Psychophysiology Center as the result of another serendipitous event. A journalist who visited our laboratory for a story on biofeedback as a medical tool asked, after a training session, if she might take a temperature meter home "to experiment with." She returned the meter a week later and said she had "got rid of" her high blood pressure. She had mild hypertension, she explained, for which she took diazepam. When she practiced hand warming at home she felt that her blood pressure decreased. "Why shouldn't it," she said, "hand warming means blood-flow control, doesn't it?" She stopped taking her medication and made an appointment with her physician for a blood pressure check at the end of the week. Her pressure was normal in his office, and he suggested that she continue without the diazepam and check with him again in a few days.

Later, to an audience of physicians at a biofeedback workshop, we mentioned this incident as an interesting "unexplained event." An elderly surgeon responded that in the years before there were appropriate drugs for severe hypertension, surgeons sometimes did a sympathectomy of the nerves leading to the legs, in order to create greatly increased vasodilation in the lower part of the body. This reduced the overall blood pressure. The surgeon suggested that if temperature training were able to increase blood flow in the lower part of the body, it might be called a "reversible sympathectomy."

No more than a week later a Menninger physician called and asked if we could help a patient with hypertension that was not satisfactorily controlled with medication, her blood pressure averaging about 190/100 mm HG. This patient, "AD" in Table 1, was woman of thirty-eight who had been on hypertension medication for sixteen years, since the birth of her first child. She was also on medication for a kidney infection. Within five months her blood pressure was normal, her kidneys healed and all her medications reduced to zero. For the first time in sixteen years she was free of drugs. This was a propitious beginning for our continuing clinical research and treatment of hypertension, without drugs.

Treatment for hypertension begins with temperature training and EMG training for management of stress and for re-establishment of homeostatic balance. Special emphasis is placed on temperature training in the feet to increase blood flow to the lower limbs, deep breathing exercises to manage stress reactions, physical exercises such as brisk walking, jogging, swimming, and information on nutrition. In addition to recording their temperature readings, hypertension patients take, and record, their blood pressure before and after each temperature training session. Seven out of eight of our hypertensive patients are able, in an average time of seventeen weeks, to reduce medications to zero (under the care of their physician), while achieving or maintaining normal blood pressure. More than 150 hypertensive patients, most of them trained in groups of six to eight, have now received treatment as successful as that of our first twelve patients, indicated in Table 1. Space does not allow the story of each patient of the table, but I hope the statistics will be of interest.

Transfer of what is learned about hypertension at the Biofeedback

TABLE 1

Biodata and Training Results with 12 Hypertensive Patients (February 1975–May 1978)

Patients	AD	ZL	AQ	CF	LI	GR	FG	FCG	AA	MR	AR	RZ
Biodata												
Sex, age at intake	F 39	M 57	F 44	M 28	F 40	M 57	F 27	M 39	F 53	F 52	F 38	F 56
Date of intake	Feb 75	May 75	May 77	Jul 77	Nov 77	Dec 77	Feb 78	Apr 78	May 78	May 78	May 78	May 78
Years of diagnosed hypertension	16	39	3	3	2	30	1	15	10	1	3	3
Years of antihypertensive medication	16	16	0	3	0	10	1	3	0	0	3	0
Starting medication index (MI)	38	25	0	58	0	50	25	19	0	0	50	0
MI at follow-up	0	17	0	0	0	0	0	0	0	0	0	0
Average blood pressure in first 10 sessions	$\frac{169}{110}$	$\frac{133}{95}$	$\frac{139}{86}$	$\frac{130}{83}$	$\frac{143}{94}$	$\frac{142}{88}$	$\frac{138}{89}$	$\frac{133}{92}$	$\frac{142}{82}$	$\frac{144}{99}$	$\frac{136}{88}$	$\frac{149}{105}$
Average blood pressure in last 10 sessions	$\frac{145}{92}$	$\frac{130}{80}$	$\frac{118}{83}$	$\frac{128}{80}$	$\frac{145}{90}$	$\frac{123}{81}$	$\frac{141}{91}$	$\frac{131}{85}$	$\frac{141}{79}$	N/A	$\frac{125}{79}$	$\frac{146}{102}$
Change in blood pressure	$\frac{-24}{-18}$	$\frac{-3}{-15}$	$\frac{-21}{-3}$	$\frac{-2}{-3}$	$\frac{+2}{-4}$	$\frac{-19}{-7}$	$\frac{+3}{-2}$	$\frac{-2}{-7}$	$\frac{-1}{-3}$	N/A	$\frac{-9}{-9}$	$\frac{-3}{-3}$
Average blood pressure at follow-up	$\frac{132}{84}$	Ongoing	$\frac{120}{80}$	$\frac{137}{84}$	$\frac{142}{94}$	$\frac{135}{83}$	$\frac{133}{84}$	$\frac{130}{85}$	$\frac{135}{85}$	Ongoing	$\frac{130}{80}$	Ongoing
Weeks to termination of drugs	25	Ongoing	N/A	19	N/A	71	1	21	N/A	Ongoing	32	Ongoing
Weeks to termination of training	26	Ongoing	16	23	13	54	21*	28	33	Ongoing	34	Ongoing
Weeks to follow-up after training	104	Ongoing	52	39	31	17	22	5	11	Ongoing	10	Ongoing

* Unable to continue training

and Psychophysiology Center to the patient's life situation is of special importance. For example, we suggest that people who drive a
car greet a red stop-light signal as an opportunity to relax their
hands, take a deep breath, and feel all the tension flow out of their
body. We suggest finding reminders, "cartoons or jokes that make
them laugh" (Cousins, 1979), a picture or poem that says "untense,"
or a smiling face to put under the glass on their desk or on their re-
frigerator door.

As patients progress we ask them to develop their own phrases,
visualizations, imagery, and other techniques for self-regulation, and
to free themselves from dependence on the autogenic phrases, the
biofeedback instruments, and the therapist. They are helped to realize that both the responsibility and the achievement are theirs.

Beyond the amelioration or healing of a physical disorder we have
found that successful biofeedback therapy usually results in increased self-confidence, self-direction, and a change in life style. At
times this becomes a "transformational" experience, as the patient
feels empowered by hope and the possibility to change, to expand
and grow.

An unusually interesting case is the hypertensive patient who took
the longest time to achieve the goal of being free of drugs and able
to maintain normal blood pressure (G.R. of Table 1). Of Jewish descent, he is now an American psychiatrist. He grew up in Hitler's
Germany and when he was fifteen, his parents, who died in the ho-
locaust, put him on a boat bound for the United States. He managed
well in the United States, completed college and medical school, and
finally went into psychiatry.

G.R. was "type A" and liked it (Friedman and Rosenman, 1981).
He liked his "norepinephrine highs," but he disliked the side effects
of the hypertension drugs he had to take. He described himself as always doing two or three things at a time, for example, talking on the
telephone while writing the notes on his last patient. A man always
in a hurry, he said, who drove his car too fast—the same man who
said, after he had been in therapy for some weeks, that he "looked
for the red stop lights" to give himself a chance to slow down.

G.R. had been on medication sporadically since medical school,
and continuously for ten years when he entered our program. By the
twelfth week of training he decided he would ask his cardiologist to

reduce his medication a little. Just thinking about it made his blood pressure rise. He lowered it again in a few days and the doctor reduced his medication. This pattern was repeated several times— each time it made him nervous. "I am a doctor," he said. "I'm used to prescribing drugs, not giving up on drugs."

Nevertheless, it was his desire to be free of drugs that brought him to psychophysiologic therapy. After having practiced the self-regulation procedures diligently for a few months he began jogging, at first around the block, but increasing the distance slowly until he was jogging three miles a day. He also adopted a more healthful and salt-free diet, reducing his weight by forty pounds. And he slowed down.

During his fifty-second week of psychophysiologic therapy he went for a check up and his doctor said, "You don't have hypertension any more. Go home and take yourself off that last bit of medication and come back in a year for your regular checkup."

When we terminated his therapy G.R. said to me, "I think at last I really know what this is all about, I have become child-like, not childish, mind you, but child-like. I notice things again. I didn't even know our neighbors had beautiful gardens—I never took time to look. Each week I make a trip out of town to do counseling. I never knew what was on the way. I just drove there and did my business. Now I drive more slowly and I notice things. You know, I had forgotten that Kansas has birds—I had forgotten that birds sing in Kansas." There are transpersonal overtones here (Green and Green, 1971).

Some patients move even more strongly toward a transpersonal orientation. The following is the story of Laura (a pseudonym), a patient with cancer. I had treated her some years before. Together we had successfully dealt with a serious bleeding ulcer, and now she had an inoperable lung cancer. She was undergoing heavy chemotherapy and radiation treatment, but the prognosis was not good. She was a woman approaching sixty, living alone and with few friends. Her only child, a son, had left home in anger years before because of her alcoholism, and because she was cruel when she had been drinking. Though she had conquered that problem, he would not forgive her, nor allow her to see the grandchildren. She was not sure she wanted to put forth the effort to live.

An intelligent and artistic person, Laura easily adapted to our procedures as she had been through them before. As she progressed in her training her feelings and thoughts began to change. She remembered that she had always wanted to shape things out of clay and she ordered a potter's wheel. She had done some painting before this illness and she ordered a new set of paints.

One day in deep relaxation (a state similar to a theta state), she said she was seeing "the face of that seductive young man, that shadowy figure wearing a black cape, that I call death." He was standing at the end of a stone passageway beckoning her to come, as he had beckoned many times before when she was an alcoholic. She had responded in those days by attempting suicide. Now, however, she told him she would not respond. She mentioned her interest in painting and pottery. He continued to smile cynically. "You know only about death," she said, "There are many things I want to do—and oh so many things I want to read—way into my old age."

There was a moment of silence, then Laura said "Mrs. Green, he's gone . . . he threw down his cape and left when I said 'way into my old age.'" She felt this symbolized her intention to live, and the figure never appeared in her imagery again.

Laura had a wonderful gift of fantasy. She had seen "Star Wars" and been enchanted with the robot 3PO, so she visualized her own robot, and called him "Robie." He was the captain, the clever and faithful leader of an army of R2-D2 robots (her white blood cells) that went to battle any time of night or day to destroy the cancer cells. She was very courageous and very diligent in her practice of all aspects of the training and after two months, X-rays showed that the cancer was reduced in size.

Three weeks later she wrote, "The immune system is right on target. For each X-ray the growth decreases and I know it will be gone in a month." And so it was. One of her doctors wrote to me, "It was truly amazing to watch so large and vicious a tumor simply melt away without a trace in the course of a few short weeks."

Her intensive chemotherapy and radiation treatments were continued, however, and Laura grew thinner and more tired, too tired to do the many things she had planned to do. She found it difficult to eat and we searched for foods that would stimulate her appetite, but with little success. This was of concern because we knew her immunological system was greatly weakened.

Laura continued to have significant imagery. She saw an old battlefield of the Civil War that symbolized the long battle with her internalized mother, but "now there was peace . . . the war was over." She had images of the potter's wheel, "looking down at a spinning ball of clay on the wheel, telling myself I had the power in my being to center it and make it grow into a bowl." Then she added, "I seem to be internalizing my desires toward clay. Hopefully I will find the right postion for centering." Another time, "I had the strange sensation of being very small and at the vortex of the clay pot I was throwing on the wheel. Just a tiny me." And again, ". . . being in the vortex of a turning pot on the wheel. It was as if I were looking down and within."

She also had recurring images of Greece that seemed so familiar she wondered if she had lived in that country in some former life. Often she would be sitting on a high rock, looking down into a green valley "a sheltered and beautiful place of peace and color. I was going down to live there. It was good and clean and ordered. I hope I can go down the somewhat rocky road into this peaceful valley." And about six weeks later, "I saw myself beginning the journey down the mountain path into my green valley. There is much luggage I have left at the pass. I am carrying only what I need."

As the weeks went by Laura's physical condition worsened and she grew afraid. She had handled chemotherapy and radiation without nausea and fear in the beginning, but now she felt they were destroying her. Dr. Carl Simonton has said, "Some cancer treatments are so potent, in fact, that patients fear the side effects . . . as much as the disease itself," (Simonton, Simonton, and Creighton, 1978). One of Laura's doctors told me it was possible her fears that treatment could destroy her were justified. I could not reveal this conversation to Laura but suggested that she confer with her physicians, attend carefully to what they said, and then make her decision, for it was her body and her life that were at stake. She refused further chemotherapy and radiation treatment.

Laura grew more cheerful and positive after she had stopped chemotherapy and radiation. Her appetite revived slightly, but she did not gain weight. Her physician put her back in the hospital to "gain ten pounds," he said. It did not happen. She grew depressed and was allowed to go home. We had two therapy sessions in her home, but she seemed very frail. Two weeks later, when I returned from a conference, she was in the hospital again. It had been decided that she should have another body scan. Her lungs were clear but there was a small cancer in her liver.

Laura could not decide at first whether, in her depleted condition, she wanted to "go to battle." (It would be difficult to describe how emaciated she was.) Finally her answer was not to battle, that she and Robie just could not get activated again, that she felt she was ready to be released from her tired body. She knew that whatever her choice, we would continue to work with her, helping in any way we could to make her more comfortable. She asked that I help her to die with dignity.

Laura remained in the hospital. She was not heavily medicated, and although she slept a great deal she was lucid when she wanted to be. Her son came to see her and they made their peace. Her attorney came and her will was made. She was proud that in spite of pain and lack of energy she was able to do these things with dignity and clarity. Our last times together were spent contemplating the Light, and moving toward the Light.

Patients can be helped to realize that just as it is possible to direct the course of living more intentionally, so it is possible to direct the course of dying more intentionally. To have the ability to call on elements of self mastery, pain control, and peace of mind in terminal illness is a valuable asset for every human. Death is an experience which we all will share, and dying with dignity is a part of living with dignity.

In closing I would like to tell you about a boy we call Gregory. He was nine years old when he was brought to the Center by his parents, after his doctors had done all they could and had estimated that he had only six months to live. He had an inoperable brain tumor, and a brain scan made about four months after termination of radiation treatment and chemotherapy showed no improvement. Gregory talked with his psychophysiologic therapist about dying, saying that he didn't want to die, and wondering why this had happened to him, "just a regular boy."

Gregory carried out the regimen of biofeedback training for self regulation and general well-being designed by his therapist (including joyous pillow fights, in spite of some impairment of movement on his left side). He had a wonderful imagination, creating and practicing his visualizations eagerly. He had a fleet of swift and powerful fighter planes. He knew exactly where his tumor was, he said, and he directed their fire with precision, with all the accompanying noise and commotion. He conceived, directed and played himself as a pilot on a Star-Wars-type tape that he and his therapist made of such a battle (Norris, 1983).

After some months Gregory began saying that it seemed to him that the tumor was gone. He continued his practice even though he "couldn't find it anymore." When a brain scan was taken after thirteen months of training, the tumor was gone as completely as if it had been removed by surgery. During the next year his visualization changed to "surveillance" and the destruction of any residual or new cancer cells that might be in his body. Now, two years later, Gregory comes to see his therapist occasionally—saying that when he grows up he wants to be exactly that kind of a therapist. Meanwhile, he has a red telephone through which he gives friendship, counsel and comfort to other young people who have cancer.

It is clear that psychophysiologic therapy may merge into transpersonal therapy, especially in cases of imminent death. There is a tendency then to penetrate beneath the trivialities of ordinary life. Values change. What becomes important, in the words of another patient with cancer, is "the love of family and friends and time to spend with them, and the beauties of nature and time to enjoy them." When the deeply quiet state is achieved in therapy, "answers from the unconscious" tend to enhance love, compassion, and peace.

REFERENCES

COUSINS, NORMAN. *Anatomy of an Illness.* New York: Norton, 1979.

FRIEDMAN, M. and ROSENMAN, R.H. *Type "A" Behavior and Your Heart,* New York: Fawcett Book Group, 1981.

GREEN, ELMER E., GREEN, ALYCE, M., and NORRIS, PATRICIA A. "Self-regusonal: some metaphysical perspectives." *J. Transpersonal Psychology* 3 (1971): 27–46.

———— BEYOND BIOFEEDBACK. New York: Delacorte, 1977 (also New York, Delta Books, Dell Publications, 1978).

———"General and specific applications of thermal biofeedback." Chapter in *Biofeedback—Principles and Practice for Clinicians*, (J.V. Basmajian, ed) Baltimore: Williams & Wilkins, 1983.

GREEN, ELMER E., GREEN, ALYCE, M., and NORRIS, PATRICIA A. "Self regulation training for control of hypertension." *Primary Cardiology* 6 (1980): 126–137.

NORRIS, PATRICIA A. "The role of psychophysiologic self-regulation in the treatment of cancer: a narrative case report." Voluntary Controls Program, The Menninger Foundation, Topeka, KS 66601, 1983.

SCHULTZ, J.H. and LUTHE, W. *Autogenic Training*. New York: Grune and Stratton, 1959.

SIMONTON, O. CARL, MATHEWS-SIMONTON, STEPHANIE, and CREIGHTON, JAMES. *Getting Well Again*. Los Angeles: J.P. Tarcher, 1978.

20

Elmer E. Green   Science and Psychophysiology,
                        Psychophysics and Mythology

As we re-evaluate the field of psychophysics, which originally referred to body-mind-spirit integration (Fechner, 1966), it seems useful to provide a rationale for recent scientific psyche-soma research
that draws together work in many areas, including education; neu-
roanatomy; neurophysiology; osteopathy; allopathic and traditional
medicine; Jungian, Freudian, humanistic and transpersonal psychologies; ethology, or comparative study of natural behavior in animals
and humans, not rat studies in mazes with extrapolation to humans;
and self regulation procedures including yoga, autogenic training,
and biofeedback. At the Menninger Foundation we have combined
much of this work under the name Psychophysiologic Research and
Therapy (Green and Green, 1977). I will focus on our scientific rationale, to the extent that modern science has the facts.

Not surprisingly, some people have said, "Rationale, who needs
it. Being is what is important, a la Maslow, not thinking." But we
need to make certain that all patients in the Biofeedback and Psychophysiology Center at The Menninger Foundation understand
very clearly how the cortico-limbic-hypothalamic brain works, because they need this understanding if they are to succeed at physiological self-regulation. Understanding satisfies the left cortex, which
in most people has veto power over everything the right cortex

240

wants to try, visualize, or hope; the right cortex, in most people, has the gestalt-like visualization facility which activates the normally-unconscious lower brain centers.

Thus the part of our brain which oversees analysis of facts, thinking, talking, and giving academic opinions but knows very little on an experiential basis, has executive control over the part of ourselves that intuitively but a-rationally knows things. This left-brain right-brain split causes suffering within individuals because initiative and enthusiasm, which generally come from, or express themselves through the right cortex, are often mistrusted by the left cortex, especially in "thinkers." (It was for this reason that Johannes Schultz, M.D., the founder of Autogenic Training, said he did not enjoy training scholars or pedants. They often could not learn in less than two years something simple as warming the hands, which a school child usually learns very quickly.)

This left-right disparity is not limited in its effects to interhemispheric problems; it also can cause interpersonal trouble. For instance, my intensely left-brained father was often wrong, but for exactly correct reasons. And my intensely right-brained mother was often right, but for the wrong reasons. You can imagine how that worked. Though it caused trouble in the family, it gave me an excellent opportunity to become the family mediator, and for several years I had valuable experience in healing rational-intuitive splits, my own as well as those in the family.

This kind of left-right split can be healed with a rationale. What I say later about the central nervous system may seem dry, but as we often tell clients after explaining the rationale of self-regulation, knowing that everything needed for achieving psychosomatic health is inside you, beautifully organized, can help you learn to operate the system. We explain that the functional parts of the nervous system are not "hard wired," or unchangeable. Because they are instead plastic, normally-unconscious habits of body, emotions, and mind can be reprogrammed in brain structures by self-regulation training, plus your own volition.

If the client is a physician, explanation of the rationale may take considerably longer than if he or she is a high school student. The physician initially has a host of left-cortex questions, but, when he succeeds in controlling his blood pressure, for example, and gets off drugs, he knows what happened and can explain it to anyone. The high school student, even though a good psychophysiologic learner, may not really understand or care about the rationale, and may not be very good at explaining to others what really happened.

Before discussing the neurophysiologic correlates of the psyche, let me explain that Alyce Green and I first developed our understanding along these lines with the aid of Dr. Will J. Erwood, a lecturer and teacher whom I soon began to think of as an "Irish yogi." As a student in physics at the University of Minnesota, I knew enough biology to know that the physiologic self-controls Erwood demonstrated were not possible. But he was doing them. After seeing and learning a few simple physiologic self-controls myself, my question was not "is he doing them?" but "how is he doing them?" Alyce and I were Dr. Erwood's students until his death in 1947, and that experiential period saved us twenty years of left-brain questioning. A small amount of personal experience can save a decade of research design and statistics, and psychophysiologic research can then be conducted like research in traditional physics, rather than in statistical probabilities of hypothetical possibilities. Standard statistical methods for research in psychology, though often necessary, are not fully satisfying because the non-experiential left cortex can never be certain of anything. That is its nature and its forte in a certain sense. The left cortex is a good servant but, speaking metaphorically, it makes a terrible chairman of the board.

In part, this is what we learned from Dr. Erwood, and strange as it may seem in 1982, he also knew (from his teachers, he implied) about the left vs right brain dichotomy. He advised me to continue practicing the piano as I continued my studies at the university, so as to properly balance my "skills and talents" in the left and right sections of my brain. I did not know then that yoga practice had for several hundred years emphasized the need for right-left, yin-yang, feminine-masculine balance in every person, and that it advocated specific exercises for enhancing sensory-motor development and balance between the sides of the body and the aspects of personality. When I asked Dr. Erwood how brain balance (through learning to be ambidexterous) would affect other talents and aspects of my personality, he merely said, "They are related." I was also told that the origin of normal consciousness is deep in the brain, not in the cortex, and volition is influenced by that region. Dr. Erwood referred to the central nervous system as an "instrument," objective rather than subjective, in the days before anything was known about its deeply buried maintenance and control-of-awareness functions. It seems particularly significant to me now, after years of study and reading brain research reports from around the world, that I am returning in thought to information given by a Western "yogi" in 1939.

There is no space to review the hundreds of animal and human behavior-brain-mind studies that have been conducted in the last thirty years in ethology, psychology, psychophysiology, and in psychoneurology, but the basic features of the diagram below are well supported by scientific research in various disciplines.

This diagram represents the entire central nervous system (CNS). To be complete it would need several billion lines, but roughly it can be divided as shown into voluntary and involuntary neurological parts, and conscious and unconscious psychological parts. To a large extent, "voluntary" and "conscious" belong together, and "involuntary" and "unconscious" belong together. The cerebral cortex, both halves of it, lies in the upper half of the diagram, and most of the remainder of the CNS lies in the lower half.

It is not improper to think of the cortex, limbic system, and hypothalamus as located in the top, middle, and bottom parts of the brain. In the diagram, though, the "limbic response" is shown at the bottom because it is largely unconscious. We are only partially aware of a few of its psychological parts (a few of its emotions). The hypothalamus is only as big as a thumb, but it contains almost all of the automatic control functions of the body, cardiac, circulatory, gastrointestinal, etc. It acts like a thermostat in a house, automatically controlling the machinery even though we are not consciously aware of it. This automatic physiologic process is called homeostasis.

Hanging by a thin stalk from the hypothalamus at the bottom of the brain is the pituitary body, half neurological and half hormonal. It is a slave of the hypothalamus (in the cybernetic sense), but the hypothalamus is controlled by signals from two places—from the body and the limbic system.

Roughly speaking, we can say that the pituitary has one master and the hypothalamus has two. That the hypothalamic-pituitary unit

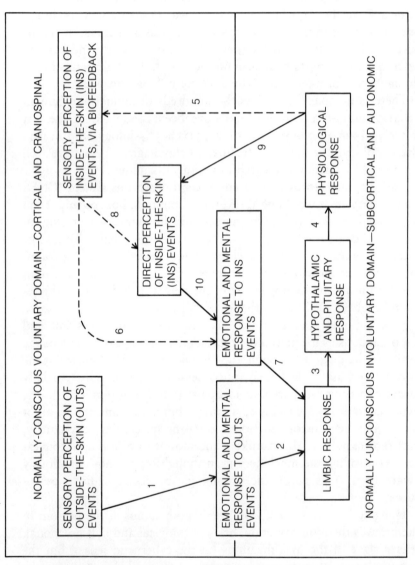

NORMALLY-CONSCIOUS VOLUNTARY DOMAIN—CORTICAL AND CRANIOSPINAL

SENSORY PERCEPTION OF OUTSIDE-THE-SKIN (OUTS) EVENTS

SENSORY PERCEPTION OF INSIDE-THE-SKIN (INS) EVENTS, VIA BIOFEEDBACK

DIRECT PERCEPTION OF INSIDE-THE-SKIN (INS) EVENTS

EMOTIONAL AND MENTAL RESPONSE TO OUTS EVENTS

EMOTIONAL AND MENTAL RESPONSE TO INS EVENTS

LIMBIC RESPONSE

HYPOTHALAMIC AND PITUITARY RESPONSE

PHYSIOLOGICAL RESPONSE

NORMALLY-UNCONSCIOUS INVOLUNTARY DOMAIN—SUBCORTICAL AND AUTONOMIC

FIGURE 20–1

has "two masters" is the cause of most of our body trouble. The two controllers, the physical body which "pulls" on the hypothalamus to respond and the limbic system which "pushes" the hypothalamus to act often are at odds with each other. The body is the physiologic self, but the limbic system is the emotional brain, and it often wants something contradictory to the body's best interests. If the clash of interests becomes violent enough, we (the often unfortunate "owners and operators" of the system) end up with psychosomatic diseases.

It is really quite simple, now that we know how the parts are constructed and interlinked. The hypothalamus-pituitary-body entity is like a computer, and the limbic system is like a set of programs. The computer carries out its BASIC body functions according to a preset pre-fabricated instruction called the genetic code, and the programs supplied by the limbic system are superimposed on it.

It is here that we can get into psychosomatic trouble because of "GIGO," programmer jargon for "Garbage In, Garbage Out." The computer's behavior will be fouled up if the program it is instructed to carry out is nonsense. Unlike electronic computers, which do not "self-destruct" when the input is garbage, but only "print out" garbage, the nervous system, being plastic, gradually shapes itself to pressure from the input, which can force "self-destruct."

"Emotional garbage" results in psychosomatic disease, some of which it seems we all have. There is a way out, however. That way is through proper visualization of what we want the mind, emotions, and body to do, and how we want them to behave in response to a variety of circumstances. Figure 1 indicates the sequence of events in this process, which works as follows:

(1) Sensory perception of outside-the-skin events (OUTS) results in emotional and mental responses. These are shown on the center line of the diagram because they are both conscious and unconscious, cortical and subcortical.

(2) Whether conscious or not, there is a limbic response to every perception from outside the skin. This response is an electro-chemical change in neurological structures of the limbic system (which has fifty-three regions, known to be connected by at least thirty-five nerve tracts).

(3) Changes in the limbic response to OUTS events are passed on

to the hypothalamic-pituitary system (HP) through nerve tracts which trigger off appropriate HP changes.

(4) HP changes always result in physiological changes in the body. This much was thoroughly known in physiological science by the time MacLean (1949) began calling the limbic system the visceral brain. It is through this route, (arrows 1-4 in the diagram), that stress literally "gets under our skin." What was known by very few scientists before 1967, however, was that we can intentionally change the response, and train the body to respond in a way we choose.

(5) Now for a crucial and profound fact: when subtle, normally-unconscious physiological changes are picked up by sensitive electronic devices and made to operate visual or auditory devices which the patient can perceive (biofeedback meters or tones), body information previously known only by the hypothalamus is made available to the cortex. Historically, this is the first time in human evolution that the cortex has been able to find out what is going on "down there." (Pain in a body organ or part by itself does not tell us specifically what is wrong.

(6) This feedback of physiological information to the cortex creates a biocybernetic control loop in which the cortex can play a determining part. This happens because the patient sees the meter as an outs, or objective event, and responds with an appropriate emotional and mental response, a subjective event. This new emotional response is reflected by a change in the limbic system. This causes an appropriate change in the hypothalamic-pituitary network, which is in turn reflected in an appropriate change in the physiological state. This change moves the meter (a new OUTS event), prompting a new emotional-mental response and, consequently, a new limbic response in a sequence that occurs until the patient begins to connect what happens in the meter reading with what he or she feels inside as subtle internal sensations that are not easy to describe.

(7) When externalized feedback information and internalized awareness begin to match, the artificial machine-aided feedback loop becomes unnecessary. The patient knows what is going on down there, and the biofeedback device is put aside. The appropriate state of consciousness for physiological self-regulation of one or another body organ, or body condition, has been achieved (see ar-

rows 8 and 9), and the patient has direct perception of inside-the-skin (INS) events.

(8) When INS perception begins to develop, no matter how difficult to describe in words (because the verbal cortex is not part of the feedback circuit), the patient finds that visualization (visual, auditory, kinesthetic, verbal, or other) can create physiologic changes as easily as does straight forward perception of outside-the-skin events.

This is a turning point, because self-regulation then becomes a fact—controlled by the patient's own visualization. Since gestalt-like visualization is predominately a right-cortex rather than left-cortex process in this left-cortex-dominated culture, the "left cortex has learned to let the right cortex do its thing." Like women's lib in the human body, the feminine half of each person, male or female, becomes a full partner with the left cortex. Integration begins and the patient's life style changes.

The capacity to visualize is apparently one of the major differences between humans and animals. Animals live in the "here and now" without much visualizing of the future or the past, as far as we know. They are Zen creatures. But humans often live in the future with great anxiety, and what some people visualize has hypo-thalamic-pituitary effects more powerful than those resulting from true outside-the-skin perceptions. We all know people who worry more about what may happen, than about what does happen or people who live in the past, visualizing guilt. That is harmful for the body as well as the psyche.

To summarize: biofeedback experience shows us that our visualizations can make body changes of the kind we want, and when that great discovery is made, we use the image-making faculty of the psyche to visualize what we want the body to do. In other words, we can use visualization in a positive way to handle the effects of a stressful environment. This is the key to healing or avoiding a psychosomatic "disease," or the unpleasant side effects of stress. Chronic environmental stress, if allowed to "get under the skin," often results in chronic physiological change, and that means damage not only to the body, but eventually to the psyche as well.

From the preceding discussion, it is clear now how biofeedback works—except for one remarkable detail. How is it that the body, in response to our visualization, is able to convert an idea into an enzyme? How does it know what to do merely because we visualize what we want to have happen (in the autonomic nervous system, for instance)? Whereas, to western science, the mind is merely a psychological reflection of the body, Eastern existentialists, such as Indian yogis and Tibetan Buddhists, have maintained for a long time that the body knows what to do because it is a part of the mind. This "mind," they say, is a form of substance, of which the physical body is only the densest part.

At the present time, considering the limitations of scientific instrumentation, it appears that the body-mind debate can not be settled in any way that is convincing to the unbiased left cortex (including mine). Therefore, for me, it is more entertaining to hypothesize that the yogic concepts propounded by Patanjali 2500 years ago (Taimni, 1967) are correct, and that the body is a substantial function of the mind.*

In our study of the self-regulation powers of yogis, the yogic concept of psychophysical "energy" came to the fore as the linking medium, or substrate in our bodies, of a hierarchy of substances (forms of matter) called body, emotions, mind, and spirit. In yogic theory the physical body is viewed as a three-dimensional perception, or brain-mind projection, of more-than-three-dimensional substance. When we extend control over the cells of our own body, we are learning (in a small test-tube way) the rules of energy control that are true throughout the cosmos. By "cosmos" is meant everything in nature which can be perceived by specific senses, or organs, of mind, emotions, and dense physical matter. By "energy" is meant whatever lies behind action in the human being or in any other section or aspect of the cosmos. This, of course, is not a definition in the ordinary sense of the word, but is consistent with the fundamental East-

---

*That theory makes room for greater human potential, which in itself is intriguing, and the cosmos to be explored in the great adventure of "breakout" from this planet is in the dimensions of mind. It is not limited to metal containers in three dimensions (space ships) which haul bodies around. But exploration in dimensions of mind is paralyzed by a fear of the unknown reflected in the funding difficulties genuinely scientific parapsychological research projects have found. This fear is part of the limbic "fight or flight" response, and is not rational regardless of the pride its possessors generally take in being "scientific." (It is interesting that the left cortex spends a good deal of creative effort trying to explain what the limbic system is doing. As might be guessed, a good name for this is "rationalization.")

ern metaphysical idea that the ultimate Mover, the ultimate generator of all motion, can not itself be apprehended by any sense of mind, emotion, or body.

In India and Tibet, this hypothesized energy is called "prana," and in China and Japan it is called "chi." In the West we are beginning to hear of "the therapeutic touch" (which can be done without touching, or even at a distance from the patient). We are beginning to hear about "psychokinesis for health." Clues for understanding these concepts are, like gold nuggets, wherever you find them.

Our study in 1971 of Swami Rama, a yogi from Rishikesh, India, produced a few self-regulation events in the lab which Rama said represented energy control (Green and Green, 1977). Before he put his heart into a state of atrial flutter Rama turned to Alyce, on her way to the lab's control room, and said, "When my heart stops, call over the intercome and say, 'That's all.'" When I asked why he wanted that, he said "Since I am not prepared in the usual way for this experiment (having not fasted for three days), I do not want to do it too long . . . I do not want to take a chance on damaging my subtle heart."

It took further discussion over a period of days to define "subtle heart," but in the swami's mind (as in Patanjali's *Yoga Sutras*) the human is an energy structure of which the "densest part" is the physical body. As the physical magnet is the densest section of a magnetic field, so the structure of the physical heart is the densest section of a subtle (energy structure) heart.

When I asked Swami how he managed to put his heart into the peculiar non-pumping state of atrial flutter, he said that a large energy center in the middle of his chest (the "heart chakra in the subtle body") was connected by a little line of "light" (prana) to a small energy center (chakra) associated with the right ear. In a state of meditation he "looked" inside himself, and when he saw the line of light he made it become "very bright," and then the heart "stopped."

A few months later, at a meeting of neurologists for whom I was speaking on biofeedback and yoga, I was pressed by one questioner to explain how the Swami did that "trick." As a psycho-social experiment, I decided to give the Swami's own explanation. After that there was a long silence. Then one of the physicians stood up and gave a neurological interpretation. There is a loop of the vagus nerve (which controls the heart) very close to the right ear; the Swami obviously had learned a way to manipulate it. "Isn't it interesting," the doctor said, "the Swami has developed a metaphor (a visualization, please note) which when thought about is able to manipulate the vagus nerve!"

I did not say it, but I thought, "Who really has the metaphor, the doctor or the Swami?" Are we in fact looking at a many-dimensioned cosmos of energy fields with our space-time brains, and seeing a three-dimensional slice which we call physical matter? That is the yogic explanation. Gary Zukov's *The Dancing Wu-Li Masters* and Fritjof Capra's *The Tao Of Physics* indicate a growing number of physicists are also thinking that way.

An interesting psychophysiologic clue for self-regulation came from our lab work with Jack Schwarz, whom I think of as a Western Sufi. Schwarz pushed a six-inch sailmaker's needle through his biceps, and the hole closed around the needle when he pulled it out, as if a tiny sphincter was in the skin. When I asked how he managed to do this, he said, "You should understand that I do not force the body to do any of these things. I had to ask my subconscious mind if it was willing to do it . . . And I had to wait for its answer . . ."

In other words, Jack had to achieve conscious cortico-limbic-hypothalamic coordination before he attempted a demonstration. Without coordination between levels of his "mind," he said, he was unable to control bleeding.

Jack's most interesting clues from an energy standpoint, however, came from what he called "reading auras." He maintained, as do yogis and many healers and psychics that the energy structure of the human is broadly divided into physical, emotional, mental, and spiritual parts, and that these different "forms of energy" are visible to a "see-er" in certain states of consciousness (Green and Green, 1977). When a "sensitive" is "seeing," unique patterns in the "body aura" are clues to the body's health. Unfortunately, it is impossible to photograph these auras (at least not consistently), but it was interesting to note that Jack's descriptions of what he "saw" coincided with what some of our research subjects in India told us about themselves, and about their own perceptual experiences.

One of the most intriguing leads in this mind-body-energy question surfaced in India. We took several opportunities along our 7000-mile route (traveling with all our equipment and nine people in a minibus), to photograph unusual temples. At Bodhgaya there is a beautiful temple erected at the place where the Buddha is said to have attained enlightenment, sitting under a Bo tree. To me, the most striking feature of the temple was the great number of gods and demons, large and small, carved into the walls, and standing here and there in the surrounding courtyard. Surely the gods should have a place by the Buddha, but what were all these devils doing in this sacred place? (For that matter, what is the significance of the carved gargoyles mounted at strategic places on Gothic cathedrals?)

Later, while viewing an old Hindu temple almost hidden in a palm jungle, we noticed the same mixing of angels and devils, gods and demons. Finally, in the town of Visakhaputnam (Waltair), on the East Coast of India by the Bay of Bengal, we took an opportunity to visit a very handsome and elaborately carved new Hindu temple. From a large rectangular base it rose in a huge rounded mass of stone against the sky.

I had just photographed a whole array of angels and devils, and was closely inspecting the sloping facade of the building when an Indian monk in an orange robe approached and said, in flawless Oxford English, "I hope you understand that when the peasants who live around here come to meditate or pray, they think they are praying to those beings out there, asking some to help them and others to not bother them. But those of us who know something, understand that those beings are in fact the various parts of our own nature, and we must integrate them before we can be whole." He named some of the beings and identified them with human virtues and vices.

As we talked, my mind began spinning through a web of myths. This rounded pile of stone was Mount Olympus; there was Zeus at the very top. Beyond him was the formless void of the Unknown. Below him was arrayed a hierarchy of gods, goddesses, demi-gods, demons, and at the very bottom, earth.

Recently it has come to my mind that not only does the temple represent the abode of the Greek and Hindu gods and demons, but the rounded rim against the sky is the cortex, and the midsection with most of the angels and devils is the limbic system. The formalized base is the hypothalamus and pituitary, and the earth on which it stands is the body. Perhaps the old religious idea that the temple of the spirit is the human frame was a prescientific intuition (or perception) of what we are just now beginning to decipher from a scientific point of view.

The Indian monk's idea corresponds with Jung's understanding of the integration of the light and the dark sides of human nature (Jung, 1963) and this "synthesis of sun and moon" (strikingly portrayed by the melding and transformation of characters in the movie, "The Dark Crystal") is perhaps what is ultimately necessary in each human being. We need this synthesis not only to become whole, as my chance acquaintance at the temple put it, but to complete our terrestrial education, to graduate and transcend the space-time system, as Tibetan thinkers would have it.

In any event, regardless of the far-reaching concepts involved in temples and myths, psyche-soma synthesis within at least a fraction of humans is necessary if the planet is to be kept whole, or made whole. As long as individual men and women are split inside themselves into hierarchies of warring angels and devils, they are easy to frighten and manipulate. To a large extent we are limbic creatures, and there is no doubt that this is a limbic planet, shown by the fact that some of the most influential leaders in world affairs are creating increasingly elaborate rationalizations for unending development of nuclear peace-keeping weapons.

My mind trip about this temple, this great symbol of human and cosmic nature, was brought suddenly to earth by the swami's voice saying something about chakras and pranas. This temple structure, he said, was symbolic of the structure of the etheric body, the subtle, pranic, energy body which was the true physical body. And all forms of energy, physical, emotional, mental, and spiritual, flowed through the chakras, whose aspects and attributes were here represented in stone. The transformation of each mind and body, and the establishment of harmony with nature, depended on which energies we allowed to flow through the chakras and thereby modulate the cells, feelings, and ideas of our composite being.

I was struck by the idea of "allowed to flow," because the monk was referring to what we have called "voluntary," in respect to physical and mental health, and he was carrying out the idea's implications for the purposeful development of hidden human potential. He seemed to be referring to transcendental states of consciousness and their manifestation in us through harmony with all beings, at all levels.

If we can integrate mind and body, medicine and myth, finding and creating a unity in ourselves from which we can project a superior kind of consciousness in which the limbic system is our ally and agent, rather than our nemesis—if we can transform ourselves in this way, perhaps there is hope for our planet. Like us individually, perhaps the planet can transform, or be transformed by the composite voluntary mind, and not disintegrate or slip back into limited consciousness in which we (and it) are puppets of great archetypal beings, the gods and goddesses whose proprietary domain in us, unless we establish control over them, is the limbic system.

In the sense of personal and global responsibilities, then, is it not possible that we are all Zeus? As temples, myths, and nervous systems, it is perhaps our task and our opportunity to integrate and synthesize the gods and goddesses, create harmony, and thus transform this planet—which is, after all, quite a good place.

REFERENCES

AUROBINDO, SRI. *The Synthesis of Yoga*. Pondicherry, India: Sri Aurobindo Ashram Press, 1955.

FECHNER, GUSTAV. *Elements of Psychophysics*. Vol. 1. New York: Holt, Rinehart and Winston, 1966. (H.E. Adler, translator; D.H. Howes and E.G. Boring, editors).

GREEN, ELMER E. and GREEN, ALYCE M. *Beyond Biofeedback*. New York: Delacorte Press, 1977. (Also Delta Books, Dell Publications, New York, 1978).

JUNG, CARL. *Memories, Dreams, and Reflections*. New York: Pantheon, 1963.

MACLEAN, PAUL D. "Psychosomatic disease and the 'visceral brain'." *Psychosomatic Medicine*, 2, (1949): 338–353.

PAPEZ, J.W. "A proposed mechanism of emotion." *Archives of Neurology and Psychiatry*, 28, (1932): 725–743.

TAIMNI, I.K. *The Science of Yoga*. Wheaton, Ill.: Theosophical Publishing House, 1967.

21

Claudio Naranjo   Bringing Eastern Meditation
into Western Psychotherapy

Meditation is a multidimensional domain that takes innumerable forms: every spiritual tradition has one or a number of them. But when we analyze these various forms of meditation we soon observe that certain components, including mental silence, attention to the breath, and visualization are pervasive. These components of meditation derive their meaningfulness, I propose, from their participation in three underlying *dimensions*. I shall begin with explanation of this theory, and then turn to an experiential demonstration of some applications of meditation to psychotherapy.

One underlying, bi-polar dimension of all meditation goes from *non-doing* to *letting go*. On one end of it is the calming of the mind, or *cittavrittinirodha*, as Pantanjali calls it, or more generally, the inhibition of activity that ranges from physical relaxation through the pacification of the emotions, to the silencing of one's thoughts, internal dialogues and fantasy. At the other end of this dimension, the letting go end, surrender to an egoless process is emphasized, as in shamanistic and prophetic trance, or in Taoistic and Zen arts. Whereas in the first case we may say that the meditator is invited to identify with the "unmoved mover," the silent center of creation, the latter is an invitation to participate in the "cosmic dance."

Contrasting as these paths may be, they are not contradictory but complementary. Nonattachment is entailed by both stopping and flowing, and the spontaneously creative activity of "expressive meditation" may be regarded as the dynamic consequence of an implicit non-doing (i.e. noninterference), just as surrender to an egoless spontaneity leads to the silencing of the mind. Any advanced meditator knows of a state where calm and inner freedom are conjoined.

Along with this bi-polar dimension of stop/go are the poles of what I call *mindfulness* and *God-mindedness*.

By "mindfulness" I mean attention to the givens of experience; attention to body, emotions and mental states, in other words, to the "here and now." God-mindedness, on the contrary, involves a withdrawal of one's attention from the body, senses and psychological processes, and a redirecting of consciousness to its transcendent center, whether this be called "God," "Self," "Nothing" or not called at all, and whether it be pursued through formless meditation, mantra or creative imagination. Great as the contrast is between the forms of meditation illustrating mindfulness and God-mindedness, it is seen as a complementarity by some spiritual schools. Not only can the forms be compatible but we may speak of a convergence of the paths at the end in the goal of a fully functioning and balanced human who stands as a pillar between heaven and earth, living in this world and also in the other.

And we can speak not only of a complementarity but (as in the case of the stop/go dimension) a movement of one pole to the other, a reciprocal feeding of the extremes. Only at the striving and honeymoon stages of the path does the sense of the divine alienate the seeker from this world. In time, we know that spiritual experience does not obliterate the here-and-now but makes it more radiant and miraculous. And conversely, attention to the here-and-now involves a process of purification that leads to spiritual perception. Those with sufficient experience in *vipassana* meditation will know how insight into the transitoriness and emptiness of the here-and-now leads to the spontaneous turning away of the mind in *samadhi*, where it takes cognizance of itself as a mirror-like emptiness in which the "aggregates" of experience are reflected. And how, when the mind detached from the object has come to rest in itself, it becomes open and appreciative.

In addition to this cognitive dimension concerning the focus of attention and conative dimension concerning activity, I envision an affective dimension in a meditation, and call its poles "universal love" and "cosmic indifference." In the case of *bhakta* and the cultivation of transcendent indifference we may speak of a complementarity, for love flows out of equanimity, spontaneously manifesting when the passions are transcended, and is also an infinite abundance, the perception of which makes up spontaneously nonattached.

If we now draw this map I have been describing to you as a graph, it could naturally occur to us to represent the three bi-polar dimensions as the three coordinates of space—two of them lying in a plane and the third at right angles to them. This would be appropriate if the three were completely independent of each other, but this does not appear to be the case. As you may have noticed throughout this exposition, there is a resonance between the "negative" and "positive" poles of each dimension and those of the two others, suggesting that the three complementarities are different projections of a single underlying "yin/yang" or "Shiva/Shakti" dimension. Also, though specific techniques of meditation may lie in any position in our map according to their proportion of the six essential components, we may discern two distinct "meditation complexes" associating the "active" and "passive" poles of each dimension: the Eastern, combining non-doing, non-attachment and mindfulness, and the Western, combining God-mindedness, surrender and love.

Because of the interrelation of the dimensions that I have outlined for the meditation domain I think that it is most appropriate not to represent them as orthogonal to each other (i.e. as the coordinates of space) but as the intersecting edges of a double triangular pyramid (that is a tetrahedron and its mirror image). For the sake of convenience I have represented them in the two dimensional writing surface at 60 degree angles.

The addition of an axis perpendicular to the hexagonal plane serves as a means to state succinctly two further contentions about meditation: first, each one of the aspects of meditation discussed converges on a common process of ego suspension; and second, in contributing to the suspension of the ego, each has the ultimate effect of unveiling spiritual perception or gnosis. If the hexagonal plane maps the "internal gestures" of meditation, or the means behind the actual techniques, the vertical axis represents the complementary aspects of meditation's result, which we may call nothing-

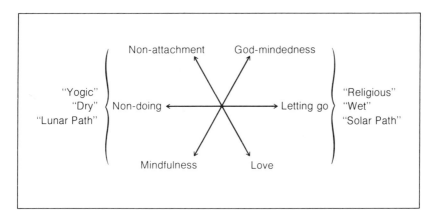

FIGURE 21–1

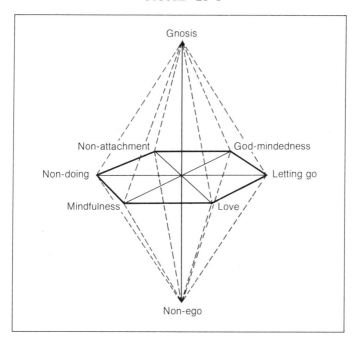

FIGURE 21–2

ness and totality, transparency and light, non-ego and being, *fana* and *baqa*, death and eternal life.

I now turn to the subject of psychotherapeutic *applications* of meditation and as a preparation for a first demonstration I will ask you to first stand up and look around. Begin to scan other people's faces, because in a few minutes I will ask you to pick somebody you want to join for an exercise of meditation in relationship.

Broadly speaking we can apply meditation to psychotherapeutic practice either as a complement to psychotherapy (as in prescribing individual vipassana practice, for instance) or as a component in the therapeutic situation. It is possible to extend the mental task involved in some forms of meditation to an interpersonal situation; we may extend mental silence to a situation of contact for instance, or the invoking of the sacred. Most forms of meditation can be carried into the world, and a most natural bridge to the world of others is *one other*. For these and other reasons I have personally been very interested in the field of silent interpersonal extensions of meditation.

Another domain open to us is that of meditation as a background to verbal interaction. By addressing ourselves to the underlying attitude of the parties involved in a psychological process (whether in a dyad or in a group situation) we may be able to refine some psychotherapeutic techniques in the light of our meditation experience. I expect to demonstrate an instance of this to you, but let us start with the simplest interface between meditation and relationship—that of silent meditation in couples. Once you arrange your chairs so as to sit face to face with your chosen partner I will begin guiding you through the process.

Begin by closing your eyes for a few minutes.

Relax your body, particularly your shoulders. Let yourselves sink into the belly.

Bring yourselves to a state of not looking for anything, just being there, letting the relaxation of your body extend to your mind.

When you open your eyes, don't look at the face of your partner.

Try to open your eyes in such a way that what internal silence you have been able to create is not lost.

Then look at your partner's chest. But more than looking, just let the visual sensations come in as if you were in a "womb with a view"—that is, being as regressive as possible.

Not trying, not pursuing anything.

There is nothing to be done.

Very slowly bring your gaze up to your partner's face, stopping for awhile at the throat, then the mouth area.

Look at the face in such a way that takes into account the space around.

Look panoramically, rather than focused.

Look not at the figure but at the ground as much as possible— *include* the ground.

And keep working on not working.

Keep working on the silence of the mind.

Not trying.

At the same time sensing that there is a person there. So, without thought, feel that there is a 'you'.

Let us allow ourselves to dissolve as much as possible, but without letting the 'other' dissolve.

If you like, you can use a sort of mantram to remind yourself: 'You—not I'; to remind yourself to get out of the way, to dissolve while focusing on the other.

Then bring up questions and comments, sharing with each other. Here are some of my responses to ITA conference participants who were involved in this exercise:

—It is very useful to have your demons projected on the other and to have to work against your distrust and fear of remaining in a state of abandon.

—What we did in silence is an instance of "I and Thou, Here and Now" in Gestalt therapy, though we didn't focus specifically on attention to the here and now. For the sake of variety, in view of what I intend to do next, I invited you to emphasize *relaxation* in the presence of the other, which also has to do with the therapeutic dimension of neutrality.

—I see a nonsystematic desensitization taking place in meditation. Instead of creating a schedule of things to confront from the calm state we may trust organismic self-regulation. I think that when we are not setting out to solve anything, we will be visited by the unfinished. And that there is a wisdom in the sequence of what surfaces in our mind.

—Spontaneous relationship arises when we are not seeking to either relate or not relate. Sometimes breathing synchronization occurs, and other parallelisms in experience, suggesting telepathic rapport.

—In the spiritual traditions the sharing of meditation has a place in the silent darshan situation or initiatory settings, between somebody who is an experienced meditator, and who can demonstrate spiritual depth through silent presence. But the principle is more general. Much nonverbal contagion takes place in every human interaction. I have been a proponent of the democratization of the old institution and sacrament.

—When the expression *karma yoga* is used, this most often refers to a situation that is a little simpler than the interpersonal one: that of working with one's hands in the company of others. In many monastic situations such as Christianity and Zen, and also in the Sufi path, handicrafts constitute important extensions of meditation or ordinary life. The interpersonal, however, tends to be left out. And I think that there is room for creative expansions of meditation to the interpersonal setting. It will also, of course, be part of karma yoga in the work of professional psychotherapists.

—The subject of the dangers of meditation is a difficult one. If I stick to the conservative view that is prompt to emphasize the potential danger of certain forms of meditation for certain people, I would say that the least dangerous will be attending to ongoing experience, contacting the here and now without avoidance or fantasy. Yet the conservative attitude may be unnecessarily restrictive, for there is something to be said for the transmutation of a healthy core of psychosis, which is a wish for transcendence. Psychosis is something like a shortcut to transcendence. We know how much there is to be said for allowing the "other worldly" consciousness of psychotics to be refined rather than discouraged. So possibly the contemplative life can be the solution to one's psychotic tendencies—a way of giving air to the fire within a constructive framework. In this way it may be possible to transmute a low level to a high level visionary experience. Mme. Alexander David Neel writes about a monk who was practicing *chöd*—a ritual and act of creative

imagination where you cut your own head and offer it, together with your blood and corpse, to the gods and spirits. She
saw the monk run screaming and become apparently crazy. Yet
she says: who are we to say "this is dangerous, don't do it"?
You can't fulfill the hero's journey if you insist on your comfort
and safety. You may have to risk your life if you seek incompa-
rable enlightenment. So this may be worth having in mind in
answer to that question.

I would now like to move on to the situation of bringing meditation into verbal communication. I will present you one among several
possible psychological exercises incorporating meditation, a refined
version of the "awareness continuum" technique of Gestalt therapy.
The awareness continuum exercise is to Gestalt therapy what free
association is to psychoanalysis. Free association is ongoing attention to and communication of the unfolding of thought without in-
terference with the thought process. The awareness continuum exercise is the ongoing communication of experience, and not thought
about one's experience. It means the ongoing communication of sensations, emotions and perhaps mental states that are not memories,
anticipation or fantasies; not elaborations, generalizations or judge-
ments—but the data of awareness. If you have not done this, you
may discover in it a profound path. It takes humility to just be with
the here-and-now as it is, and not with the data that may want to
confirm an ideal self. It takes patience if your experience is not right
now as alive or as meaningful as you would like it to be. It takes au-
thenticity to share the here and now with another. It takes courage
to be open to whatever comes while in the presence of another. It is
really *work*—work on oneself.

So please get together again with a partner, ideally not the same
person with whom you just did the past exercise.

For the listener, this time practice attention to your experience of
the other; awareness of your partner's gestures and voice.

Practice relaxation, particularly relaxation of the face. You will be
hearing somebody speak, but don't respond in any way; do not en-
gage in a facial dialogue. Make it your only task to be present and
aware, neutral and relaxed; let yourselves be inwardly as you are—
natural and aware.

For the partner who does the speaking, this will be a ten minute long experience. The content of the speaking is the ongoing experience. For the first five minutes or so focus on sensations and feelings. Be sure you do not leave the feelings out. Do not turn the exercise into an inventory of sensations, but pursue the feeling state in addition to body sensations, and perceptions of the environment and the other. After a while start bringing into your awareness what you *do*—not only what you do with your gesture and your voice, but what you do internally, such as waiting for something to say or internally deciding a course of action. I will give you a signal at some point to begin to bring awareness of action into the communication. Remember to abstain from considerations, explanations, etc. Resist that temptation. And listeners, resist the temptation of verbal or gestural feedback.

Let us start now. I will tell you when to switch, in about ten minutes.

And now, as you continue with sensations and emotions, communicate also your awareness of gestures and observations about what you do with your voice, and what you do otherwise. Just continue in the three tracks observing and sharing your sensing, feeling, doing.

When the ITA conference group reconvened, we again shared questions and comments. Here are some of my responses.

To the question, "How do you use this in therapy?" I responded that in Gestalt therapy, where it originated, the awareness continuum exercise may be regarded as a point of departure for therapeutic interventions. Interventions in Gestalt may invite focusing attention in one direction or another, or constitute directions for expression and dramatization. From what is going on when the client opens up to the experience of the moment you take your cues for suggesting the client become such and such, re-live a certain past experience, act out a catastrophic fantasy, etc. The awareness continuum exercise is the beginning, the end and the middle of Gestalt therapy and tends to be forgotten in Gestalt practice. There is much talk about the here-and-now in Gestalt, and in practice much of what goes on in the sessions is the prescribed reactualization of the past, dramatization, and the enactment of fantasy. The awareness continuum is a somewhat neglected technique, especially valuable if refined in the light of meditative experience, emphasizing a combination of openness and awareness, attention and organismic spontaneity.

—I think it is important to have in mind that there is such a thing as an avoidance of the here and now. When you do not confront that avoidance you are bound to get into the trap of talk for talk's sake.

—I did not intend you to exclude the perceptions that are not body perceptions. The ideal is to develop a panoramic awareness in which sometimes you will focus on the person with you, sometimes attend to the room, sometimes look at the rug, sometimes hear a car passing by. The more choiceless the awareness, the best.

—Analytic neutrality, originally tackled by placing oneself behind the couch, becomes more potent than upfront neutrality when it is not merely an outer neutrality but an inner state. I like to think that it is the creation of a meditation field. If you really manage to sustain a sense of being present, a sense of being focused on your own awareness of the other and yourself, this has a contagious effect. It is as if there is an energetic aspect to awareness and what happens in a therapeutic interaction to some extent consists in this "x" factor of the energy transaction. We do not always talk to the same kind of silence. There are different qualities of silence. We know the experience of talking into certain silences that are like deep wells, or certain silences that are challenging, because we cannot get away with phoniness in their presence. Or we cannot get away with meaninglessness in the presence of silent meaningfulness. And then there is "ordinary" silence, and silences that suck at us like hungry ghosts.

—Keeping our eyes open in meditation is conducive to the practice of meditation in the world. It is a challenge to sustain a state of peace and lucidity in spite of reality, in the full presence of all of our sensory input, That is the test of meditation, to be able to bring it into the world. Yet since that is difficult to do, there is a temptation to make the task a little easier.

—In the therapeutic situation I take any avoidance of contact as a cue of anxiety or a cue of something being off. Avoidance of the here-and-now manifests in the avoidance of I and You. Looking into the avoidance of contact you come upon something that is hot. There is a discipline involved in sustaining the contact—a discipline of nonavoidance.

—There is such a thing as music therapy, yet there are more dimensions to music than ordinary listening. It sometimes makes a difference how we listen and if we know what to listen for. There is a potential contemplative dimension in music, and when what is called music therapy is expended to include meditative audition, it becomes a rich field because of the combined variety of music and of ways of listening. Since music is a part of everybody's life, we can be helpful to clients in at least giving a stimulus to the intentional use of music as a device of meditation.

Some of the highest spirits of the West have spoken through music, expressing through sound something of the upper reaches of consciousness. I think, for instance, of the music of Bach as the supreme expression of the Christian sense of God-the-Father. The romantics in music have been the rediscoverers of the Mother, and they are the worshipers of the night, the unconscious and the feeling side of our nature; they have expressed the Dionysian side of the spirit, the yin or shakti side. Each great musician contributes a specific quality of experience. Hans von Büllow, German pianist and conductor of the late 19th century, likened Bach, Beethoven and Brahms to the Father, the Son and the Holy Ghost. There is much truth in that, though we can put it even better by saying the Father, the Son, and the *Mother*. Music can be an important support for what the Sufis call *dhikr*, a word that translates as "repetition" and "remembrance." In verbal dhikr, the repetition is a means for remembering; but we can use music too as a remembrance of the different facets of the consciousness that we want to evoke. I have with me a recording of the second movement of Brahms' First Symphony, a paen to the universal Feminine, and I propose that one use it as an occasion for dhikr, evoking not God-the-Father, of whom the churches have been reminding us throughout our lives, but God-the-Mother. Let us contemplate in the mirror of music an oceanic and womb-like depth. As we evoke the holy, let us do so calling to mind the attributes of creative, sustaining and devouring origin.

22

Swami Sivananda Radha   Women's Place
in Today's World

It is good to be back in India. This is where my spiritual birth took place. My spiritual journey started in the Himalayas, under the guidance and blessings of my great Guru, Swami Sivananda. His compassion was boundless, for sick people helped through his free clinic and medicine, for those afflicted with leprosy, and for the orphaned children he took into the Ashram to give a home, food and care, at least temporarily. In his special way he would coax his devotees to take these orphans into their families to care for them and give them a life in the future. He would always make enquiries about the children's well-being later. There seemed never to have been a moment of temptation in Swami Sivananda to use these children for his own ends, for the Ashram, as laborers, or servants. In all ashrams there is more work than helping hands.

Many women came to him to seek help and guidance. He encouraged them to seek an education or training so they could go into employment, or even a career. He taught them emotional independence. Thousands of women have laid at his feet their pains and agonies, their lost hopes for a meaningful life for their remaining years. With unfailing discrimination he encouraged them to enter specific careers that he found suitable to their basic inclinations and talents. He also encouraged them to accept leading positions and to stand up for their rights.

A few women who visited the Ashram while I was there resorted to tears, the old female game to extract pity, but Gurudev would have none of that. He gave them sound advice and encouragement, and sometimes he even promised to stand behind them. Like other women of my generation, even though I came from the West where education and certain careers were opening up to women, I still was very shy, timid and my self-respect was at a very low key. For this reason he suggested, when he gave me the name Radha, that he put his name, Sivananda, in front of it, saying: "People will know that what you do, you do with my approval." That was a splendid move psychologically. It did the trick for quite a number of years. Traditionally, of course, I am Swami Radhananda.

It seems to me that Swami Sivananda, at that time, already had an awareness of the coming political and economic world situation, which would naturally bring along a revolution among women. I do not belong to any Women's Liberation Movement, but I believe the second step, which is woman's purpose in life, is far beyond the competitive struggle between the sexes. Woman must look at her position in relation to her religion, whichever it is, and to the ambiguity in that aspect of her life that needs clarification. For example, women who study with me in the west have said, "Why is it wrong to have an abortion, when the church does nothing to prevent my child being killed at 18 years of age? Why must we women sacrifice our children for a small group of powerful, ambitious people in every country, who are the rulers of the world?" In *On Human Nature*, Edward O. Wilson of Harvard University writes that "The noblest among them are sure that humanity migrates toward knowledge by logotaxis, an automatic orientation toward information, so that organized religion must continue its retreat as darkness before enightenment's brightening dawn."[1]

In a workshop I conducted, a woman wrote: "There are so many men who are said to be in possession of great intellect, to have luminous minds, who are capable of a logic almost as cool as mathematics, and yet they cannot settle their affairs among themselves without killing millions of people in the struggle to come out on top in their competitive games." We were discussing at the time the survival of religion, with the development of the new sciences, especially socio-biology, and whether women could, through special training, contribute more positively to future generations.

I wish Gurudev was alive and had an answer for that question. There are very few people of his calibre left these days. He had the courage not only to involve himself in women's problems, but also to initiate a woman, and a Westerner in particular, into Sannyas. So I think it is suitable to make women's place in today's world the topic of my presentation.

When I look at the films made during my stay at Sivananda Ashram in 1955 and 1956, I am very grateful to my Guru. I was at the time 44 years old, yet people complimented me, saying "You look so young, like 19." I no longer take that as a compliment because my immaturity at that time is evident to me every time I see the film. It is due to my Guru that I learned I had a right to be my own person. In order to have Liberation I needed to set myself free from the various dependencies, particularly emotional ones, hinged to my survival. And I like to tell all other women today, like an older sister, "Be strong, be courageous. Pain is not ended by putting on an ointment, but by dealing with the festering boil underneath."

I did not think I could take more pain than two wars and the times between had brought to me, the economic breakdown and the lack of food, the loss of loved ones—to be the widow of two husbands and a grieving mother of two babies, how could I possibly deal with more pain? It was the yoga philosophy of maya and illusions that showed me that the apparent cruelty of clearly looking at the facts was the gateway to a freedom where the newly acquired tool of awareness would prevent the continuation of pain.

And so I would like to say to my women sisters of today: You must assume responsibility for yourself. There is no merit for you to turn the other cheek, to swallow your pain and tears, and fight to survive in your family, in your marriage, in society. I have all the compassion for you that your pain right now is big enough, you have no need to look for more. And yet, that particular surgery, the last one to be performed on you, you will conduct yourself, in your own time, in your own way. You can come into your own if you are willing to look clearly into the deepest depths of yourself. You will start having a dialogue in that place with yourself, to know what is going on, and carefully avoid simply imitating what your male partners are doing. It is here in your innermost depths that you can find yourself. No doubt it is harder to do this kind of work in the family setting than if you were all alone. But let me warn you, financial independence and equality are not enough, although they are a very important part in the struggle for your emotional freedom. You must stop dreaming of the prince that will carry you, take care of you, love and look after you. Remember the Kangra painting of Radha when she had found Lord Krishna—she was ready to be carried by him, piggyback, when he vanished into nothingness.

This is a classic example of how women, in their devotion and worship, transfer even into the spiritual field those emotional desires to be carried, and it is here that your ambiguity lies. You transform your dream lover into the God that you worship, a redeemer who will save you from yourself. I am afraid that God will work with you, but not for you. It is a hard job to let go of all these dreams and illusions. You will slip and fall many times, but you will have to pull yourself up by your own bootstraps.

The enlightened ones in any religion have pointed to the god within, and that idea has survived in many myths and even fairy tales—the sleeping princess, the sleeping giant, and so on. Consider yourself to be the Handmaiden of the Divine Mother and you may have Her constant help and reminder, to awaken to your own divinity that is within.[2]

For most people at this time, the evolution of consciousness is more of a guessing than a knowing, a speculation that hopefully roots a deep desire inside the heart, and recognition of the importance of consciously cooperating with the forces given to us.

Woman must find her place, fulfill herself through none other. She is the Handmaiden of the Great Goddess, the Divine Mother. Because of the Goddess, life renews itself[3]. History has often shown women that when technological man has finished the creation that is peculiar to him, it becomes destruction. Man is focused on his principles, his order, as he sees it. It is she, the woman, who picks up the pieces to give life a new beginning after each monstrous destruction. That observation brings many questions to mind. Is there a competition between man's scientific creations and woman's ability to create life? If that is the case, then the avoidance of such destructiveness of life on a large scale can only be accomplished when competition between the sexes stops completely.

History also shows us that when cultures reach a peak they subside into mediocrity, or they vanish altogether. The female aspect of creation, the Goddess Shakti, starts a new cycle. But most women function on an unconscious, instinctual level, and the new woman I speak of must be very aware to be the Handmaiden of the Great Goddess. She must accept the burden of renewal after destruction. Through her the Divine Mother transforms the barren land into fruit-bearing growth and the bleak world becomes once again dazzled by a million colors of Her creation. Through woman the Great Goddess lets new life emerge and be tenderly cared for.

That is the service women have always given, but without awareness of their accomplishments. There is much women can take credit for; now, however, with even a greater threat of destruction, perhaps lasting longer than anything before, women must increase their skills for service. The women who are superior in their contribution have not been trained to achieve that superiority. Their development came more by accident than by intent.

The development of women's intelligence, talents and skills must have been given greater importance at one time, because Plato tells us that a young man should look for a suitable partner for the procreation of children, and choose a wife of good breeding and education. He must look at her as the future mother of his children, for which she needs to have many talents. He also warned that one should regard the preventive mistakes as a matter of supreme importance[4].

Fred Hoyle, the well-known British astronomer, laments that there are too few women like his own mother, who awakened him to the love of mathematics, instead of being fearful about it. She would bounce him on her lap and teach him the multiplication tables. His conclusion is that if we had more such mothers, attitudes towards mathematics would be dramatically different. Or, there is the example of one of my own students, a single young mother: "I feel like I am being buried alive, to be with the mentality of a 3-year old every day, and have no nourishment for myself." One day she found the solution. She used her subscription for the *National Geographic*, which often includes maps of different countries, to show her little boy the clothes, hairdos, and customs of people in various parts of the world. Suddenly she realized that while training her son she learned much about the world herself, and was sure that one day she would be able to see it. Now, 15 years later, he is considered one of the brightest students at the university and has a relationship with his mother that is heart-warming to witness. More women need to use their creative resources to come up with such solutions for their children as well as themselves.

Psychology has always stressed the formation of character and intelligence in early childhood. The importance of this development has always been obvious, but nothing has been done to train young girls to become superior women and mothers. Instead, the development of the future mother has been left to chance, and when her children do not turn out right, she is the source of all that went wrong. She is responsible for any tendencies that the children display, be they emotional, criminal, homosexual, violent or dishonest. It seems that any mother is the worst enemy that anybody could have.

In all other professions we make a job assessment and a requirement of excellence before giving a degree or promotion. We expect no such thing of mothers. In fact, one nurse at the cerebral palsy hospital, a mother herself, said to me, "Animals are well-bred for domestic purposes. We humans are still wild, and when we are young we have no clue what our responsibility as a future mother is. We do not treat mothers during their pregnancies very well either. All the young mother's emotional distress is picked up by the fetus . . . The 4 or 5 month fetus [has been seen] sucking its thumb, affected by the stress of the mother. We can monitor the unborn, [and] operate on the fetus, but we close both eyes to the need of helping prospective mothers to become complete, harmonious and well-balanced in themselves."

The nurse pointed to the children that surrounded her. "Their mothers were unable to take care of their sickly children, and to assume responsibility for them. Properly trained, they could have sought medical advice before getting pregnant, or even married. If the chances were too great of having an abnormal child, the right choice would have been made by a woman who in the formative years of her life had been given the proper direction, education, and advice to wisely handle her future with its ensuing decisions."

If no changes are implemented, the continuation of an inferior human race is ensured and the development of any outstanding men or women is left to chance. Thereby it is no wonder that we have so few enlightened people and so few geniuses.

In some cultures girl children are not counted and women are barely considered human. A sociobiologist quotes from a great epic of the past, ". . . we have heard women crying when war was declared, 'Now we will be sold into slavery, myself and my daughters be raped.'" These tendencies to violence, the sociobiologist tells us, are all rooted in our biological past, and discrimination against ethnic groups, homosexuals or women is based on the theory of natural selection developed by Darwin. Wilson (of Harvard University), in his *On Human Nature*, says: "I have tried to show sociobiology can account for the very origin of mythology by the principle of natural selection acting on the generically evolving material structure of the human brain."[5]

"Humanists," Wilson says elsewhere, "are not interested in spiritual conversions and what goes with it, and scientists cannot in all honesty, serve as priests." A scientist, Wilson poses a question: "Does a way exist to divert the power of religion into the services of the great new enterprise that lays bare the sources of that power? We have come back at last to the second dilemma in the form that demands an answer." Whatever the biological facts are, we have to make choices, preferably of an ethical nature. We must choose, particularly as women, how human we want to be.

Robert Trivers, another Harvard biologist, has this to say, "Sooner or later, political science, law, economics, psychology, psychiatry and anthropology will all be branches of sociobiology." It is too early to accept such a statement, even though it may be true for the first three stages of six stages of human development that Ernest Wood suggested in his *Practical Yoga*, a commentary on the sutras of Patanjali. He called the first five stages mineral-man, vegetable-man, animal-man, man-man and being truly human, while the sixth is beyond description.

I suggest to my women sisters not to be confused by scientists, who often state something, only to recall or at least correct it, sometime later. But let us assume there is some truth in the findings of the sociobiologist. The first three stages of man may indeed be reflected in lack of awareness, and living in the dark of instincts. However, if there had never been any growth of the intellect, and everything had developed perchance, would scientists have come into existence? Perhaps, then, women should look at what their potential could be, since all does not depend on the genes.

There may not be complete free will for the human race. For example, one is not free not to eat at all, but the choice of what to eat still belongs to the individual. The choice of how to conduct one's life is made by many, but some women have to discover that choice is indeed theirs.

This should not be confused with what is generally called "free will." Alternatives and variables can influence the choice to be made. We can predict the outcome of a choice more often than not, taking into consideration all the genetic variables and all the operations and influences that take place in the human brain. However, factor X, the unknown, influences the ordinary as well as the most highly-trained individual. There are many findings about the power of the human brain to gather and process information, but no special attention has been given to the woman's brain.

It is appropriate that terms like "programming or reprogramming ourselves" have entered into daily language use, and it is inviting to compare the processes of the brain to spoken and written language. To compare the way information is recorded in the brain in women, or in people of different backgrounds, can only enlarge our present limited knowledge about reflexes, electrical waves, and so on, and enhance our understanding of human nature in general.

It is not certain when language was first written down. Supposedly the Sumerians invented the cuneiform symbols to catalogue events that took place in the skies. Agricultural developments had also necessitated keeping accounts of the harvest and other mundane transactions. These accounts vanished as other cultures were moving towards their peak, also to vanish in due time. Only tiny fragments are left of the mythologies originating from those observations of the starry skies.

Written language is made up of symbols, and communication is complicated because each word is a symbol standing for more than one idea. Are those ideas part of the functioning of the brain, particularly in regard to processing information? Is the brain more than a complex machinery of electrical currents, nerve cells, and other complicated activity? Until recently, psychologists and philosophers have not given enough credit to the research the neurologist has done, and no agreement has been reached about where the brain begins and ends, where the mind begins and ends, and where consciousness has its place.

In the yoga system symbolism and metaphor are used to explain the otherwise unexplainable, and it is interesting to note that some of the texts use the term, "The Devi of Speech," and other versions use "The Lord of Speech." It seems that competition between the sexes, which I have lightly touched on, had its beginning way back in time.

Ideas like love have developed from an intense degree of attachment. If this kind of reductionism has a place, then where shall we look for love, selflessness, self-sacrifice, caring, tenderness, or protection? Are these, then, the irrational tendencies, particularly connected with women, which might be discovered by a study of the way information is recorded in their brain?

From early childhood all children learn to fit into the social world in which they were born, because it is here they must survive. Is it by observation that a little girl learns to smile and charm the great gods that are her family? And does she, as time goes by, acquire more and better skills to elicit from others what she needs for her survival?

We talk about cattiness, seduction, or temptation as particularly female characteristics, while men have often been compared to predators, conquerors, heroes. And, of course, there is also a positive aspect of Woman as the Great Mother, the nourisher, or protectress, and Man as the warrior, crusader, creator of gods, provider, or scientist. This pair of opposites on various levels, if accepted as complementary to each other instead of contrary, could open up a new dialogue between the sexes, giving each one its place. There is no need to get into fierce competition.

From the simple aspects of religion helping humans with the problems nature provides, to the complicated structure of religious, social and scientific life today, we can see that more confusion than order has been produced. Robert Graves helped to untangle the confusion by saying, "It must be explained that the word *lex*, 'law', began with the sense of a 'chosen word', or magical pronouncement, and that, like lictor, it was later given a false derivation from ligare. Law in

Rome grew out of religion: occasional pronouncements developed proverbial force and became legal principles. But as soon as religion in its primitive sense is interpreted as social obligation and defined by tabulated laws—as soon as Apollo the Organizer, God of Science, usurps the power of his Mother the Goddess of inspired truth, wisdom and poetry, and tries to bind her devotees by laws—inspired magic goes, and what remains is theology, ecclesiastical ritual, and negatively ethical behaviour."[6] Graves also aptly states that myth and religion are clothed in poetic language; science, ethics, philosophy and statistics in prose.

Robert Graves' writing concerns the re-establishment of the Mother Goddess in religion that only accepts the Father, the ruler, the judge, the destroyer, the punisher. His position is secured with so many laws and regulations that today's lawyers have to specialize. The scientist is in no better situation. His field has grown so monstrous that he must court people in high government, industry or business office, and only if he has a talent for showmanship will he win in the competition for scientific research money.

Out of all these complexities woman has become important in the management of finances for the household, but only in the way a typist or secretary is important to the boss. The field of orthodox religion is still closed to her. That has not deterred many women from starting their own church. Maybe that is a signal from the Great Mother, the Goddess, that Her time eventually will come when the predicaments of the rational world will burst into a chaos of destruction. Only She will be the preserver of the pieces, and only She can recreate a new era of life. And it is for this reason that I tell you, my women sisters, to turn your gaze to Divine Mother and be Her Handmaiden, but in your own right, with new strength, power and wisdom that you have for so long denied yourself. Refuse, and if necessary, even protest to be just a symbol of the soul that was created by the Greeks, making you the holy virgin to protect man from his own sexuality.

You, the women, have put men into heaven as God the Father to protect yourself from your own sexuality. Do not allow yourselves to be used as a sex goddess, even in the most disguised ways. Rather explore the power of regeneration and reproduction to the fullest, to which nature has already pointed the way. Use your intuitive forces, treasure your irrationality, and once again dive into the deepest depths of yourself.

In many parts of the world people have been wondering why Westerners, particularly Canadians and Americans, are so preoccupied with self-development. Women participating in growth workshops outnumber the men by far. Are they not being very narcissistic? I am sure that some are, but the majority have an intuitive perception that their lives are not quite right, that they have not reached their potential and want to find out what it is and what their chances are to fulfill it. In the traditional schools of psychology many questions are still unanswered. Some who have gone through therapy feel that they have just shifted from one personality aspect to another.

Most problems within the individual or in interaction with others lie in often fierce competition among the many personalities playing their roles, or being at war with each other. Who has not experienced the frustration of being of two minds? Clarity of thought is needed. Most women know enough about their body, less about their mind, and wonder what "power of speech" means. I have heard many a woman saying, "I don't know what I think until I hear myself say it." "Mind," says B.K.S. Iyengar, "is the king of the senses. One who has conquered mind, senses and passions, thought and reason, is a king among men. He has Inner Light."[7]

The first light is insight into the need for a psychology that will deal with the rational as well as the irrational, with an external and internal reality, and with the intuitive, symbolic, and poetic. Such psychology would also point to the source from which happiness and joy grow. The importance of the inner subjective and meditative, as well as introspective capacities, has been rejected by the orthodox psychologist. The Eastern and, the transpersonal psychologists have always known and accepted that all experiences are worth remembering. Maslow paid attention to all, calling some "peak experiences." Yogic practice is the key to freedom and liberation only when it embraces the human being in its totality, be it male or female. Dependency, interdependency and interaction of the body, the mind and speech have to be seen in this larger context to fathom their formidable power.

Lack of security, fear, or a sense of helplessness, are often the result of uncultivated imagination, and it is necessary to get hold of the culprit of these feelings and their origin. Maslow pointed out that to learn more about oneself means to learn more about human nature, and therefore more about people in general.

He extended that knowing to other fields such as law, history, philosophy, and religion, all of which are essentially human products. The more you know about the human being, the more you know about the products. "By psychologist I mean all sorts of people," Maslow said, "not just professors of psychology. I mean to include all people who are interested in developing a truer, clearer, and more empirical conception of human nature."

Transpersonal psychologists are such people. Because they are patient, understanding, loving and tender-minded, even humble, it as if they are less than scientific. They do not have the scientific attitude which often expresses patronizing arrogance, more interested in executing beautiful, precise, elegant experiments from which the members of the guild could benefit, than in helping the clients and patients. But, like scientists, the transpersonal psychologists are cautious, careful, accurate, observant to avoid making mistakes. Searching within unorthodox methods they do not react to hostility with self-importance and self-protection. Deep compassion has made many stick their necks out, pursuing new ideas to first get results, then mapping out a methodical way that can be taught to others.

A new breed of scientist in the field of psychology, the transpersonal psychologist, has boldly pushed the windows open, allowing a vision that embraces all of life, both what is directly in front and what is beyond. Transpersonal psychology can perhaps be called the youngest school of thought; it is still open-ended and, like the bee that gathers honey from many sources, it draws from the East—yoga, reflection, meditation and the workings of the mind—as well as building on traditional psychology. I have been involved for at least seven of its ten years. I have seen transpersonal psychologists moving courageously into once-forbidden areas to bring about a more holistic development into their own lives as well as those of their patients and clients.

Transpersonal psychology has been able to incorporate cultural transitions in religions, intellect, and education, and it is open to gray areas that are awaiting their completion in the future. It is to transpersonal psychology that women can turn, not only for help, but to make a significant contribution.

Psychology so far has been the science of the man and the few women psychologists who have been trained by them have not developed a psychology especially for women. By looking into the depths of their being, women can convey what they are all about and help to develop that much-needed psychology of woman.

Women are concrete thinkers, using metaphor and symbolism, and have a greater capacity to understand and experience what is generally termed the irrational, mystical or visionary state. Although symbolic or metaphorical functioning usually surpass reasoning, it is desirable to be able to transcend at will, not only different aspects of personality, but also the visionary state, to reach an analytical functioning. Women have been classified as living in a world of feeling and dreaming. But many men have acknowledged they live in the sense of feelings, translating what they feel into the mental, thereby stimulating their imagination. Bypassing the rational, they arrive at the intuitional to achieve a stronger feeling of security in the making of extraordinary decisions. Through various types of spiritual practices, women can also learn to achieve these states of mind and emotions.

Although the use of symbolism or metaphor to enter the visionary state at will, and later to transcend it, is still frowned on by many scholars and scientists, scientist John Z. Young, in *Programs of the Brain*, emphasizes the need to expand the use of symbols and metaphor: "This brings us again to the question of language and symbolization . . . The concept . . . is not simple, and the concept of symbolism is used in various ways . . . a symbol is a special sort of signal because it represents the features of the surroundings in such a way that the organism immediately recognizes its significance and acts accordingly. . . . Furthermore these activities themselves depend on the symbol system of heredity, the code of the DNA. Symbols are indeed the core of life. They provide the 'knowledge' of what the world is like, which is essential for survival. . . ."[8]

It seems that children, by experiencing first and then speculating possible results, slowly become thinkers who determine an outcome. In other words, they no longer need to have personal experience, but anticipate on the basis of what they have already experienced. We see here a process that, in yogic terms, means that in later life there is difficulty in learning something new or even foreign like yogic spiritual practices, because there are not prior experiences on which to base one's anticipation.

Knowledge acquired by theoretical anticipation is only considered information in regard to yogic practices. Students often become frustrated, wanting to understand before experiencing. Pure theory is not too helpful (otherwise scholarly works would be of much more practical use). Information is gathered from theoretical structures and, when it comes to yogic practices to attain Liberation, experiences and observation are a stepping-stone to assessment/analysis.

Speculation and possibilities do not need to be excluded, but they are like the cart which cannot go before the horse. Correct assessment is often difficult anyway, and room for error would be too great if expectations are created. Clarification about what has been experienced is indeed very necessary to avoid self-deception, and it may be difficult at times to verbalize non-material unusual happenings.

The brain can be trained and the mind can be disciplined, a difficult job for women who have lived, shall we say, "untamed" in reasoning for most of the years of their life. For those who are "born analysts" and live entirely by the power of reasoning, the difficulty is equally great when it comes to developing intuition. Listening and thinking with intuition is an important difference between the Eastern and Western mind.

The early training to develop and balance both these faculties is similar to that of early childhood, and when people become frustrated in courses I suggest that they think of themselves for the present as spiritual babies. The mind is too complex to make easy abstractions, which lead only to generalizations and entirely lack the very necessary personal experience. It is like learning to write the letters of the alphabet and to form words and sentences, so that someday the poetry that has always been there will find its expression. But you need the tools to do so.

The tree is already in the acorn, the seed of the oak. It does not go in search of itself, or wonder what it will become. It does not need to muster courage to be what it is meant to be. It just is.

By transcending the multitude of personalities with their residing egos, you can become what you essentially are—your innate nature, the core, the very essence that is You, which has always been there.

REFERENCES

1. Edward O. Wilson, *On Human Nature*. (Cambridge, Mass.: Harvard University Press, 1978), 169.

2. Swami Sivananda Radha, *The Divine Light Invocation*. (Kootenay Bay, B.C.: Shiva Press, 1966).

3. Swami Sivananda Radha, *Kundalini Yoga for the West*. (Spokane, Wa.: Timeless Books, 1979).

4. Plato, *The Laws*. Translated by Trevor J. Sunders. (Middlesex, England: Penguin Books Ltd., 1970), 250–251.

5. Edward O. Wilson, *On Human Nature*, 192.

6. Robert Graves, *The White Goddess*. (New York: Vintage Books, 1959), 532.

7. B.K.S. Iyengar, *Light on Yoga*. (New York: Schocken Books, 1977), 22.

8. J.Z. Young, *Programs of the Brain*. (Oxford: Oxford University Press, 1978).

Biographical Notes

CECIL E. BURNEY, Ph.D., is a Jungian psychologist in private practice. He did his postdoctoral studies in Zürich, Switzerland, with Aniela Jaffé and Dora M. Kalff. He has lectured widely on the Jungian sandplay and other topics of transpersonal psychology in the United States and abroad. Currently, he is President of the International Transpersonal Association.

FRITJOF CAPRA, Ph.D., studied theoretical physics at the University of Vienna in Austria and has done research in high energy physics at several European and American Universities. He is presently working at the University of California at Berkeley. Dr. Capra is the author of two revolutionary books, *The Tao of Physics* and *The Turning Point*, in which he explores the philosophical and social implications of the new physics.

ALYCE M. GREEN, Ph.D., is Co-Director of the Voluntary Control Program in the Research Department of the Menninger Foundation in Topeka, Kansas. Her special area of interest has been the relationship between creativity, reverie, imagery and alpha-theta brain wave feedback. She is a pioneer in the field of biofeedback, first president of the Association of Transpersonal Psychology, and co-author of the book *Beyond Biofeedback*.

ELMER E. GREEN, Ph.D., is Director of the Voluntary Control Program in the Research Department of the Menninger Foundation in Topeka, Kansas. With a background in optics, electronics, computing and biopsychology, he is a pioneer in the area of biofeedback and voluntary control of internal states, president of the Biofeedback Society of Amer-

281

ica and co-author of the book *Beyond Biofeedback*. With his wife, Alyce, he has done extensive research with Indian yogis.

FATHER BEDE GRIFFITHS, is a writer, philosopher and Benedictine monk, who also holds a degree in English literature. Since 1955, he has been living in India, attempting to integrate the tradition of sannyasa with the Christian monastic tradition. He is the author of the books *The Golden String* and *Marriage of East and West*.

STANISLAV GROF, M.D., is a psychiatrist who in the last twenty-five years has done extensive research in the field of non-ordinary states of consciousness induced by psychedelic drugs and non-drug techniques. Former Chief of Psychiatric Research at the Maryland Psychiatric Research Center, past President of the International Transpersonal Association, and currently Scholar-in-Residence at the Esalen Institute in Big Sur, California, he is author of *Realms of the Human Unconscious* and *LSD Psychotherapy*.

DASTOOR MINOCHER HOMJI is the high priest of the Parsee community of the religion of Zoroastrianism. Born in 1921, he holds an M.A. from the University of Bombay and has completed a thesis entitled "The Philosophy of Atman in the Avestan scriptures." He is also a keen student of Gandhian philosophy and has participated in international conferences such as the Human Rights Conference of UNESCO, "Peace Through Religion," and four spiritual summit conferences in different parts of the world.

YASHPAL JAIN is a prominent Hindi writer dedicated to the idea of non-violence as expounded in Gandhian philosophy and Jainism. He is the author of eight collections of original stories, two biographies, many poems, and books in which he describes his world-wide travels. Some of his works have been awarded prizes by the Central and State Governments of India. He also twice received the Soviet Nehru Award for his books *Forty-Six Days in Russia* and *The Bridge Builder*. He is the editor of "Jeevan Sahitya," a Hindi monthly magazine advocating non-violent evolution of society, and secretary of "Sasta Sahitya Mandal," a society publishing Gandhian and related literature.

JACK KORNFIELD, Ph.D., is a psychologist and former Buddhist monk, practitioner and teacher of the Buddhist Vipassana meditation, and Director of the Insight Meditation Center in Barre, Massachusetts.

He teaches at Naropa, Esalen and other centers worldwide and is the author of *Living Buddhist Masters.*

SWAMI KRIPANANDA, was formerly a professor of Spanish at San Jose State University in California. She has been a disciple of Swami Muktananda since 1972 and took the vows of sannyas in 1978. She lectures on Kundalini Yoga in the Siddha Yoga courses and intensives.

AJIT MOOKERJEE, Ph.D., scholar, author and lecturer, the world's foremost expert on Tantric art, science and ritual, and collector of yoga art. He is the author of the books *Tantra Art, Tantra Asana, Yoga Art, The Tantric Way,* and *Kundalini.*

SWAMI MUKTANANDA, born in 1908 into a wealthy family in Mangalore, India, began his spiritual journey at the age of fifteen. A few years later he took the vows of a monk, and was given the name Muktananda. For twenty-five years he travelled around India on foot, spending time with many of the renowned saints and meditation masters of his day. He mastered the classical systems of Indian philosophy, as well as Hatha Yoga and many other branches of spiritual and worldly science. In 1947 he met Bhagawan Nityananda, one of the great modern saints of India, and a master of the Siddha tradition. After nine years of intense study under Nityananda's guidance, Muktananda reached the goal of spiritual practice, the state of Self-realization.

When Nityananda took *mahasamadhi* (died) in 1961, he passed on the power of the Siddha lineage to Muktananda. During the next 21 years Swami Muktananda travelled widely, making several tours of the world, and introducing Siddha meditation to hundreds of thousands of people. Swami Muktananda's students have established several hundred meditation centres around the world, and his disciples number in the hundreds of thousands. In October 1982, Swami Muktananda himself took mahasamadhi. His work is now being carried on by his successors, Swami Chidvilasananda and Swami Nityananda.

CLAUDIO NARANJO, M.D., a psychiatrist of Chilean origin who has been active in psychoactive drug research, psychotherapy, spiritual learning and guidance, community building and writing. He was an associate of the Esalen Institute in its early days, has taught at Nyingma Institute, the University of California and at the California Institute of Integral Studies and is a Fellow of the Institute for Cultural Research in London. Among his books are *The One Quest, The Healing Journey* and *Techniques of Gestalt Therapy.*

JOSEPH CHILTON PEARCE is an educator and philosopher who has received awards and honors for his outstanding dedication and achievements in the field of humanities. He is renowned for his books on consciousness: *The Crack in the Cosmic Egg, Exploring the Crack in the Cosmic Egg, The Magical Child*, and *The Bond of Power*.

SWAMI PRAJNANANDA is one of the foremost disciples of Swami Muktananda. Formerly a professor of Sanskrit, she taught Vedanta in postgraduate classes at Bombay University. During her twenty years with Swami Muktananda, she has written many articles and edited a number of books on Siddha Yoga. She has taught classes in Siddha Yoga and Indian philosophy at Swami Muktananda ashrams during his world tours. Author of Swami Muktananda's biography *A Search for the Self*.

KARL PRIBRAM, M.D., a neurosurgeon, scholar, author and lecturer, who formulated the revolutionary holonomic theory of the brain function. Over the last three decades, he conducted brain research at Yale and Stanford Universities. He is the author of over 100 articles and books including *Languages of the Brain*.

RUPERT SHELDRAKE, Ph.D., is a biologist and biochemist, who also studied philosophy and history of science at Harvard University as a Frank Knox Fellow. From 1974 to 1978, he worked in India on the physiology of tropical crops at ICRISAT (International Crops Research Institute for the Semi-Arid Tropics) in Hyderabad, where he is now Consultant Plant Physiologist. He is the author of the ground-breaking book *A New Science of Life*, which he completed during his stay of a year and a half at Shantivanam in South India.

JUNE SINGER, Ph.D., is a Jungian analyst in private practice and lecturer at the California Institute of Transpersonal Psychology, who is currently interested in transpersonal aspects of sexuality and its relationship to creativity. She is the author of *The Unholy Bible, Boundaries of the Soul and Androgyny*.

KARAN SINGH, former Regent and Sadar-i-Riyasat of Jammu and Kashmir, Chancellor of the Jammu and Kashmir University and of the Benares Hindu University, is a unique figure in the public life of India who combines active academic, intellectual and spiritual pursuits with a full involvement in political life. He received his Ph.D. from Delhi University after completing a thesis on the political thought of Sri Aurobindo. His books include writings on political science, philosophical essays, travelogues, translations of folk songs, and original poems and autobiography *The Heir Apparent*. He is also a keen student of Indian music.

SWAMI SIVANANDA RADHA is the founder and spiritual director of the Yasodhara Ashram, a yoga retreat located at Kootenay Bay, Canada. She received her training in Risikesh, India, and at the request of her Guru, Swami Sivananda Saraswati, returned to the West as a yoga teacher. She is the author of *The Divine Light Invocation, Kundalini: Yoga for the West*, and *Radha: Diary of a Woman's Search*.

MOTHER TERESA, a Roman Catholic nun and founder of the Sisters of Charity, is one of the world's most honored humanitarians. Born in Yugoslavia in 1910, she has spent the last thirty years in Calcutta, dedicating her life to caring for the poor and dying. In 1979, she was awarded the Nobel Peace Prize for her life work.

FRANCES VAUGHAN, Ph.D., is a transpersonal psychologist, psychotherapist, writer and lecturer, core faculty of the Institute of Transpersonal Psychology, and past President of the Association of Transpersonal Psychology. Her publications include *Awakening Intuition* and *Beyond Ego* (with Roger Walsh).